Spiritual Warfare

Spiritual Warfare

A Charismatic Baptist Theology
of Participating in Divine Conflict

ALISTAIR J. CUTHBERT

Foreword by Gregory A. Boyd

RESOURCE *Publications* · Eugene, Oregon

SPIRITUAL WARFARE
A Charismatic Baptist Theology of Participating in Divine Conflict

Copyright © 2025 Alistair J. Cuthbert. All rights reserved. Except for brief quotations in critical publications or reviews, no part of this book may be reproduced in any manner without prior written permission from the publisher. Write: Permissions, Wipf and Stock Publishers, 199 W. 8th Ave., Suite 3, Eugene, OR 97401.

Resource Publications
An Imprint of Wipf and Stock Publishers
199 W. 8th Ave., Suite 3
Eugene, OR 97401

www.wipfandstock.com

PAPERBACK ISBN: 979-8-3852-3000-6
HARDCOVER ISBN: 979-8-3852-3001-3
EBOOK ISBN: 979-8-3852-3002-0
VERSION NUMBER 07/28/25

Dedicated to

My wife Lynsey and children Nathan, Amaris, Rebekah, and Hannah

For our struggle is not against flesh and blood, but against the rulers, against the authorities, against the powers of this dark world and against the spiritual forces of evil in the heavenly realms.

—Eph 6:12 (NIV)

Contents

Foreword by Gregory A. Boyd | ix
Preface | xi
Acknowledgments | xv
Abbreviations | xvii
Introduction | xix

Part One: The Theology of Paul Fiddes

1. Fiddes' Doctrine of God | 3
2. A Fiddesian Account of Evil | 32

Part Two: A Doctrine of God

3. Knowledge—God's Omniscience in a Context of Spiritual Warfare | 63
4. Power—God's Omnipotence in the Realm of Spiritual Conflict | 86
5. Panentheism—The Spiritual Combat Situation Within the Omnipresence of God | 108

Part Three: Theological Construction

6. Theological Construction: A Doctrine of God for Spiritual Warfare Theology | 135

Conclusion | 173
Bibliography | 181

Foreword

THE WORK OF ALISTAIR Joseph Cuthbert in *Spiritual Warfare: A Charismatic Baptist Theology of Participating in Divine Conflict* is nothing short of a landmark contribution to contemporary theology. In an era when systematic theology is often accused of failing to engage with the lived realities of Christian communities, Cuthbert has crafted a book that bridges the gap between rigorous academic scholarship and the dynamic, lived spirituality of the Baptist-Charismatic tradition. This work stands as a testament to what theological inquiry can achieve when it dares to address complex and contentious topics with intellectual humility and boldness.

At its heart, this dissertation is a dialogue—one that is both interdisciplinary and interdenominational. Cuthbert engages critically with the theology of renowned Baptist theologian, Paul S. Fiddes, whose work is widely recognized for its depth and breadth, addressing issues as varied as the nature of God, the suffering of Christ, and the relational dynamics of the Trinity. By drawing upon Fiddes' theological insights, Cuthbert develops a robust framework for understanding spiritual warfare, a topic often relegated to the periphery of theological discourse. The decision to ground this exploration in Fiddes' kenotic theology—his vision of God as self-emptying and relational—is both innovative and profoundly resonant with the pastoral and doctrinal concerns of the global church.

What makes this work particularly compelling is Cuthbert's ability to navigate and synthesize diverse intellectual traditions. The book is firmly rooted in the Baptist tradition, yet it reaches far beyond denominational boundaries. Cuthbert engages with charismatic theology, process thought, philosophy of religion, and biblical studies, weaving these strands together into a cohesive theological tapestry. This interdisciplinary approach allows his work to address questions of immense significance: How can Christians understand the presence of evil in a world governed by a loving God? What role does human agency play in the divine drama of redemption? How can the church engage with spiritual realities in ways that are intellectually credible and spiritually enriching?

Cuthbert's work is not merely an academic exercise; it is a deeply pastoral project. The themes of suffering, evil, and divine conflict are not abstract concepts for this author—they are realities that resonate with the struggles of faith communities worldwide. By articulating a theology of spiritual warfare that is both biblically grounded and theologically sophisticated, this text offers hope and guidance to believers grappling with the complexities of modern life. It reminds us that theology is not only about understanding God but also about participating in God's mission to confront and overcome the forces of darkness in the world.

The significance of this book extends beyond its immediate context. It challenges scholars and church leaders alike to rethink the relationship between theology and praxis and to embrace a God who is both transcendent and immanent, sovereign yet self-emptying, powerful yet vulnerable. In doing so, it exemplifies the best of what Baptist-Charismatic theology can offer to the wider theological community.

It is with great admiration and gratitude that I commend this book to readers. Alistair J. Cuthbert has given us a theological treasure—a work that I believe will inspire, challenge, and edify for years to come.

Dr Greg Boyd, Senior Pastor, Woodland Hills Church, author of *God at War; Satan and the Problem of Evil*; and *Crucifixion of the Warrior God* (vols. 1&2).

Preface

Given the western world inhabits what some refer to as a "post-Auschwitz reality," many question the classical description of the biblical God of the Christian faith in the light of events that took place in the extermination camps in Poland and elsewhere during the second world war. Moreover, the constituent nature of evil (a word we regularly use but fail to understand) is open to all manner of definitions now that the biblical narrative about evil has been jettisoned from popular western culture and is no longer taken seriously. This is reflected by the significant lack of any serious systematic theological work being done on evil, the demonic, et al by academic theologians and biblical scholars when compared to other subject matter or pursuits.

Considering this lack of systematic work on the demonic-spiritual realm, the purpose of this book is to construct a doctrine of God which is commodious and coherent enough to locate a theology of divine conflict and evil (better known as "spiritual warfare"). The specific question that guides the work is *"does the contemporary theology of Baptist theologian Paul S. Fiddes offer a better framework than traditional theologies to explain the nature and character of God that best fits with a theology of spiritual warfare?"* Indeed, this book argues that at variance with traditional doctrines of God, a critical evaluation and reconstruction of Paul Fiddes' theology—with emphases on God's kenotic sovereignty, passibility, openness to the created order and panentheistic reality—offers a better structure to construct a doctrine of God to best imbibe a theology of spiritual warfare.

Part one (chapters 1–2) broadly delineates and analyses Fiddes' doctrine of God and his understanding of the demonic realm and nature of evil. To use Fiddes' theology to construct a doctrine of God that is congruent to the biblical paradigm of spiritual warfare, it is imperative in chapter 1 to analyze his body of work on God's ontological reality, including key themes such as the passibility of God, the impact of passibility on other theological ideas, the nature and character of God and the use of experience as a theological source. In chapter 2 I formulate a specific theological definition of evil which arises from interlocution with Fiddes. This understanding emerges from Fiddes' work on both the doctrine of God and the relationship of literature and theology in which he often analyses evil, pain and sorrow through analogy with the written genre of tragedy. Questions pertaining to the nature of evil, its ontology and personifications, and implications for atonement and theodicy will be discussed and debated. Subsequently, a default-nuanced explication of evil is formulated on which to a build a doctrine of God.

Part two (chapters 3–5) critically examines three incommunicable attributes of God,—divine omniscience, omnipotence, omnipresence—which are explicated using Fiddes' corpus and salient debate partners. The chosen attributes are central to a doctrine of God that helps make sense of the spiritual world, especially the demonic, as attested to by scripture, reason and experience. Concerning divine omniscience, given the current semi-realized eschatological reality means that, despite biblical claims regarding the origins of evil and teleological accounts of the existence of evil, there is a significant openness, and an ambiguous fog, about current and ongoing spiritual conflict. Therefore, this raises several questions about God's omniscient knowledge together with other concomitant corollaries. Again, using Fiddes as a key primary source, all matters pertaining to God's omniscience including his foreknowledge, aseity, passibility, immutability, relation to space, time and an open future, nature of freewill, and knowledge of counterfactuals are analyzed and critiqued.

Regarding divine omnipotence, questions that emerge from the study of theodicy such as why does God, if he is all-powerful, not simply destroy evil, and relatedly, given the fact that he does not eradicate evil, what does this say about his nature and character including the nature of power that he operates with, are examined and answers posited. Central to the discussion on omnipotence is Fiddes' writings on power, especially kenosis and his specific view of the atonement—*a subjective view which has an objective focus*. Then on the subject of divine omnipresence, Fiddes' panentheistic vision is outlined and then developed in order to make sense of the presence of evil (even territorial presence) within God's panentheistic presence. This involves interaction with Moltmann and others about *where* evil exists within the reality of God. Central to this understanding is Fiddes' use of Von Balthasar and the fact that spiritual beings and human persons can say "no" to and rebel against God within the "yes" of the Son to the Father.

Finally, in part three (chapter 6) the overall findings of these five chapters are used to build a constructive theology of spiritual warfare; a dialectical theology operant on the planes of the individual and corporate which is theologically congruent with the critically adapted doctrine of God presented in the previous chapters. This articulation of a unified theology of spiritual warfare in light of Fiddes' doctrine of God uses the recent work of key scholars, both similar and different to Fiddes, and takes the form of a dialogue between Fiddes and this author.

The conclusion contains a brief justification made of choosing Fiddes to answer this research question before a summary of all the chapters and main points, a succinct theological account of spiritual warfare, and finally mention of areas of future potential research not covered by this book.

Acknowledgments

EMBARKING UPON A JOURNEY to explore the unlimited expanse of the spiritual realm that constantly interacts with earthly life could not have taken place without fellow travelers and encouragers along the way. I am very indebted to all those who have aided and inspired me to pursue this investigative work from its embryonic beginnings while travelling around the world as a peripatetic missionary & Bible teacher until graduating at the University of St Andrews with a systematic theology doctorate, an award I received for the thesis that is the content of this book.

That said, there are some who deserve special recognition for their ongoing assistance and encouragement. First and foremost, I would like to thank my wife Lynsey for the years of supportive love and continual sacrifice she willingly made in order to allow me the time for research and writing. Also, huge thanks to my children—Nathan, Amaris, Rebekah, and Hannah—for their ongoing patience with me during the many times I was unavailable, and they were robbed of 'dad time.' This book is dedicated to you all.

Moreover, many thanks to my parents, Colin & May, for their continual interest in and support of this project that continued through the most difficult of seasons we had as a family following the premature and tragic death of my little sister Fiona. I miss you wee sis!!

Very special thanks are due to Stephen R. Holmes, my doctoral supervisor throughout, for his wisdom, encouragement, guidance, availability and friendship. I'm especially grateful for his willingness to take me on as a part-time doctoral student, his initial suggestion of using the theology of Paul Fiddes for this thesis, and his advocacy of me—both as my academic supervisor and elder colleague at St Andrews Baptist

Church. Thanks also goes to Paul S. Fiddes of Oxford University for his interest, support, and generosity of time and publications. Last, but certainly not least, I would also like to convey much thanks to Gregory A. Boyd for taking the time to engage with the work and write a very positive commendation of the book in the foreword.

This research and writing project would not have been completed without the significant assistance and support from the two churches I've had the privilege of serving as pastor over the last twelve years. First, many thanks to St Andrews Baptist Church and the then senior pastor, Andrew Rollinson. Their discernment and willingness to call me as their part-time assistant pastor made the start of this journey possible. Then, there is the ongoing support and encouragement I have received from the church I'm currently pastoring, Falkirk Baptist Church. Their willingness to call me knowing my intention to continue the PhD was ideal, and they have backed up that commitment via study weeks and mini sabbaticals over the last eight years.

And finally, many thanks goes to my friends and acquaintances who have supported me in different and creative ways while on the journey: Lindsay and Anne Glasgow, for their amazing and lovely hospitality and fellowship every time I needed somewhere to stay when in St Andrews; Steve and Fiona Downs for the use of their lovely flat in Campbeltown each time a writing week in solitude was needed; Paul and Ruth Taylor, for their wonderful and kind hospitality during my research time in Oxford; and finally, my theological brothers-in-arms, Stuart Weir and Tim Allen, for their encouragement, many theology discussions over coffee, meal or zoom, as well as critical comments on the published articles that have come from this research.

Abbreviations

CD III/3	Karl Barth, *The Doctrine of Creation*. Vol. 3.3 of *Church Dogmatics*. Edited by G. W. Bromiley and T. F. Torrance. Translated by G. W. Bromiley and R.J. Ehrlich. Peabody: Hendrickson Publishers, 2010.
CD II/1	Karl Barth, *The Doctrine of God*. Vol. 2.1 of *Church Dogmatics*. Edited by G. W. Bromiley and T. F. Torrance. Translated by T.H.L. Parker, W. B. Johnston, Harold Knight and J.L.M Haire. Peabody: Hendrickson Publishers, 2010.
CD II/2	Karl Barth, *The Doctrine of God*. Vol. 2.2 of *Church Dogmatics*. Edited by G. W. Bromiley and T. F. Torrance. Translated by G.W. Bromiley, J.C. Campbell, Iain Wilson, J. Strathearn McNab, Harold Knight and R. A. Stewart. Peabody: Hendrickson Publishers, 2010.
CD IV/1	Karl Barth, *The Doctrine of Reconciliation*. Vol. 4.1 of *Church Dogmatics*. Edited by G. W. Bromiley and T. F. Torrance. Translated by G. W. Bromiley. Peabody: Hendrickson Publishers, 2010.
CD IV/3.1	Karl Barth, *The Doctrine of Reconciliation*. Vol. 4.3.1 of *Church Dogmatics*. Edited by G. W. Bromiley and T. F. Torrance. Translated by G. W. Bromiley. Peabody: Hendrickson Publishers, 2010.
CSG	Paul S. Fiddes, *The Creative Suffering of God*. Oxford: Clarendon, 1988.

FAL	Paul S. Fiddes, *Freedom and Limit: A Dialogue between Literature and Christian Doctrine*. Basingstoke Macon: Macmillan, 1991.
PIG	Paul S. Fiddes, *Participating in God: A Pastoral Doctrine of the Trinity*. London: Darton, Longman, & Todd. 2000.
PEPS	Paul S. Fiddes, *Past Event and Present Salvation: The Christian Idea of Atonement*. London: Darton, Longman, & Todd, 1989.
TPE	Paul S. Fiddes, *The Promised End: Eschatology in Theology and Literature*. Oxford: Blackwell. 2000.
SWKG	Paul S. Fiddes, *Seeing the World and Knowing God: Hebrew Wisdom and Christian Doctrine in a Late-Modern Context*. Oxford: Oxford University Press. 2013.

Introduction

SETTING THE SCENE

IN 1993 THE INTERCESSION Working Group (IWG) of the Lausanne Committee for World Evangelization met in London to discuss the rapid advancement of "Spiritual Warfare" (SW hereafter) teaching and practice among Evangelicals and Pentecostals around the world. This meeting resulted with a written statement on "spiritual conflict" in The Lausanne Covenant.[1] The statement is an expansion on the original statement on spiritual conflict in clause 12 of the 1974 Lausanne Covenant.[2] By 1993 many voices from Asia and Africa were stating to the western church of the constant reality of dark powers and SW where they live. These voices catalyzed the discussion that led to the forming of the 1993 statement, which, while recognizing that the influence of the enlightenment had dulled the western mind to spiritual realities, acknowledged that the overall global context of the mid-1990s was one of increasing openness to and interest in the occult and dark arts.

Two factors precipitated this rise and interest in SW according to the Lausanne committee. First, the growth of the church in the global south, situated in cultures explicitly open to the dark side of the spiritual realm; this church and its worldview is then exported around the world via mass migration of people from the global south to the west. Second, the decline of Christianity in the west has resulted in an increased interest in eastern religious practice, a sensationalism of the occult, and a

---

1. "Lausanne Statement on Spiritual Warfare (1993)," Lausanne Movement, accessed February 18, 2025, (https://www.lausanne.org/content/statement/statement-on-spiritual-warfare-1993)

2. Padilla, "Spiritual Conflict," 205.

progressive reversion back to pre-Christian pagan belief. Collectively this has prepared the ground to receive a nuanced Christian gospel message that emphasizes the spirit realm and a semi-dualistic struggle between good and evil.[3] These factors collectively lead to an ever-increasing juxtaposition of contrasting worldviews ubiquitously present around the globe and in the world-wide church, especially Evangelical, Pentecostal and Catholic-charismatic expressions.[4]

This means that in western culture, as enlightenment-modernity is replaced by the current late-modern milieu, there is a greater openness to spiritual ideas such as angels and demons than in the past. No longer will the mention of the devil, angels or demons bring the social conversation to a halt.[5] Rather, angels are one of the main comeback tales of recent times,[6] and evil characters are central to many blockbuster films.[7] Indeed, a brief perusal of a modern book shop will make one aware of the ever-increasing availability of books on witchcraft and the occult.[8] Therefore, as interest in the supernatural rises in western culture and the epicenter of Christianity shifts towards the global south, there has been a concomitant rise of intrigue within the church of matters pertaining to spiritual beings; their ontology, purpose and role in the spiritual war behind the scenes. With that has come much debate concerning the nature of SW, Christians and demonization, demonization and mental health,[9] whether Satan is a personal being or mythical-malevolent force, and whether or not there are demonic spirits over geographical or sociological territories.[10]

The situation that now exists is the culmination of a number of decades of researching, writing and practice of the spirit realm, both in the

---

3. "Lausanne Statement." The statement notes the sizeable popularity of Frank Perretti's three fictional novels about SW, *This Present Darkness, Piercing the Darkness, The Prophet*, widely held to be the Christian equivalent of the film *The Exorcist* in raising awareness of SW in the psyche and zeitgeist of Christian sub-culture.

4. Jenkins, *The Next Christendom*.

5. Wink, *Unmasking*, 1.

6. Noll, *Angels of Light*, 11.

7. For example, Dr Hannibal Lecter in "Silence of the Lambs." Delbanco, *The Death of Satan*, 19.

8. A cursory search on the Waterstones website reveals over 1000 titles on the occult. Accessed February 18, 2025, (https://www.waterstones.com/books/search/term/occult).

9. Virkler, "Demonic Involvement in Human," 96–101.

10. Wagner (ed.), *Territorial Spirits*; Lowe, *Territorial Spirits and World*.

church and culture. For the Lausanne statement of 1993 reflected a time period many consider to be the zenith of the SW movement. In fact, by the 1990s there had already been at least two decades of popular teaching on the subject as the charismatic renewal movement spread through different Christian denominations. To illustrate, in the UK Anglican church renewal movement a few decades after the ministry of the first British Anglican-charismatic pioneer, Alexander Boddy, Pentecostal happenings took place among a number of Anglican curates in the 1960s and 70s which resulted in a large number of charismatic Anglican clergy getting involved in SW teaching and praxis. Of this large group, three—namely Michael Harper, David Watson and Michael Green—published books specifically on the subject of SW.[11]

These three texts were part of a deluge of popular texts on SW that appeared in the years from the 1970s to mid-1990s, with the sole intent of raising the level of awareness within churches regarding the heavenly realms, especially the sphere of the demonic.[12] Many of these texts cover similar ground: a definition of SW,[13] biblical data on demons and evil spirits,[14] and practical guidelines on SW and deliverance ministry.[15] Indeed, there has been a steady flow of general texts on SW from the 1990s to the present day covering similar themes.[16] Questions about SW, evil, theodicy, angels and demons, and so on, are now so prevalent across the world, that it is a subject within doctrine which is constantly in need of research, examination, development and sermonic address.[17]

---

11. Harper, *Spiritual Warfare*; Watson, *God's Freedom Fighters*; Watson, *Discipleship*, 167–86; Green, *I Believe in Satan's*; cf. Smith, *The Church Militant*, 30–44. Perhaps because of its narrower focus on deliverance and exorcism, Smith omits John Richards' well known text *But Deliver Us From Evil* from the list. Also, Collins, *Exorcism and Deliverance*, 76–80; Young, *A History of*, 131–32.

12. "Classic" texts include Anderson, *Victory Over*; Mae Hammond, *Pigs in the*; Horrobin, *Healing Through*; and Koch, *Between Christ*.

13. Gross, *Miracles, Demons*, 111–23; Arnold, *3 Crucial Questions*, 17–72.

14. Murphy, *The Handbook for*, 192–425; Wagner, *Spiritual Warfare Strategy*, 117–241.

15. Sherman, *Spiritual Warfare for*, 179–97; MacNutt, *Deliverance from*, 167–255.

16. For example, Beilby and Eddy, *Understanding Spiritual Warfare*; Beck, *Reviving Old Scratch*; and Hallowell, *Playing With Fire*.

17. Keller, *Preaching: Communicating*, 154–55.

SYSTEMATIC THEOLOGY—AN INTEGRATIVE APPROACH

Broadly speaking, this thesis is a systematic theology of SW. As the title states, it is a construction of a Baptist-charismatic systematic theology of SW in dialogue with the Baptist theologian Paul S. Fiddes. However, as will become clear throughout the thesis, for two reasons the theology articulated will be as interdisciplinary as systematic. First, SW is a concept that a number of theological disciplines debate. The multidisciplinary nature of the subject is seen in the copious amount of work that seeks to tackle this broad matter from different perspectives. In addition to the above-mentioned general and popular texts on the subject, there are academic works exploring the various ways one can approach the subjects of evil, suffering, the demonic, and Satan, which can all fit under the rubric "SW."

To illustrate, biblical scholarship. Old and New Testament scholarship have been researching, in-depth, the cultural context, worldview and belief systems of the Ancient Near East and first century Palestine when it comes to the spirit realm. For instance, questions are asked about the only four places in the Hebrew Bible that the noun הַשָּׂטָן (*the śaṭân*) appears and what it signifies in those contexts.[18] Or what influence did the surrounding neighbors, with their own beliefs about evil beings, have on Israel's development of The Satan.[19] Moreover, passages about "divine councils" such as Deuteronomy 32 and Psalm 82 have led to exegetical investigation about the implications of this concept for Israel's understanding of Yahwistic monism.[20] Research into certain passages has revealed Old Testament theological themes such as the "divine warrior" motif of Yahweh,[21] and even caused some scholars to explicate the corollaries of Old Testament texts on systematic questions such as divine omnipotence.[22]

---

18. Numbers 22; Job 1–2; Zechariah 3; 1 Chronicles 21. Scholars conclude that because of the pronoun used with "Satan" it cannot refer to a name but to forensic imagery of an accuser who opposes divine plans. Breytenbach and Day, "Satan," 1369–80; Forsyth, *The Old Enemy*, 107–23.

19. Wray and Mobley, *The Birth of Satan*, 75–94.

20. Laato, "The Devil in the," 5–17; Heiser, "Co-Regency in Ancient Israel's," 195–225.

21. Longman III and Reid, *God is a.*

22. Levenson, *Creation and the Persistence.*

Within New Testament scholarship much is made of the discovery of the Dead Sea Scrolls at Qumran.[23] From these ancient texts scholars have unearthed an abundance of information about the development of a systematic demonology in the Qumran tradition, providing "a rich vocabulary for the prince of the evil demons."[24] From Jubilees and the Enoch books comes the claim that the origin of the demonic is the rebellion and lust of the watcher angels, via an in-depth account of the Genesis 6 narrative involving the sons of God marrying human women and producing giants, the Nephilim, as their progeny.[25] Much of this second temple scholarship lays the groundwork for the first century Palestinian Jewish attitudes and beliefs regarding the realm of the spirit world, and some of the texts appear to be in the background of 2 Peter 2:4 and Jude 6.[26]

According to Wright, via Jesus of Nazareth's announcement about the coming kingdom of God, the gospels delineate a multitudinous account of the problem of evil and how the kerygma and praxis of the kingdom confronts the darkness.[27] Indeed, because of the multifarious nature of evil, it has been argued that Jesus operated as an exorcist, much like other exorcists of the time.[28] Perhaps this role was birthed during Jesus' 40 days of temptation in the wilderness, which in the contemporary Jewish imagination was a haunt for demons.[29] As an exorcist, this influences the content of Jesus' teaching by often using parables with a Godward view in order to counter the Satanward view of the Jewish culture.[30] This belief in and exercise of exorcism continued, so it is claimed, by many of the New Testament koinonia and ecclesia,[31] as well as many of the churches of the 2nd century.[32]

---

23. Most of the focus has been on Jubilees and 1 and 2 Enoch, fragments and translations of which were discovered in the Qumran caves.

24. Ferguson, *Demonology*, 76–77.

25. According to both Jubilees and 1 Enoch demons originated from the Watchers. They are the spirits of the giants, and they happen to be evil spirits, i.e. demons. Ferguson, *Demonology*, 70; cf. Frohlich, "Evil in," 33–35.

26. Kelly, *Towards the Death*, 19–23.

27. Wright, *Evil and the Justice*, 45–63.

28. Twelftree, *Jesus the Exorcist*, 136–56; Twelftree, *Jesus The Miracle*, 281–92.

29. Ferdinando, *The Message of*, 74–81.

30. Kallas, *Jesus and the Power*, 141–51.

31. Twelftree, *Christ Triumphant*, 85–134. Some claim that exorcisms only happened in the Gospels and Acts, see Thomas, *The Devil, Disease*, 307–9.

32. Twelftree, *In the Name of Jesus*, 209–75; Daunton-Fear, *Healing in the Early*, 40–67.

If we take biblical scholarship into SW and frame it as "research and systematization," then "meaning ascription and implementation" could be housed within the theological encyclopedic domains of practical and pastoral theology. In these disciplines there are no shortage of texts containing various claimed phenomenon concerning SW, claims that I will not critique but rather accept as existent and use as described.[33] Much of it focusses on anecdotal accounts of deliverance prayer and exorcism rites, especially from Catholic and Anglican authors since there is a long history of exorcism and deliverance in these church traditions, and they have their own international association of exorcists (AIE) and ministries of deliverance.[34] Also, in light of some fatal consequences of exorcisms,[35] some practical theology texts helpfully target safeguarding implementation.[36]

As well as biblical studies and pastoral theology, much ink has been spilled considering evil in all its forms within philosophy of religion. What is termed "the problem of evil" is consensually held to be arguably the most potent challenge to theism and has been called the "rock of atheism."[37] Indeed, it is by far the most written about subject in the last few decades within the discipline.[38] The standardized format of the "argument from evil" has a long history. In the sixth century Boethius asked, "If God indeed does exist, what is the source of evil?"[39] Twelve hundred years later, Hume expanded and developed Boethius' question to ask of God, "Is he willing to prevent evil, but not able? Then he is impotent. Is he able, but not willing? Then he is malevolent. Is he both able and willing?

---

33. A selection of texts includes Amorth, *An Exorcist Tells*; Linn and Linn, *Deliverance Prayer*; MacNutt, *Healing*; MacNutt, *Deliverance from*; Martin, *Hostage to the Devil*; Richards, *But Deliver Us*.

34. The AIE's statutes were recognized by the Catholic Church only in 2014. Of course, the Catholic church has always assumed the existence of angels and demons since the Lateran IV council in 1215. Quay, "Angels and Demons," 20–45. The aforementioned John Richards was instrumental in establishing the "Christian Exorcism Study Group (CESG)" with recommendations on ecclesial authority structures and permission in cases of genuine possession. Young, *A History of Anglican*, 129–30. In 1987 the CESG changed its name to the "Christian Deliverance Study Group" as a reflection of how rarely demonic possession is discovered and actual exorcism needed.

35. Allen, *Possessed*; Goodman, *The Exorcism of*.

36. Church of England Working Party, *A Time to Heal*, 167–81; Duffey, *Lessons Learned*.

37. Astley, Brown and Loades, *Evil*, 1–3; Davis, *Encountering Evil*, 1–6;

38. Hasker, *The Triumph of God*, 15–16; Hick, *Evil and the God*, 365–86.

39. Boethius, The Consolation of, 11.

Whence then is evil?"[40] More recently, moral philosopher McCloskey asserts, "The problem of evil is a very simple one to state. There is evil in the world; yet the world is said to be the creation of a good and omnipotent God. How is this possible? Surely a good, omnipotent God would have made a world free of evil of any kind?"[41]

However, as has been pointed out, the problem of evil, i.e. theodicy, as articulated above is fundamentally a philosophical and logical problem. It does not consider the probabilistic, epistemological or existential approaches to the problem.[42] The multilateral challenge is why Ricoeur dubbed the question of evil as one that resists reflection and remains inscrutable.[43] Types of evil are delineated into different categories: moral, natural, diabolical, and gratuitous or dysteleological which collectively create different questions in theodicy such as, is this the best possible world; do we need first order suffering in order to experience second order positive goods; or what is the cost-effectiveness of evil and how are we to quantify suffering in theodicy? Some philosophers re-articulate Augustine's scheme defining evil as *privatio boni* whereas others follow an "Irenaean theodicy" as more recently advanced by Schleiermacher.[44] Still others proffer a different approach, such as Kelsey's argument that since rationalistic theology will not produce the needed answers there needs to be a great level of ability to discern what is going on in the spirit realm; there is a real need for the spiritual gift of discernment.[45] As we will see a constructed theology of SW routinely considers and engages with philosophy of religion questions of theodicy and their implications for theology.

The second reason why the constructed theology will be as interdisciplinary as systematic is because of the choice to engage with the written corpus of Paul S. Fiddes, a theologian whose theological *oeuvre* is commodious. While Fiddes holds a professorial role in systematic theology at the University of Oxford, he prefers the nomenclature "constructive" theologian over systematic since he has spent his entire academic career

40. Hume, *Dialogues Concerning*, 198.
41. McCloskey, "The Problem of Evil," 187.
42. For an overview of the approaches to the problem of evil, see Peterson, *God and Evil*. The logical problem of evil for the philosopher is different to the existential problem of evil for the pastor—both belong to the complex called the problem of evil. Inwagen, *Christian Faith and*, viii–ix.
43. Ricoeur, *The Symbolism*, 151–57.
44. Hick, *Evil and*, 35–235; and Hick, "An Irenaean Theodicy," 39–68.
45. Kelsey makes this claim, not from 1 Corinthians 12:10, but from depth psychology and his reading of Jung. Kelsey, *Discernment*, 51–85.

writing connectional theology between disciplines.[46] In order to locate a Baptist-charismatic theology of SW within a doctrine of God, it is imperative to draw on, engage and critique a theologian who writes with breadth, is inter-connectional, and baptistic. Fiddes is that theologian and has amassed a significant amount of theological work on the doctrine of God in a career of approximately 50 years. Since his appointment in 1972 as a research fellow at Regent's Park College he has had a prolific scholarly career of immense proportions.[47]

The nature of his theological enterprise demonstrates congruence with the three proverbial hats he has worn within Regents Park for the last half-century: as a professor of systematic theology he has published extensively on different doctrines of theology; as a graduate and lecturer of mediaeval language and literature, as well as one of the founders of the Oxford Centre for the Study of Christianity and Culture, he has written widely on the relationship between theology and literature; and as an ordained minister in the Baptist Union of Great Britain he has contributed greatly to Baptist scholarship.[48] For these and other reasons that will become apparent throughout the thesis, he makes a suitable dialogue partner for the interdisciplinary subject of SW.

THIS STUDY

Historically relatively little systematic-doctrinal work on evil forces and SW has been done.[49]

Until the turn of this century when, so it is argued, Gregory Boyd raised "the current discussion of spiritual warfare to a new and unanticipated level of scholarly investigation,"[50] theologians rarely wrote dogmatic or systematic theology on the evil spiritual realm. There are some

---

46. Fiddes, personal communication with the author, 15 & 16 March 2016.

47. His published monographs, journal articles, book reviews, edited volumes (as both editor and contributor), and reports number to date more than 200. For an in-depth biographical account see Clarke and Fiddes, *Dissenting Spirit*, 153–221.

48. Clarke and Moore, "Introduction," 1–6.

49. Famously, having spent 150 pages developing his angelology and kingdom of heaven thesis, Barth finally turns his attention to give a "momentary glance at demons," for only 13 pages. *CD* III/3, §51.1–3, 369–531.

50. Wagner and Greenwood, "Response to Gregory," 169, cf. Boyd, *God at War*, interior flyleaf. Others who agree with Wagner concerning *God at War* and Boyd, *Satan and the Problem of Evil*, include Anderson, Review of *God at War*, 128–29; Long, Review of *God at War*, 125; Hall, Review of *Satan and the Problem*, 90–91.

possible rare exceptions in the 20th century,[51] but in comparison to the substantial amount of work that has come from the above-mentioned disciplines—as well as popular-general texts—there is still very little systematic theology work addressing this somewhat controversial area of Christian belief and praxis.[52]

This thesis, therefore, is a Baptist-charismatic contribution to the debate in order to build upon the small amount of systematic-theological work that has already been done.[53] The specific research question answered is whether or not the contemporary Baptist theology of Paul S. Fiddes offers a better framework than other theologies (traditional and modern) to construct a doctrine of God that best underpins a theology of SW? For, as will be shown below in chapter seven, the theological problem this thesis seeks to address is whether or not Fiddes' baptistic theology offers a contemporary, capacious, effective and dynamic doctrine of God into which a theology of SW can be situated, without succumbing to the weaknesses of other accounts.

Stated slightly differently and with more exactitude, will a critical evaluation and reconstruction of Fiddes' theology—with emphases on God's kenotic sovereignty, passibility, openness to the created order and panentheistic reality—offer a more effective schema to construct a doctrine of God that best explicates a unified theology of SW than the strong sovereignty account of Powlison, the dualistic rationale of Wagner, the neo-molinist justification of Boyd, or the Jungian integrative case of Wink?

METHOD AND SCOPE

Methodologically, this thesis will be a scholarly conversation between Fiddes and me. As his main interlocutor, I will bring into the dialogue alternative ideas gleaned from other theologians and contributors from the literary corpus of systematic theology and SW thinking. With regard to scope, establishing a Fiddesian doctrine of God commodious enough

51. Thielicke, *Between God*; Torrance, *The Apocalypse*; Cox, *On Not Leaving*.
52. Warren, *Cleansing*, 23.
53. It is over 20 years since a British Baptist scholar last published a theology of SW. Nigel Wright's *A Theology of the Dark Side* is an updated version of his original 1989 publication *The Fair Face of Evil* and close reading and analysis reveal some significant theological adaptations in the 14 years between the editions. Wright, *The Fair Face*, 17–52, cf. Wright, *A Theology of*, 29–61. More recent works include Kay and Parry, *Exorcism & Deliverance*; Warren, *Cleansing*; Torr, *A Dramatic*; Smith, *The Church Militant*; Bradnick, *Evil, Spirits*; Löfstedt, *The Devil, Demons*.

to locate a theology of SW into, is the major priority of this thesis. Therefore, only theological issues common to both Fiddes' doctrine of God and SW theology will be analyzed and discussed. Areas of discussion in divine conflict studies not addressed by Fiddes will not be considered. Once Fiddes' doctrine of God is delineated, then the main theological-constructive section of the thesis will follow, situating a unified SW theology into the doctrine of God.

The thesis logically separates into three distinct, yet interrelated, parts. In part one, the reader is introduced to the theological world of Paul S. Fiddes. A general introduction and overall summary of his doctrine of God is followed by an assembled Fiddesian doctrine of evil, one that is both systematic-connectional and interdisciplinary. Part two explores the three main incommunicable and necessary properties of a doctrine of God, namely omniscience, omnipotence and omnipresence, which centrally pertain to a coherent theology of SW. This then leads onto the final part of the thesis, an operation of constructive theology in which a theology of SW, one that can be located within the established doctrine of God, will be delineated and situated into a nuanced articulation of God's nature and character.

PART ONE

The Theology of Paul Fiddes

1

Fiddes' Doctrine of God

INTRODUCTION

THE PURPOSE OF THIS chapter is to elucidate the key themes in Paul S. Fiddes' theological work on the doctrine of God. The above-mentioned separation of Fiddes' theological corpus into three areas of interest is for didactic clarity only and should not be seen as a suggestion that there is little interconnectedness in his work. Indeed, like all sophisticated theologians, most of what he says is ultimately grounded in the doctrine of God.[1] However, for the purpose of this chapter, I will draw upon those key works of Fiddes that focus primarily on analyzing, discussing and contributing systematically to the Doctrine of God.[2] Other writings of Fiddes on the doctrine of God will be used to buttress the main texts where appropriate. Focus on these key sources will not only allow for elucidation of Fiddes' doctrine of God but also possibly reveal whether or not there has been any change or development in his thought over the thirty years covered by these texts.

---

1. Fiddes' conviction that the Christian God is passible who suffers in love with his creation is used in order to better understand literature such as Gerald Manley Hopkins' sonnets and is also a strategic doctrine that is significant for Baptist believers. CSG, cf. FAL, 138–45; Fiddes, *Tracks and Traces*, 57–61.

2. CSG; PEPS; PIG; Fiddes, "Relational Trinity," 159–85; Fiddes, "The Atonement," 103–22.

This chapter will bifurcate into two halves. Before attempting to critically delineate Fiddes' doctrine of God, some historical and methodological issues will be examined. First, the reasons for the increased popularity of the concept of a passible God which concomitantly infers problems with the traditional-historical position, and second, a shift regarding the appropriate sources used to formulate a doctrine of God with special reference to Fiddes' strong advocacy that spiritual life *experience* should be a more influential source for theological formulation. Following these considerations attention will then turn to Fiddes' doctrine of God: specifically looking at the nature and character of the triune God of the Christian faith; the claimed fact of, and the way in which, God is a passible God of suffering love; the impact of God's suffering on salvation and atonement theology; and the ways in which a central divine attribute of suffering redefines other divine attributes.

THE CONTEMPORARY NEED FOR A PASSIBLE GOD

As other theologians have identified, a number of factors have driven the current suspicion in some quarters concerning God's impassibility.[3] Many who critique the traditional doctrine of impassibility, especially the impassibility of God's feelings,[4] have become convinced that God suffers and is therefore passible with humanity.[5] These scholars hold the belief in a suffering God axiomatic for modern theology,[6] a kind of "new orthodoxy."[7] Fiddes concurs and argues that there are some very good reasons for adapting our understanding of God's nature and character, both ontologically and immanently, in order to speak coherently into the contemporary *zeitgeist*. He lists four central developments that drive the need to articulate a passible God: a new understanding of love;

---

3. Weinandy, "Does God," 35; McGrath, *Christian Theology*, 273–79.

4. Creel, *Divine Impassibility*, 113.

5. Weinandy lists scholars who defend the full passibility of God including Jüngel, a very influential theologian for Fiddes. Fiddes criticizes Webster for claiming that Jüngel is not a divine passibility scholar whereas Jüngel actually describes God facing both death and non-being. Weinandy, "Does God," 35, cf. Fiddes, "A Review of *Eberhard Jüngel*, 265–69.

6. Lee finds it incredible that so little has been written on the suffering of God. Lee, *God Suffers*, 1.

7. Bauckham, "Only the Suffering God," 6–7.

Christology and a theology of the cross; theodicy and human suffering; and a new worldview about the nature of the reality of the world.[8]

First, there is insight from modern psychology regarding the nature of love, a movement away from love being defined as an attitude of will and mind that is devoid from emotion to a posture of suffering love that involves empathy for and vulnerability with the sufferer. As process theology portrays "God is the great companion—the fellow sufferer who understands."[9] This change in understanding helps reiterate the often-ignored biblical theme found especially in the prophets that Yahweh's pathos means that he suffers when his covenant people reject his covenant *hesed*. In fact, the Old Testament describes Yahweh as not simply sharing in the suffering of his people but actually a God whose *hesed* summons all humans to enter into and share in the suffering that he already feels for humanity.[10] The book of Hosea quintessentially tells this tale: Hosea, Fiddes argues, marries the known prostitute Gomer in order to partake in the suffering that God is already enduring due to the covenant unfaithfulness of his people Israel.[11]

Secondly, the suffering of Jesus Christ on the cross, which has always been central to understanding the Christian faith (1 Corinthians 1:18–31), is now understood in a different, less-dichotomized way than that inherited from Chalcedon. No longer can we define personhood in a compartmentalized way but rather if Christ is one with God and humanity, then he must be so as a complete person. Starting at Luther's "theology of the cross," we need to go further and understand that the suffering of Christ on the cross creates a theology *from* the cross (*kreuzestheologie*), an actualized event in human history that explicitly reveals God's triune, eternal nature.[12] Rooted in the centurion's response after Christ died (Mark 15:39), Fiddes states "God suffers in the cross in *oneness* with the

---

8. Fiddes, "Suffering, Divine," 634.

9. Whitehead, *Process and Reality*, 351. In CSG, Fiddes makes little reference to scripture (only key texts such as Exodus 3:14, Jeremiah 31, Hosea 11 and Mark 15:39) whereas both Whitehead and Hartshorne are among the most cited authors. This offers a marked contrast with other passibilists who base their arguments in "divine repentance" type texts such as 1 Samuel 15. For example, Fretheim, "The Repentance," 47–70.

10. CSG, 19–25.

11. Fiddes, "The Cross of Hosea," 176–78. This paper well illustrates the influence on Fiddes' thinking of H. Wheeler Robinson, especially his two key texts *Suffering Human and Divine* and *The Cross in the Old Testament*.

12. CSG, 25–31.

person of Christ; God suffers *eternally* in the cross; God is most *Godlike* in the suffering of the cross."[13]

To further develop his point, Fiddes suggests that this change in our understanding of Christ crucified and the theology that comes from the cross will alter the meaning of the atonement for this modern era. Indeed, argues Fiddes, this is not unprecedented since church history clearly shows us that ideas regarding the atonement have changed from era to era in order to make the atonement communicable to the current milieu. Therefore, viewing God as suffering in his entire being through Christ on the cross helps the church today communicate the atonement in ways that offer answers to a modern society struggling under the weight of personality fragmentation and loss of social relationships.[14]

Third, "there seems little doubt that the problem of human suffering has been the most powerful motivation in recent years for affirming the suffering of God."[15] Ubiquitous media has created an ever-increasing global consciousness of suffering, pain and evil among humanity which renders the impassibility of God more tenuous in a growing awareness and context of theodicy. When affliction and torment avail "it is a consolation to those who suffer to know that God suffers too, and understands their situation from within."[16]

The genocide at Auschwitz, more than any other historical event, took evil and suffering to an unprecedented level, according to Fiddes. In fact he asks whether it is at all possible to do theology after Auschwitz?[17] In the face of such tragedy and evil the most satisfying (though not perfect) theodicy is the "freewill defense" by which God passes onto creation a radical freedom that is irrevocable and which places limits on himself. To morally justify this, Fiddes claims, it is imperative that God also share in the suffering caused by evil human actions located in the irrevocable freedom given to creation. In suffering with creation, God is both present with and also protesting against the pain befalling creation, which

---

13. CSG, 31.

14. PEPS, 3–13.

15. Fiddes, "Suffering, Divine," 636; Other passibilists come from countries or racial groups that have experienced much pain and suffering in the twentieth century. Weinandy, *Does God*, 2–6.

16. CSG, 31.

17. Aguilar asks similar questions in a post-Rwandan genocide era. Aguilar, *Theology, Liberation*.

he often does in silence and hiddenness, and this serves as a pattern for humans to imitate with each other.[18]

Fourthly, Fiddes asserts that the way in which humanity thinks about the world will influence the way we think about God the creator of the world. Unlike past worldviews that saw God and the world as static and immutable, today the world is viewed as being in a state of flux and decay, a living organism instead of a machine.[19] Within theology much of this view has been developed by process theology that posits that God is the designer who has to work *inside* the organism and experience its growing pains. God the co-creator of the universe suffers just like the creatures in the world and this means that God can only *cause* by persuasion and influence, that everything in the universe enjoys some kind of experience or feeling, and that there is a place for sacrifice in the world systems.[20]

Defining reality as "event" and "becoming" in which there is potential that grows into actual entities, significantly changes the doctrine of God. As Fiddes summarizes, Process theology holds that God is di-polar in nature consisting of an immutable primordial-nature pole and a pre-hending, interactive and mutable consequent-nature pole and this redefines divine omniscience as God's perfect knowledge of possibility and actuality, not possibility *as* actuality, and omnipotence in terms of persuasion.[21] However, despite accommodating into his doctrine of God elements of process thinking, Fiddes is no process theologian. He fundamentally disagrees with process thought that creativity is *the* supreme value and instead argues that God's limitations and suffering are rooted in his freedom, desire, will and decision as creator. He also takes issue with the di-polar nature of God as it is insufficiently trinitarian, insulating part of God's being from the suffering of the world instead of allowing God in his entire being to be changed by the world.[22]

The above reasons for why Fiddes believes that we need to hold a conviction about a passible God of suffering love not only present a positive case for change but negatively render the historical tradition of impassibility as erroneous and not an accurate representation of the God of the Hebrew and Christian scriptures. For this charge centers around the Harnackian "history of Dogma" thesis which claims that

18. PEPS, 207–20.
19. CSG, 37–39.
20. CSG, 39–42.
21. Fiddes, "Process Theology," 472–74.
22. CSG, 44–45.

Greek philosophical ideas increasingly influenced Christian thinking in a negative way and this needs to be admitted and addressed. However, no serious scholar denies that the early Church Fathers used Greek philosophical concepts;[23] rather the debate centers on whether the use of philosophy was legitimate, and did it aid or impede articulation of a doctrine of God?

Some passibilists hold to a strong form of the ruination by philosophy theory.[24] Pollard is scathing in his polemic against the tradition of impassibility arguing that the acceptance of Greek concepts radically changed Semitic ideas to the point of being completely unrecognizable which resulted in a gradual reduction of the living God of the Old Testament into a transcendent and nameless absolute of Greek philosophy.[25] In contrast, Fiddes holds to a softer version of this theory and argues that while the doctrine of God does need re-articulation into a passible framework, there are some understandable reasons why the early Fathers proposed an impassable God and there is a need to deconstruct the case for divine impassability and offer a more careful and nuanced alternative.

To begin, Fiddes states that the fickle gods of the Greeks and Romans created a cultural context that drove the need to conclude God as a necessary being. However, now in a current post-holocaust context this calls for a God who suffers through his participation with the world.[26] Second, this drive for a necessary God meant that perfection and simplicity were fundamental to God's being and so any suggestion of *change* or *complexity* was immediately condemned as this would infer that God was not complete and needed some kind of improvement. Subsequently, this disqualified any conceptual form of divine suffering since—despite the best efforts of Tertullian and some modern scholars to create a one-dimensional definition of divine suffering that involves *no* change—to suffer, either internally or externally, means to go through some sort of experience of change.[27] Yet there is a need for caution in the way that we talk about "change" and, even though Fiddes disagrees with

---

23. Advocates of God's impassibility such as Weinandy and Hart have no problem at all admitting that the Fathers used Greek philosophy. Weinandy, "Does God," 38 and Hart, "No Shadow," 205–6.

24. Gavrilyuk, *The Suffering*, 176.

25. Pollard, "The Impassibility," 353–56.

26. PIG, 176–79.

27. CSG, 57–63; cf. PIG, 170–76. Little difference in Fiddes' thinking on this subject in the twelve years between the two texts.

his conclusions, it would be advantageous to follow Aquinas' example of careful speech when stating that God is unchanging and that he only changes *in certain ways*.[28]

One way Aquinas is adamant that God does not change, and thereby suffer from, is in the kind of change that humans grow in experiential knowledge of. Conversely Fiddes states the opposite, suggesting that our understanding of God and his ability to change and suffer *has to be* grounded in human experience of change and suffering, especially the experience of inner feeling suffering and outside impact suffering.[29] This raises the question of human experience as a source of theology, a subject to which I now turn.

THE PLACE OF EXPERIENCE IN FORMULATING A DOCTRINE OF GOD

"Even if Fiddes' proposed understanding of God makes for creative and imaginative philosophical theology, unfortunately it makes for poor biblical theology. This god is hardly the God of the Bible."[30] Ware's candid criticism betrays the fundamental conflict over what sources should be used when formulating doctrine, especially a doctrine of God. As is clear, Ware believes that scripture should be the main source, and all other sources are subservient to the supremacy of scripture. This understanding undergirds judgment of Fiddes' work as a philosophical treatise or philosophical theology, not biblical or systematic theology.[31]

Fiddes does not hide which sources he draws upon in creating a doctrine of a suffering God. There is no denying that he draws mainly on German theology *from* the cross (including Luther, Barth and Hegel), process philosophy and theology (especially the work of Whitehead and Hartshorne), death of God theology (Altizer and others), and finally classical theism.[32] He uses these four strands in an interweaving and interpenetrating way to construct a theology of a suffering God. Indeed, some

---

28. CSG, 49–57.
29. CSG, 52–53 cf. 47–49.
30. Ware, Review of *The Creative*, 238.
31. Tripole, Review of *The Creative*, 381–82.

32. CSG, 12–15. Fiddes states that most of his theology is drawn from the six "greats" of twentieth-century protestant, catholic and process theology: Respectively, Barth, Tillich, von Balthasar, Rahner, Whitehead, & Hartshorne. Fiddes, personal communication with author.

reviewers have noted the strong dialectical conflation of the four traditions with much conversation, cross-pollination and synthesis. This is especially true of Fiddes' disproportionate use of process theology which he aligns with Barth's insistence on the concept of the *freedom* of God in order to formulate a God who freely chooses to be in love and wants to receive love from creation.[33]

For Fiddes German theology *from* the cross acts as the central conduit, bridging the real-life faith-historical event of the crucifixion of Jesus of Nazareth to the *experience* of God in the heart of his triune nature. This drives the central thesis of his doctrine of divine suffering love which is to "speak consistently of a God who suffers eminently and yet is still God, and a God who suffers universally and yet is still present uniquely and decisively in the sufferings of Christ."[34] The title "Son of God" has to be acknowledged in any doctrine of the atonement as it grounds the fact that the son-ship of Jesus to the Father has eternal significance for God's nature and character. Jesus' oneness with the Father means that the cry of dereliction on the cross reveals the forsakenness in the center and heart of the Trinity.[35]

Forsakenness, dereliction and death at the cross, which are therefore in the very center of God's nature, naturally raise the question of how to appropriately speak of the suffering and, ultimately, the death of God? Fiddes suggests that, though the death of God movement is past, the questions asked, and answers given are still salient today. Altizer et al were dealing with the general conscious loss of a sense of God, especially now that God is not necessary in order to answer many of life's fundamental questions. They were also reacting to certain caricatures of God and so this is why it is imperative to understand God in his passibility, vulnerability and kenosis. Fiddes argues that we need to face up to God's absence and hiddenness without concluding that he no longer exists.[36] The key to understanding dereliction and death in the heart of God without concluding that he no longer exists is to take Hegel's *real* death of God seriously, that dialectically God's death is at the same time his living presence. The death of the living God means that God enters into the realm

---

33. Ware, Review of *The Creative*, 233–35; Sponheim, Review of *The Creative*, 217.

34. CSG, 3. It has been asked just how reasonable and justifiable is it to claim that humans are able to probe into the character of the divine being? Pailin, Review of *The Creative*, 60.

35. PEPS, 51–58.

36. CSG, 174–89.

of death, defeats it while facing non-being and ultimately overcomes it through the resurrection of Jesus. We can talk of degrees of perishing and relationlessness with the cross of Christ as the most extreme type of relationlessness possible. Hence, through the cross God experiences alienation in his own relationships and this brings those relationships closer. In experiencing death, God is alive.[37]

Not only did the suffering and death of Christ on the cross bring dereliction and forsakenness into the center of the triune God, it also radically changed the way Christ's disciples thought about and understood God in light of their *experience* of God's self-revelation in the crucifixion and resurrection.[38] Some of Christ's disciples were present and witnessed the pain and suffering of the crucifixion (John 19:25–27). As noted by Fiddes, Jesus pre-empts his ultimate demonstration of love when going to the cross by stating that "greater love has no one than this: to lay down one's life for one's friends" (John 15:13).[39] The cross has the power to move hearts and minds but not by compulsion or individual election. By revealing the love of God on the cross, God infused love into humanity in a way that exceeds a mere exemplarist theory of atonement.[40]

The quintessential demonstration of the redemptive power of love is the cross of Christ, a love undergirded by God's suffering and anguish. Fiddes argues that the contrast between Judas Iscariot and Jesus in the entire passion narrative amplifies God's self-sacrificing love. In his death on the cross not only was God's love put on full display, but so was the Lordship of Christ since in freedom Jesus of Nazareth chose to love, suffer and die in order to realize God's strong desire to be in fellowship with humanity.[41] Moreover, this demonstration of love was accompanied by divine forgiveness, as highlighted in Jesus' statement "Father, forgive them, for they do not know what they are doing" (Luke 23:34a), and so the death of Christ on the cross perfectly exemplifies forgiveness as a journey of endurance and anguish. Witnessing the endurance of divine

---

37. CSG, 189–206. As stated below, Fiddes asserts that all God-speech is highly metaphorical and thus inevitably lacks metaphysical exactness. Strong metaphors such as "degrees of perishing" and "relationlessness," for example, are Fiddes' attempt to understand the death of God incarnate on the cross without concluding that God is dead.

38. Fiddes, "Relational Trinity," 162–63.

39. PEPS, 155–58.

40. PEPS, 141–50.

41. PEPS, 140–68.

love and forgiveness speaks into our experience of guilt, shame, anxiety and unforgiveness.[42]

The suffering love of God, as demonstrated in the human and divine Jesus of Nazareth, offers understanding of the nature of human suffering and opens to us the use of human experience of suffering as analogous to divine suffering. Fiddes pleads that we need to avoid "one dimensional" suffering ascribed to God like in the past tradition. Learning from the human experience of *active suffering* to attribute suffering to the divine consists of both fate and action, suffering that is chosen and that which befalls in a dialectical manner; otherwise, all talk about suffering becomes largely meaningless and foreign.[43]

If, Fiddes maintains, we treat seriously human experience as analogous to divine nature and experience, and do not simply reduce it to anthropomorphic and anthropopathic language, then this opens up a whole new theological horizon for exploration into who God is and the nature of his relationship with creation.[44] It also permits treating stories outside of scripture and tradition as potential source material that allows God to speak to us through those accounts as we participate in him.[45] Seeing experiences such as living in community, having dependency in relationships, intercessory prayer, and forgiveness and reconciliation as participation in God will take those experiences to deeper and richer levels.[46]

We should note that the place of *experience* in the formulation of doctrine appears to have become more central in Fiddes' thinking as time has progressed. An early strong critique made by Fiddes about the charismatic renewal movement was that its main evidence and source material was experience and therefore it was difficult to conclude it was theologically coherent and made a contribution to the doctrine of God.[47] It also has a tendency to diminish the normative place of water-baptism in favor of the less-regular and manifestation-based "baptism in the Spirit."[48]

---

42. PEPS, 171–89.
43. CSG, 57–63.
44. PEPS, 190–206.
45. Fiddes, "God and Story," 5–22.
46. Fiddes, "Relational Trinity," 182–85. It appears that later Fiddes emphasizes that not all experiences can become normative but only those which witness to the revelation of God in Christ. Fiddes, "A Response to Andrew."
47. Fiddes, "The Theology," 19–40. Moore has the same problem with using experience either as a source or a norm. Moore, "Experience and the," 65–66.
48. Fiddes, *Charismatic Renewal*, 35–37.

However, by the turn of the century Fiddes was adamant that we need to follow the early church who spoke of the Trinity out of their experience and therefore delineate an experienced and pastoral doctrine of the Trinity; one that has been shaped by pastoral experience and also a belief in our participation in God.[49] As we will see, Fiddes' panentheistic vision of participating in God is the warp and woof of his doctrine of God.

THE NATURE AND CHARACTER OF THE TRIUNE GOD

Fretheim laments that the Christian church in the western world has relied on monarchical images of dominance and masculine power for too long. There is a need for the non-monarchical biblical witness of God to be brought to the fore.[50] Fiddes concurs and explores ways to communicate the God of scripture in ways that resonates with the contemporary and cosmopolitan cultural milieu. The way to do this is to describe God's triune nature in terms of personhood, relations, participation and a perichoretic inter-penetration both within God himself and between God and creation. This can be best articulated within a panentheistic framework. While the early church theologians managed to find language that expressed the oneness and diversity of God, as well as the distinctness of persons in the Trinity and the freedom of both divine and human persons, there is still a need to go further.[51] Fiddes avers that participation in the relations of the Trinity is the way forward since the idea of "participation" treats the triune relationships very seriously.[52]

Personal language rooted in pastoral experience is vital and very promising in helping humanity understand its relations both with God and with each other. Participative language is not subservient to analogic language proper, but rather an appropriate image for the personalness of God.[53] Seeing God as an event of relationships grounded in the language of participation can, insists Fiddes, allow us to retain the Thomistic language of "subsistent relations" so long as we raise our gaze to a "third level

---

49. PIG, 3–10.
50. Fretheim, *The Suffering of God*, xiii–xvi.
51. PIG, 13–16.
52. PIG, 11–13. Participation in the "relations," not persons, of the Trinity is arguably the unique, centripetal idea of Fiddes to which all his theology migrates. Fiddes, "Creation Out of," 184–91; Fiddes, "The quest for," 51–55; Fiddes, "Participating in the," 375–91.
53. PIG, 28–33.

of meaning"[54]: God's relations are as ontic and real as that which is either created or uncreated and their ground of existence lies within themselves.[55] This understanding is what sets the foundation for a so-called "radical" trinitarian model,[56] one that consists of genuine perichoresis thereby mirroring Jesus' high priestly prayer in John 17:21.[57]

Moreover, a genuine understanding of our participation in the divine nature (Acts 17: 28; Col 1:16–20; 2 Peter 1:4) will, asserts Fiddes, help us more effectively close the post-enlightenment gap between ontology and epistemology since we know God as we participate in life. It will also help with ecological theology and inter-personal relations since all of creation—because of its covenant with God (Genesis 9:8)—shares in the divine dance and responds to God, and participation in the Trinity closes the gap between the subject and object which will impact, intensify and deepen our relationships with each other.[58]

Fiddes believes that this social, perichoretic, panentheistic understanding of the Trinity that *actually* places human beings in participation with the relations of the Godhead also has a number of significant advantages that offer solutions to perennial problems unearthed in church history. First, it strongly counters the above-mentioned images of dominance, power and monarchical superiority that have led to subordination and abuse.[59] The divine dance that emphasizes interpenetration and focus on the movements, not the dancers, removes domination of the Father, so often used to justify oppression. It throws open relational language allowing us to talk about a motherly father or fatherly mother which, without undermining, brings equality to our understanding of the Trinity.[60] This egalitarian dance flattens out authority structures both within the state and the church and it redefines authority in terms of kenotic, humble service as modelled by Jesus in John 13. Vicious cycles of domination, power-plays and scapegoating cease when we focus on our

---

54. PIG, 34.

55. PIG, 34–46.

56. A model that has come in for significant criticism in recent years. Holmes, "Response to Paul," 186–90; Molnar, "Response to Paul," 191–96; McCall, "Response to Paul," 197–203.

57. PIG, 46–56.

58. Fiddes, "Participating in," 375–91.

59. PIG, 62–71.

60. PIG, 71–96.

participation in the Trinity and the completeness of fellowship we have with the triune God.[61]

A second advantage is a new understanding of the role and experience of intercessory prayer. Fiddes is highly critical of the traditional "two-cause" theory of prayer held by Aquinas and others suggesting that it makes the world appear to have no freedom and that God appears to be the cause for everything that happens.[62] If he is the irresistible first cause of everything that happens then is there any point making requests to him? Instead, avers Fiddes, if we view time as situated "in God" and our prayers "participating in God" then, to borrow from Barth, "God's creation of our time" happens while being influenced by our prayers.[63] By taking the process theology idea of divine action as persuasion Fiddes suggests that instead of seeing God as an object to be grasped, it is better to conceive of persuasion as part of the divine dance, a working partnership between God and the world in which God has perfect and eternal knowledge of all possibilities. Like God in the Old Testament, since God knows the power of persuasive love he can make open-ended promises that involve slight risk with regard to the *content* of the fulfilment of future promises while having assurance about the attunement of creation's choices into the divine purpose.[64]

Another helpful improvement that participating in God's movements of love creates concerns the practice of forgiveness and potential reconciliation. Forgiveness is a two-stage journey of discovery and endurance. It seeks to win the offender back into relationship and in the process overcome hostility, anxiety and self-indulgence.[65] Therefore, "when salvation is understood as an act of divine forgiveness," a journey of forgiveness that became part of God's journey when uniquely demonstrated by Christ on the cross, and realized in moments of inter-human forgiveness and possible reconciliation, this negates the need for an atonement theory to be based on legal pardon, commercial arrangements or divine wrath appeasement. Therefore, pastorally, claims Fiddes, if viewed from a

---

61. PIG, 96–108.

62. PIG, 116–20.

63. PIG, 121–26 cf. *CD* II/1, §25.2, 61–62. Holmes is highly suspect of claiming that intercessory prayer is participating in God since Fiddes embeds this claim in a "normative" experience of prayer. Holmes rejects any concept of a "normative" experience of prayer. Holmes, "Response to Paul, 187.

64. PIG, 131–44.

65. PIG, 192–97.

participation in the divine perspective, speaking forgiveness over people *before* they repent could unlock repentance and possible reconciliation since people are set free from guilt. Christ did this from the cross (Luke 23:34) as well as at other times in his earthly ministry (Matt 9:2; Luke 7:36–50; Luke 19:1–10).[66]

A final significant corollary of our participation in the divine perichoresis is greater understanding of the contentious area of bodily healing. In dialogue with a medical-missionary doctor Fiddes differentiates between three forms of the unknown in healing: the unknown in the known, the not as yet known, and the completely inexplicable type of healing that has no knowable explanation in scientific terms. Fiddes purports that the category of "supernatural healings" as the third kind and these events point to a kind of new possibility in which God is doing something *new* in nature. This can, he claims, only happen when there is cooperation and synergy between God and creation, divine initiative and creaturely response. Since the world is complex and a suffering God is on the side of victims of sickness, then the only plausible explanation of these unique healings is the conflation of divine purpose and creation's response. If there is a breaking down of that cooperation, then healing will not take place.[67]

There are other aspects of Fiddes' doctrine of God that bolster his panentheistic vision of participation in the divine perichoresis, which need mentioned. In the divine dance within God himself and between God and creation, Fiddes argues that the Spirit of God should receive greater recognition than has historically been the case. While acknowledging some ambiguity as to the anonymity and self-effacing nature of the Spirit, it is imperative to see the Spirit as a distinct mover within the triune God whose movement is represented through Old Testament images of fire, water, oil and wings.[68] Juxtaposing East and West Spirit traditions also creates the understanding of the Spirit as a *disturber*, disturbing the relationship and common life between the Father and Son, resulting in life and love constantly being renewed. Lastly, creation-ward movement

---

66. PIG, 197. Fiddes counters Swinburne's logical objection to forgiveness *before* repentance by asserting that the transformative power of salvation lies in the untidy and extravagant nature of forgiveness. PIG, 197–220.

67. Fiddes and Lees, "How are People," 12–22.

68. PIG, 251–64. Elsewhere Fiddes claims that through the same images we understand the relations of eternal generation and movements of self-giving. Fiddes, "The quest for," 51–55.

of the Spirit also creates spiritual gifts; gifts that should be fundamentally viewed as coming from the being of God, kenotic in nature and therefore not to be used as spiritual collateral in order to dominate while subordinating other gifts and persons.[69]

Other facets of the triune God in whom we participate which help us to understand him and explain him to others include his creative force of love, his fuller presence due to his inimitable relationship to time, and within that fuller presence his hiddenness within the triune relations without being absent. To state "God creates out of love" may well have a place within science as well as theology, which starts from the religious experience of love demonstrated by Jesus of Nazareth, and has significant consequences regarding God's omniscience, divine risk and openness in continual creation, use of evolution, and creation *actually* indwelling divine life.[70]

Also, to counter all visions of the future within postmodernity, Fiddes argues that one needs to view the millennial hope as an eternal dwelling of God, a kenotic humility of the incarnation that heals and fills the now while keeping the future open-ended.[71] Finally, regarding the perceived absence of God by many, Fiddes develops a theology of divine presence and place by taking the hidden wisdom of Job 28 and juxtaposing it with Plato's concept of the *Khora* (that primordial space which is both absent and present, a place and yet not-a-place). Then using highly metaphorical language, human inter-personal relationships can be viewed as analogous of the participatory relations of the triune God and so those "no-places" that exist between the human self and other selves analogously represent the places-that-are-no-places in the divine relations in which God can be present but hidden.[72]

Having sketched the grand panentheistic vision of Fiddes' doctrine of God, it is now necessary to hold up the proverbial microscope to the engine of this vision—divine pathos and suffering—in order to better understand the way Fiddes articulates it, and also unveil its impact on

---

69. PIG, 264–74; Fiddes, "The Theology of," 32–38; Fiddes' focus on the presence of the Spirit in the world and his kenotic reality may have come from Moltmann. Fiddes, Review of *God in Creation*, 262–65.

70. Fiddes, "Creation Out," 167–91.

71. Fiddes, "Millennium and Utopia," 7–25.

72. Fiddes, "The quest for," 35–55; SWKG, 218–65. Another example of Fiddes using strong metaphors and connections from elsewhere, this time to try and articulate the apparent hiddenness of an omnipresent God.

the atonement and salvation as well as on other divine attributes. The rest of the chapter will address these matters.

DIVINE PASSIBILITY OF SUFFERING LOVE

Fiddes believes that there are a number of reasons why it is vital to formulate a coherent and communicative doctrine of a passible God.[73] Of the four listed, the most prevalent in his writings focusses on a practical theodicy undergirded by a sound philosophical "freewill defense." To repeat, his argument is that the best way to elucidate and construct a solution to the theodicy problem is to advocate that it is only a suffering God who could create a world in which suffering and misery are significant aspects of reality. To suggest otherwise—i.e. that only an impassable God who is immune from change can create this kind of world—is according to Fiddes a residual "negative transcendence" of platonic philosophy.[74]

Absolutely integral to this insistence of divine passibility is the Barthian pillar that God's sovereignty lies specifically in his freedom (Fiddes would also add "desire") to *choose* to empty himself and be conditioned by the world.[75] While God is of course self-existent, he chooses not to be self-sufficient but rather open to affection and impact from creation without necessary conditioning *by* the world.[76] The theodicy problem of suffering, both human and creation, demands a God who suffers through participation with the world. Given that God gifted the world with irrevocable freewill which will inevitably lead to evil and suffering, necessitates that he must be a God who participates in it himself both externally and internally since his self-revelation determines that all external activity to God must have some analogy to his actual essence.[77]

On this basis it is plausible to hold to a doctrine of a passible God that significantly answers the current challenges of theodicy. Fiddes

---

73. See "The Contemporary Need" (pp. 4–9) section above.

74. Fiddes, "Suffering, Divine," 634–35. A good example of a contemporary impassibilist who holds to Fiddes' description of negative transcendence is John Webster. Webster, "Non ex aequo," 95–107. Fiddes responds stating it is an erroneous understanding of divine aseity, especially confusing self-existence with self-sufficiency, which feeds this negative transcendence tendency. Fiddes, "A Response to John."

75. *CD* II/1, §31.1–3, 440–677.

76. Fiddes, "Suffering, Divine," 634–35. Fiddes' emphasis on divine choice sets him apart from process theology.

77. Fiddes, "Suffering, Divine," 636.

proffers a theodicy of four different types. First, a theodicy of consolation means that in the midst of suffering the sufferer can be assured of God's suffering presence with them. Second, a theodicy of story allows for appeals to the stories of others who have suffered to be made, with Christ's passion narrative being the most effective. Third, a theodicy of protest which reinforces the conviction of injustice and wrongdoing by insisting that God is on the side of the victim and protesting against the dealers of pain. Then finally, a theodicy of freewill that moves the philosophical questions beyond any doubt that the only free world God was able to create is one in which there was the potential of both good *and* evil.[78]

In a specific comment on the "freewill defense" theodicy, Fiddes argues that any coherent appeal to it must contain two vital aspects of God's passibility. Firstly, if it is the case that, because of the freewill of creatures, evil happens from the created universe then it has to be something that befalls God. Indeed, in creation, God takes the risk of the emergence of nothingness and he suffers its impact. Secondly, this emergence of non-being unearths the matter of divine responsibility for a broken world. Even though God indeed shares in the consequence and does everything possible, especially in the cross of Christ, to overcome the brokenness, any freewill theodicy *ultimately* traces responsibility back to God.[79]

The main reason for the urgency to formulate an acceptable and cohesive freewill defense theodicy with a suffering God as its kernel is the post-enlightened and western understanding of suffering and pain that has raised new questions. There are now, according to Fiddes, three main forms of the phenomenon of suffering that western culture is acutely aware of. First, the theoretical paradigm that associates the status of evil in the universe with the causation and consequences of evil. Secondly, the practical conundrum of how to live authentically in the face of mass suffering which is followed lastly by the aesthetic concerns in which human suffering has been placed within the context of tragedy. These three forms of understanding, together with the modern idea that suffering is both an inner feeling and result of impact from causes beyond our bodies, means that there is a need for a theodicy proper built upon divine passibility.[80]

This new kind of post-Auschwitz theodicy—moving beyond the eighteenth and nineteenth centuries' theoretical, practical and aesthetic approaches to suffering of Leibniz, Schelling, Schopenhauer, Nietzsche,

78. PIG, 155–70.
79. Fiddes, "Something will come," 99–100; PIG, 164–70.
80. Fiddes, "Suffering in Theology," 169–70.

and Unamuno—needs at its core a trinitarian theology which has been ruptured by the victims (the main vessel of which is the death of Christ rupturing the heart of the Trinity) and makes space for both God's presence and empathy with those who suffer.[81] Therefore, accepting this particular world as the highly probably outcome of a creation full of irrevocable freedom to be used for good and ill, and assuming that pain and suffering is not a first cause of God for some higher decretive will, Fiddes argues that the only option for God was to limit his own self, a universal act of kenotic cruciformity (Philippians 2:5–11), which means that God can only persuade, not coerce, and so humanity and wider creation have genuine freedom to choose to partner with him or not.[82] Obviously, a God with suffering humility at the center of his triune being radically changes the nature and understanding of his attribute of omnipotence and this undermines domination, power, superiority, hierarchy and oppression within creation, the very factors that cause and perpetuate suffering and pain.[83]

Indeed, purports Fiddes, the triune God of scripture has suffered in his entire being since the rupturing of creation through the fall. As the Hebrew Bible attests, once God enacts his salvation history plan through divine purpose and desire, this is often frustrated or thwarted by the freewill rebellion of his people. In Hosea we read of a vulnerable God full of divine pathos who calls his prophet to act out sexually the spiritual adultery taking place with his beloved people. There has to be an openness to the *way* God achieves his purposes with the path open to judgement as suffering and a specific blend of wrath and love conflating as the pathos of God. Ultimately, the suffering does result in transformation as the suffering of the empathetic forgiver becomes redemptive for the offender because the offender realizes that their life is under judgement and so turns to receive this redeeming love.[84]

This suffering through chosen self-limitation also exacerbates the humility of God because it allows something alien and strange to emerge from creation. From Barth's influence, Fiddes sees evil—another significant cause of pain and suffering—as "nothingness";[85] a parasitic non-being entity that emerges from creation and manifests itself in all forms

81. Fiddes, "Suffering in Theology," 170–88.
82. PIG, 164–65.
83. PIG, 62–112.
84. Fiddes, "The Cross," 175–90.
85. CD III/3, §50.1–4, 289–368.

of both moral and natural evil. The entire creation is no longer what God intended it to be, and the malevolency of creation is what befalls God and causes him to suffer.[86]

While Fiddes believes that divine passibility offers the best framework for a more plausible theodicy, he is not blind to its limits. Taking his cue from Dostoyevsky's Ivan Karamazov who asked, "is the whole universe worth the tears of one tortured child?" Fiddes acknowledges that the question remains largely unanswered as to whether God's initial decision to proceed with creation was worth the ongoing cost.[87] The other significant weakness of divine passibility raised by critics is whether or not the specific and uniquely efficacious crucifixion and suffering of the Son on the cross simply collapses into a general doctrine of divine suffering, contrary to scriptural witness and church tradition. Let us now address this specific critique.

DIVINE PASSIBILITY'S IMPACT ON ATONEMENT AND SALVATION

Since Fiddes' doctrine of God centers upon a description of a passible God of suffering love, a love that is analogous to some extent with human love, then it should come as no surprise to discover that the love of God is the central impetus for Fiddes' understanding of both salvation and the atonement. Using Aulen's three "types" of atonement theory (Christus Victor, objective, subjective) each of which addresses a different fundamental obstruction which prevents salvation,[88] we see that Fiddes claims a slightly nuanced atonement theory, one he calls a "subjective view which has an objective focus."[89]

Rooting the cross of Jesus as the catalyzing event, Fiddes agrees that the modern orientation in atonement theory, which begins at the subjective end by focusing on the present response to God and is then *followed by* affirmation of the objective event of the cross for a response, is a superior atonement theology for today's western culture.[90] There have been different ways of understanding the objective and subjective poles

---

86. PIG, 166–68.
87. PIG, 187.
88. Eddy and Beilby, "The Atonement," 11–20.
89. Fiddes, "A Response to Stephen."
90. PEPS, 28–29.

of the atonement: salvation as a process in present human experience (subjective) versus salvation in the past event outside of our experience and feeling (objective) or salvation as an act of God (objective) versus salvation including a human response (subjective). However, the problem in these theories is a framing of the objective and subjective in a zero-sum game relationship, in which accentuation of one results in a lessening of the other. Rather, states Fiddes, what is needed is an account that integrates the past event of the cross and the constantly current process of salvation.[91]

The best attempt, according to Fiddes, lies in a reversal of some of the strongly objective atonement theories (e.g. Anselm) and propose some kind of change in God and also, once God is satisfied, in human attitudes. A subjective theory with an objective focus in which both the human and divine go through a process of change is the most satisfactory way of dealing with human alienation and estrangement as well as fragmentation of social relationships which need healing and reconciliation.[92] Ideally, there should be a juxtaposition of divine suffering with human change, a serious picture of God who goes through some kind of change in the act of at-one-ment. Holding the human response of the Son to the Father when on the cross as the aimed norm stresses the power of the cross to change human hearts within a context of open obedience to the Father and empathetic divine suffering love towards the human.[93]

Underlying this preference for a subjective view with objective focus is Fiddes' commitment to understanding salvation as a *process of transformation*. Starting with his baptistic commitment to community and relationship within an eschatological reality, he applies the more eastern concept of progressive divinization which is identified by being increasingly molded into the likeness of God. Within a committed and faithful community, salvation is defined as a moving away from sin towards a more divinized existence that in the process effectively deals with aspects of residual fallenness such as estrangement, anxiety, hostility, fear and idolatry.[94]

When Fiddes takes this conviction of salvation as transformation and conflates it with the kernel of his atonement theory, the love of God, this firmly places him within the stream of Abelard, but one less traditional. For he purports that Abelard, who centrally emphasized Christ as

91. PEPS, 26–28.
92. Fiddes, "Salvation," 178–80.
93. PEPS, 27–28.
94. Fiddes, "Salvation," 176–78.

the great teacher and example and the one who arouses responding love within humanity,[95] has been misunderstood. Yes, Abelard attacked the classic objective imagery of the atonement with its dualistic perspective, believed that the atonement should not be focused on overcoming the devil, and rejected Anselm's objective theory. However, he did not simply develop "Christ as the example of love" model for Christian believers to emulate but instead viewed God's love as transformative, a love that God revealed and poured out on us as an act of fulfilling his own being.[96] The ultimate demonstration of this love happened objectively in the death of Christ when God himself entered the bitter depths of human experience to the utmost degree.

The fundamental purpose of God's transformational love is to heal broken relationships in acts of divine-human reconciliation. God is constantly seeking out people to save (1 Timothy 2:3–4; 2 Peter 3:9) and perennially offering forgiveness and reconciliation to the sinner in a process which is costly to God. This must happen in the here and now and involve response from humanity: the reciprocal movements in the process of salvation is the intimate act of atonement.[97] This reconciliatory act with humanity also has its place within a greater quest of unity of creation through redemption. Salvation in the present is enacted by God as creator and redeemer seeking to bring oneness to a chaotic and disharmonized creation, often symbolized in the Hebrew Bible as sea monsters of chaos.[98] Like forgiveness and reconciliation with humans, this harmonization of creation involves much pain, suffering and cost to God and causes him to adopt a continual kenotic posture of vulnerability.[99]

Fiddes' atonement idea which places the present process of salvation prior to the past objective event of the cross, together with the insistence that God continually suffers through vulnerable love in the process of salvation and reconciliation, could potentially be susceptible to the danger of reducing the specific and unique suffering of the son on the cross into a broader and more general divine suffering. However, as one recent interlocutor of Fiddes' atonement theology has pointed out, he manages to avoid this and does not collapse Christology into divine passibility in

---

95. Aulen, *Christus Victor*, 95–96.

96. PEPS, 141–50.

97. PEPS, 14–17.

98. Some claim these monsters are demonic beings. Boyd, *God at War*, 93–113; Day, *God's Conflict*, 87.

99. PEPS, 17–22; cf. Fiddes, "Creation Out," 167–91.

a way that other divine suffering accounts do.[100] In fact, despite locating himself firmly within a reinterpreted Abelardian tradition on the atonement which was often accused of underplaying the cross of Christ,[101] Fiddes is adamant that the cross of Christ is not only the sublime example of who God always is in creative-redemptive work but moreover is a totally unique and ultimate event in the story of the human and divine.[102] The cross is the most intense event of divine suffering because God goes the furthest he ever will into a world alienated from its creator in order to achieve reconciliation.[103]

Therefore, if the death of Christ on the cross is the greatest demonstration of who God is and defines God's very ontology, then the cross is, suggests Fiddes, the "primary word" in God's *ordo salutis* as well as the full conceptualization of the doctrine of the Trinity. The crucifixion fully reveals the nature of the relations of the triune God: the abandonment and forsaking of the Son by the Father; the suffering and total sense of forsakenness experienced by the Son and the Holy Spirit; and the divine hypostasis who incorporates us into the universal cruciform nature of God by drawing us into the atonement event.[104] It unpacks the sequence of revelation and fuses the word of the cross and Word of eternal begetting within the very being of God. Consequently, this more closely aligns with the Orthodox tradition's view of "the heart of the atonement in the identification of the divine Logos with human nature in all the circumstances of human fallenness,"[105] thereby demonstrating God's willingness to enter into the muck of the human predicament, offer forgiveness, seek out reconciliation and open up participation in the divine being in and through the subsistent relations of the Trinity.[106]

This location of the cross of Christ in the very center of God's being unearths innumerable corollaries that need to be explored when trying to articulate salvation and atonement theology in today's cultural milieu. Fiddes primarily focusses upon three, which he believes

---

100. However, Holmes claims that Fiddes is less successful in keeping the cross the objective focus in his critique of various soteriological images. Holmes, "Who Can Count," 124–33.
101. Aulen, *Christus*, 96–97.
102. PEPS, 24–26.
103. Fiddes, "A Response to Stephen."
104. Fiddes, "The Atonement," 103–8, 117–20.
105. Fiddes, "The Atonement," 113.
106. Fiddes, "The Atonement," 108–17.

are non-negotiable: sacrifice, justice, and evil. Sacrifice, he claims, was the first primary image that the early church used when it was trying to understand salvation.[107] As most Old Testament scholars attest, sacrifice was not seen as an act of propitiation to placate the anger of Yahweh, but rather an act of expiation designed to cover over sins through cleansing. Therefore, the death of Christ is recognized in scripture as a sacrifice, a sin or gift offering that is both substitutionary and representative but not in a penal way.[108] When understood this way, a path is paved for development of other sacrifice language-type metaphors for atonement, such as Girard's mimetic theory and scapegoating, Kristeva's female sacrifice through kenotic self-sacrifice, and Von Balthasar's triune mutual self-giving and Christ's separation experience,[109] all of which can aid but not replace the use of sacrifice to understand salvation.[110]

With regards to justice, it is vital to remember the above-mentioned point that views of justice in atonement theology are heavily influenced by their historical epoch.[111] When it comes to Jesus, Fiddes reminds us that Jesus was rightfully guilty of blasphemy in Jewish eyes and sedition in Roman minds. However, human judgement against Jesus does not equate to divine judgement against him. Instead, as a subjective view demands, the Father identifies with human fallenness which outworks itself in allowing sinful behavior take its natural course (Romans 1). This naturally leads to the condemnation of Jesus by a corrupt court, and he painfully experiences the alienation and forsakenness of the Father who also suffers greatly in the process.[112] Contra Calvin and Luther, the atonement responds to the demands of justice by seeking out restoration and reconciliation as God participates in human estrangement and alienation. Punishment has the aim of reform, and forgiveness is offered *before* repentance.[113]

107. Fiddes, "Salvation," 183.

108. PEPS, 61–82. "I make clear that, understood in this way, the language of penal suffering is biblical and appropriate, as is the language of substitution, since Christ goes further along the road towards non-being than we need ever do. What is not appropriate, I argue, is penal substitution understood as paying a penalty in our place." Fiddes, "A Response to Stephen," cf. Schreiner, "Penal Substitutionary," 67–98; Craig, *Atonement and the Death*.

109. Fiddes, "Sacrifice, Atonement," 48–65.

110. Fiddes, "Salvation," 185.

111. See "The Contemporary Need" (pp.4–9) section above.

112. PEPS, 84–96.

113. PEPS, 96–111.

Finally, Fiddes advocates a transformational victory over evil, one with an Abelardian root in which the victory of Christ over evil through the atoning love of God has the power to move human hearts into action and impact against the evil at work in the world. We enter into cooperation with God's saving action via the power of revelation, creative power of the community of the crucified, the unveiling of God's own self, and the power of the story, especially stories of victory over evil.[114]

THE CHALLENGE OF DIVINE PASSIBILITY ON OTHER DIVINE ATTRIBUTES

Intrinsic to all discussion and language used for God is its metaphorical and analogous nature, with an awareness that it all falls short in actually describing exactly who God is. Fiddes agrees that all God-talk is metaphorical and so the job of the theologian is to decide on the most appropriate form of language to be used of the God of the covenant.[115] As widely recognized, scripture says very little of God's ontological reality but rather describes him in the context of relating with his covenant partners. This creates a discussion about who God is and what his divine attributes are. In short, what qualities or attributes make God God and are there any divine attributes that could be changed or discarded and would still leave God as exhaustively divine?

Fiddes is acutely aware of the need for a doctrine of God that sails a central course maintaining a refined definition of God's sovereignty and control while avoiding the Scylla and Charybdis of God as controll*ing* or not-in-control. For him it is possible to portray a suffering God, without this being simply a projection of human experience, who suffers and remains God. In this God's immanence and transcendence need to be firmly juxtaposed.[116]

While there have been some serious and well-thought-out attempts to do this in the recent past, Fiddes identifies some theological problems within these attempts that need addressed and corrected. Barth's insistence that God freely chooses to be a suffering God and remains impassible while also becoming passible is to be applauded. Yet there is still

---

114. Fiddes, "Christianity, Atonement," 222–26; cf. PEPS, 135–39. In the near-30 years between these two works of Fiddes there has been little change concerning his ideas on the atonement and evil.

115. Fiddes, personal communication with author.

116. CSG, 110–12.

too great a wedge between the being and action of God in the immanent Trinity. God is more complex than Barth allows.[117] The di-polar approach of process theology creates a way to convey God as both immersed in the processes of the world while completely independent of it through his immutable grasp of actuality and possibility. Yet God is still too absorbed in creation and too subject to it, whereas divine suffering is possible because of the completion of who God is and his free decision to become self-limited.[118] Moltmann, it seems, finds a way to satisfactorily articulate a suffering God who remains transcendent. He does this by focusing on the necessary love response within the inner life of the Trinity whilst also taking seriously the analogous connection between divine and creaturely persons and relations. However, claims Fiddes, he does not go far enough about creation's participation in the divine which reveals the complexity of God. For if he did this would allow maintaining transcendence and otherness *within* suffering thereby avoiding transcendence *beyond* suffering, as normally held by traditional theology.[119]

Fiddes is mainly interested in the divine attributes intrinsically linked with a concept of a suffering God. Seldom in his corpus does he address or challenge the moral characteristics of God predicated in scripture (1 John 1:5, Luke 18:19; 1 John 4:8). Rather it is the key classical incommunicable attributes of God (omnipotence, omnipresence and omniscience) and their corollaries (eternality, simplicity, self-existence, self-sufficiency, and immateriality) which are his main focus. Given the salience of these three omnis and inferences to theologically understand God's ontology during SW and conflict, and in preparation for the chapters below, a brief delineation of Fiddes' divine attribute theology at this point is warranted.

In the light of both divine passibility and the cross of Christ, Fiddes desires to re-define omnipotence. His key point is that true divine power is grounded in divine vulnerability, self-limitation, persuasion, sacrifice, feeling, and forgiveness.[120] There is little doubt of process theology's influence on Fiddes regarding divine power; however, Fiddes takes the emphasis upon divine persuasion and vulnerability and centers it within the triune divine dance, those movements of love that creation participates in. This, he claims, solves the perennial problem of process theology

---

117. CSG, 112–23.
118. CSG, 123–35; cf. Fiddes, "Process," 474–75.
119. CSG, 135–43.
120. CSG, 144–73; PEPS, 75–82; PIG, 131–51.

with God portrayed as an object to be grasped.[121] The use of persuasion does not mean that God is potentially impotent as his influence is still powerful while devoid of domination and omnicontrol. God's activity is persuasive, luring, often aligns with the hopes and wishes of creation, and results in dependence upon God without subjugation.

In answering the usual criticisms of this view, namely that God is not powerful enough to be both the creator and sustainer of the world, and God cannot be sure of fulfilling his divine purposes, Fiddes acknowledges that the risk is real though minimum since God acting in "weak power" is far more fruitful in bringing people along with him by being malleable in his divine will through attunement of our choices into the divine purpose which increases God's persuasive love and power.[122] Primarily God does this through three main conduits: the story and situation of a suffering God, in which the story of the Jesus' suffering becomes the kerygma for the church that helps the marginalized identify themselves with it and places God in a situation where he opens up through suffering to embrace what we suffer. Then the feelings of God, where God transcends rationalism, uses intuition and is able to both anticipate the experience and receive the actual experience into himself once it occurs. Finally, the creative journey of forgiveness, analogous to forgiveness between humans, in which divine forgiveness reconciles both feelings and love having come through the fires of judgement and transformation.[123]

Fiddes' wider panentheistic vision of participation means that creation's experience of death, a movement from something to nothing, is analogous to God's omnipresence, which without contradicting scriptural texts of God's total presence (e.g. Psalm 139), allows space for death and non-being within God himself, especially in light of the "death of the living God" on the cross.[124] Since in the fallen world existence is constantly threatened by alienating non-being, God as creator suffers as he exposes himself to the hostile ontology of *das Nichtige* which arises primarily via evil, both moral and natural.

Of course, argues Fiddes, God is ultimately responsible for creating the conditioning factors (such as irrevocable freewill) which made both natural and moral failure within creation a distinct possibility and so he has to be able to confront, expose and absorb negation into himself in

---

121. PIG, 131–36.
122. PIG, 139–44.
123. CSG, 146–63.
124. CSG, 193–200.

order to overcome nothingness.[125] Hostile non-being represents the alien nature of suffering that arises from free creation which befalls the sovereign God. It could not be otherwise, and it is something God endures and deals with. This he has done by the cross where, through Christ, God conquered non-being and took death into his very being and transformed it so that it is no longer an instrument of hostility affecting creation.[126] This closely aligns Fiddes with Hegel's self-negating God theology that sought to counter ideas of negation being alien to God, while differing somewhat from both Altizer's death of God thinking where there is a total immersion of God into the finite world and Tillich's dialectic of opposites theory which needs to deny the historicity of Jesus of Nazareth in order to work.[127] What all these different understandings of nothingness that befall God have in common is, as Macquarrie helped develop, the need to construct a trinitarian model of the triune God in which the relations of God can be ruptured and disturbed because of the vulnerability and kenotic self-emptying reality at the heart of God's very being.[128]

Thirdly, Fiddes' drive to understand how to speak coherently of God's omniscience is not due primarily to his desire to understand the mutability of God in scripture (e.g. Genesis 6:6) but rather a progressive elucidation of a suffering God concept in conversation with process theology. He not only believes that process thought can offer helpful insights into understanding how the particular factual event of Jesus of Nazareth can transform lives today but that their definition of divine omniscience as God's perfect knowledge of both possibility and actuality without ever treating them synonymously is worthy of note.[129] Indeed, this idea helps when seeking to develop language that takes divine suffering seriously and involves talking about "the future" since suffering involves waiting, participating in time, and moving into new states of change from potential to actual. We have to somehow convey that there are new reality states ahead for God but not in a way experienced by humans.[130]

Fiddes' reformulation of God's omniscience in this way leads to him purport the "perfect incompleteness of God." This means a distinction between God's perfection and completion holding that God is perfect

---

125. CSG, 207–29.
126. CSG, 261–67.
127. CSG, 233–60.
128. Fiddes, "On God the Incomparable," 182–86.
129. Fiddes, "Process," 474.
130. CSG, 77–78.

but his completeness lies ahead. Since God has perfect knowledge of all possibilities, then something new to him is not new and surprising as it is to us but when potential becomes actual this contributes something fresh to his experience. In order to make this concept coherent Fiddes further distinguishes between the nature of possibilities. Those that arise from creator and creature interaction, God fully knows as possibilities whereas for those possibilities he conceives from his creative imagination and desire for creation, there lies a knowledge gap between possibilities and actual experience.[131] Considering how difficult it is logically to articulate humans' relation to time, past, present and future, then it is infinitely more difficult to understand God's relation to time and so we need to explore what this means for temporality and eternity, certain and unknown aspects of future, divine desire, and divine suffering and change.[132] Only then will we move nearer to understanding divine passibility and also God's self-revelation of his name "I will be who I will be" to Moses and his people (Exodus 3:14).[133]

CONCLUSION

The objective of this chapter is twofold: to examine and analyze Fiddes' methodological and historical presuppositions which ground his doctrine of God, and to delineate his doctrine of God with specific focus on the ontology of the triune God, especially his passibility of suffering love, and the impact divine suffering has on the doctrine of salvation and atonement and other attributes of God. As demonstrated, Fiddes remains a stalwart defender of divine passibility. While he understands the reasons why divine impassibility was the traditional norm, today's post-Auschwitz western culture demands a different vision of God, one that is present in scripture, tradition and experience but has been a minor theological stream in the past.

Certain influences, primarily German theology *from* the cross and less-so death of God theology, have resulted in Fiddes viewing human experiences as definite sources and, if they align with the revelation and witness of Christ in God, possible norms. Hence, humanity can learn much about divine suffering *inter alia* from human experience of tragedy and pain. Once divine passibility of suffering love is established as the

---

131. CSG, 91–98.
132. CSG, 100–109.
133. CSG, 98–100.

warp and woof of the doctrine of God then this has significant impact on other areas of doctrine: a more subjective understanding of the atonement and salvation and rearticulated definitions of the incommunicable attributes of God and their deductions.

A secondary question, mentioned in the introduction, to be answered in this chapter is whether or not there has been any significant developments or changes in Fiddes' vision of a doctrine of God in the thirty years of published theological work. Given that some consider Fiddes' *Creative Suffering of God*—the earliest monograph to be discussed in this chapter—to be his magnum opus,[134] then it comes as little surprise to conclude that there has been some development of ideas over the years but without any significant change in vision. The following vision facets have remained: his understanding of divine passibility that involves change; divine power characterized by vulnerability, kenosis and persuasion; re-assessed atonement theory of Abelard as transformation; and the relationship of evil and the atonement. Secondly, he actively reiterates certain features of his theological vision throughout his writings, namely the participation of all creation in the relations of the triune God,[135] the relational nature of the Trinity, and the presence of punishment and substitution in scripture without support of a forensic penal substitution understanding of the atonement.

Finally, despite there being few significant critical engagements of Fiddes' work by interlocutors and critics over the years,[136] this has not prevented him specifically developing his conviction that experience can be a theological source and possible norm. This is clearly seen in the significant corpus of work exploring the relationship between literature and theology, in which he seeks to unearth the voice and presence of God in literary works not traditionally used by the church. This body of work will be the main source for the next chapter since much of it explores the human experience of tragedy, suffering and pain in relation to evil and so will facilitate a critical appraisal of the doctrine of evil and demons in conversation with Fiddes.

134. Pool, Review of *The Creative*, 471.

135. Fiddes accepts that what divine suffering of the Spirit entails is something that needs developed. Fiddes, personal communication with author.

136. In 2016 Fiddes could only think of five serious critics of his written work: Thomas Weinandy, Frances Young, Stephen Holmes, Paul Molnar and Thomas McCall. Fiddes, personal communication with author. The contributors in Clarke and Moore's *Within the Love of God,* and Gregory Boyd, could also be added to the list. Boyd, *Crucifixion of the Warrior*, 776.

2

A Fiddesian Account of Evil

INTRODUCTION

IN CHAPTER ONE it was repeatedly noted that one major *modus operandi* of Fiddes' theology is to delineate theological doctrines in ways coherent to the current milieu, which will likely involve significant reconstruction of certain doctrines.[1] This includes constructing a superior understanding of the atonement, i.e. Abelard's atonement theology of transformation, that not only makes sense of the modern fracturing of personality but also best explains God's victory over evil.[2] In doing this Fiddes is continuing along the well-worn path of contextualizing systematic theology in order to make it coherent and communicable to those in the contemporary epoch.[3]

Fundamentally, the imperative to recast theology using new constructs and ideas in order to communicate today is rooted in the existential tension between the closed nature of the past and the open reality of the future, one full of possibility and potential.[4] Fiddes argues that this reality offers the perfect opportunity to juxtapose theology and literature

---

1. See "The Contemporary Need" (pp.4–9) and "The Nature and Character" (pp.13–18) sections above.

2. See "Divine Passibility's Impact" (pp.21–26) section above.

3. Fiddes claims that the early church's emphasis on *Christus Victor* and views of justice were epochal driven. See "Divine Passibility's Impact" (pp.21–26) section above.

4. FAL, 3–7.

in a way that releases doctrine from its usual path moving from mystery to the world, and thereby closure, and instead move from the story or world to mystery, which leads to openness.[5] Future openness, as often found in literature, is congruent with the self-opening of God through his capacious self-revelation.[6] The practice of aligning theology with literature's movement towards openness only works if both God's revelation and creation's response to that revelation are located within a framework of participation in the triune God. When this is the case, states Fiddes, it means that we have a theological basis for including story, metaphor and non-scriptural analogy into works of systematic theology. We can, therefore, draw upon literature and art in different ways in order to further articulate divine revelation and theology in ways understandable to contemporary culture.[7]

By using this methodology Fiddes seeks to analyze and understand the nature and location of evil. Claiming to follow Jewish and Christian tradition, as well as Derrida and Jones, he posits that God is a supreme sign-maker and has created a world which is a text and full of signs.[8] Therefore much literature, especially tragic literature, reflects the fallen nature of the world and all its pain, evil and suffering. So these texts are full of signs which can not only illustrate a theology of evil but *make* a theology of evil.[9]

So, the main objective of this chapter is to formulate a theology of evil in conversation with Fiddes in order to establish a kernel understanding of evil that will be used throughout the rest of the book. Drawing primarily on his work concerning the relationship of literature and theology, as well as salient texts from his doctrine of God corpus, I will analyze and critique Fiddes' explication of evil and corollaries in ways coherent for western late-modern culture. This will be used to arrive at a formulation and definition of evil which will be the understanding upon which to construct a doctrine of God that can coherently explain a SW theology. The rest of this chapter will explore these main facets.

---

5. FAL, 8–15.

6. This is why for Fiddes apocalyptic eschatology envisages an end of history and the cosmos with surety about the "event" of the eschaton while maintaining an openness concerning the "content." TPE, 1–28.

7. Fiddes, "Concept, Image," 11–17.

8. Fiddes, "The Sacramental Modernism," 61–64; Fiddes, "Dystopia, Utopia," 17–18.

9. Fiddes, "Concept," 5; Fiddes, "Story and Possibility," 29–37.

WHAT IS EVIL? ITS ONTOLOGY

"For what is that which we call evil but the absence of good?"[10] Fiddes aligns firmly with Augustine's definition of evil as a *privatio boni*,[11] a slipping away towards an absence of the good, which leads to a corruption of the good and eventual moving away from God back to nothing.[12] Like Augustine's argument that animal disease has no substance or intrinsic existence but is rather the absence of health, Fiddes avers that evil, be moral, human or natural, has no ontological standing at all but instead has a fundamental ambiguity to it.[13]

Defining evil as movement away from the good towards nothingness and ultimately death places Fiddes alongside theologians and literary writers who superimpose metaphysical categories such as being and non-being onto this definition of evil as nothingness. Indeed, notes Fiddes, Augustine clearly defines two types of non-being: an absolute non-being—Plato's *ouk on*—which, while intrinsically not evil, is the slipping back towards it, and a malevolent and aggressive non-being which is hostile to the Good; Plato's *me on*.[14]

Fiddes concurs with Wright's definition and critique of evil as nothingness, which though not a necessity of creation, does exist and has far-reaching implications for other areas of theology.[15] Rejecting Moltmann's *zimsum* and Barth's account of *das Nichtige*, suggesting that they both imply that evil is necessarily part of creation, Fiddes applauds Wright's following of Niebuhr and his proposition that since existence is basically the tension between freedom and anxiety, there is always the possibility of evil; a practical inevitability without the logical necessity.[16]

Extrapolating this understanding to the macro-level of creation means that since creation was created *ex nihilo* it is always under threat of

---

10. Schaff, The *Enchiridion*, 240.

11. Augustine took the *privatio boni* theory from the Platonists in order to defeat the widely held Manichean dualistic view of evil at the time. Hebblethwaite, "MacKinnon and the Problem," 132.

12. Fiddes, "Something will come," 94–95; Fiddes, "Tragedy as Rhetoric," 170; Fiddes, "Is this the Promised End? Fiddes, "Question and Answer"; Fiddes, "Christianity, Atonement," 213.

13. Fiddes, "Tragedy," 169–73.

14. Fiddes, "Christianity, Atonement," 213; Fiddes "Can God Face Up"; cf. Fiddes, personal communication with author.

15. Fiddes, "Something will come," 87–88.

16. Fiddes, "Something will come," 93–95; cf. Wright, *A Theology*, 77.

collapsing back into chaos as humans exercise their immature freedom in order to freely rebel against God and give evil a chance to "posit itself."[17] Significantly, Wright, following Niebuhr, refers to "sin," not "evil" positing itself and this, it seems, demonstrates Fiddes' contention that sin has a particularity whereas evil is universal. For if we understand sin as an attitude and action of covenant breaking and rebellion against God, and a failure to actualize the potential that human beings have received from God, then behind this lies a wider reality of cosmic and universal estrangement and opposition to the Good. This, we can define as evil.[18]

Besides, this universal hostility of evil which consists in part of human rebellion and sin means that evil is something that befalls God.[19] Consequently, if this is something that happens *to* God then this raises the question—discussed below—about *where* evil is located.[20] Fiddes also notes the obvious criticism against process theology that if evil is ever-present within God's being, specifically in his consequent nature which is thoroughly immersed into the flow of time and the world, then this gives no explanation of evil and no possibility of its judgement or eradication. Moreover, evil acts and experiences can have the same everlasting state as beautiful and good experiences.[21] Fiddes replies that all branches of process thinking promote the *transformation* of all experiences God has in his consequent nature thereby not bestowing evil with either a subjective or objective immortality: "we can surely approve the basic idea that if all experiences can be preserved in God, then they can also be transfigured, and evil need not triumph."[22]

Furthermore, in accordance with other literary writers, Fiddes' use of literature to make theology leads him to develop further Augustine's *privatio boni* definition of evil. As part of a larger discussion on transcending the perennial Augustine versus Pelagius debate,[23] Fiddes analyses

---

17. Fiddes, "Something will come," 94–95; cf. Wright, *A Theology*, 77–79.

18. There is however some overlap of evil and sin according to Fiddes. They are intertwined in the demonic principalities and powers mentioned in the New Testament, and in taking Barth's definition of nothingness as that which God *does not will* means the actualizing of nothingness is sin and this gives non-being its own evil identity. Fiddes, "Christianity, Atonement," 212–14; cf. *CD* III/3, §50.3, 302–12.

19. See "Divine Passibility of Suffering" (pp.18–21) section above.

20. See "Ontological Evil and" (pp.123–130) section below.

21. TPE, 206–8.

22. TPE, 208. Fiddes however believes that trinitarian, not di-polarity, theology is the superior way to explain this transformation. CSG, 125–35.

23. FAL, 196–202.

the nature of evil from which humans need to be saved by theologically critiquing Golding's writings, especially *Lord of the Flies*. Fiddes largely supports Golding's use of Heidegger and Barth, in which he postulates that the antidote to human darkness and movement towards a non-being *das Nichtige* is to acknowledge that God, as being-himself, kenotically enters the realm of nothingness, endures the consequences and overcomes in order to call human beings back to him and have the courage "to be."[24]

Charles Williams, notes Fiddes, proffers a more radical understanding of Augustine's definition of evil in human life in his writings. He negates any concept of evil as a created force by noting that evil is "nothing"; very parasitic and extracts from the good. His interpretation of the Edenic fall introduces a unique and helpful answer as to *why* Adam was drawn to evil and disobedience. Combining Augustine and Aquinas, Williams purports that Adam wanted to know the good but could only know it through experiencing evil. Using the phrase "this is and is not" all the characters in Williams' books embark on a way of exchange in order to discover that the nothingness of evil mixed with part-good is, in fact, the path towards the good.[25] Unfortunately, Williams' suggestion does not answer the theological conundrum of justifying the presence of evil in the world. Instead, argues Fiddes, the image of the perichoretic dance will help disqualify the idea of the necessity of evil not by unifying good and evil but rather acknowledging the messy interweaving of good and evil. This image of a dance, together with the Christian story of suffering love which we all can indwell and relate to our own story, can also help avoid polarizing good and evil which often leads to the demonizing of others through scapegoating and perpetuation of the redemptive myth of violence.[26]

The messy interweaving of good and evil means there is an ambiguity to evil. To best understand this, claims Fiddes, we need to look to tragic theology, a theology rooted in tragic literature and playwrights, and is best extracted from Shakespeare, not Greek tragedy.[27] Tragic theology best deals with the intractability of evil and suffering in the contingencies of everyday, normal life. It helpfully divides "evil" into three different types: "moral," when human behavior rebels against moral categories; "human fragility," the failure of humans in a hostile world; and "natural,"

24. FAL, 224–28.

25. Fiddes, "Charles Williams," 65–73.

26. Fiddes, "Charles Williams," 83–85; Fiddes, "The Story and the Stories," 87–89; cf. Girard, *The Scapegoat*.

27. Fiddes, "Is this the Promised"

those natural disturbances that are caused by the randomness in creation. All three types of evil are portrayed best by Shakespeare since his plays are shaped by the Christian culture of the time.[28]

It is the Christian milieu of the time of Shakespeare that catalyzes his definition of tragedy as the clash between individual persons and the surrounding society,[29] especially in the area of values and morals and the discerning of good from evil.[30] In King Lear, the story centers on a man who is reduced to nothing, an *ouk on* which aligns with the strong reformation principle of the time that humans are made from nothing. In most works of Shakespeare, claims Fiddes, evil as *privatio boni* is the inability to survive a clash of values, unless the character is able to feel love and grief in the moment for this will ultimately be the value that will conquer evil.[31]

Overall, what impression do we receive from Fiddes regarding the ontology of evil? Since he is a systematic theologian who constructs theology primarily by making connections,[32] I want to suggest that Fiddes does not arrive at tight, systematic theological definition of evil but rather, via his discussions about evil in his analyses of tragic literature,[33] he arrives at a number of conclusions without necessarily addressing the question of coherence of these concluded ideas.

The clear conclusions reached are as follows: Fiddes is Augustinian in his understanding of evil as *privatio boni*; he rejects the idea of ontic evil since evil is fundamentally ambiguous because of its non-ontological state; he views sin and subsequently evil as rooted in creation's freedom and rebellion against God, hence evil *befalling* God;[34] and despite his apparent rejection of a Barthian definition of nothingness,[35] he still defines evil as a Niebuhrean freedom-anxiety movement towards non-being whether that is absolute non-being (*ouk on*) or nefarious non-being (*me on*).

---

28. Fiddes, "Tragedy," 165–73, cf. Hebblethwaite, "MacKinnon," 131–45. Fiddes raises the question of why, especially in art, moral evil is labelled tragic whereas natural evil seldom is? Fiddes, "Is this the Promised."

29. The subject of Fiddes' monograph, Fiddes, *More Things*.

30. Fiddes, "Tragedy," 178–79.

31. Fiddes, "Tragedy," 179–83.

32. Fiddes, personal communication with author.

33. Only his critique of Wright's theology has evil and the demonic as the main subject matter. Fiddes, "Something will come," 87–104.

34. See "Divine Passibility of Suffering" (pp.18–21) section above.

35. A definition which has been heavily critiqued. Warren, *Cleansing*, 65; Rodin, *Evil and Theodicy*, 166–67; Mallow, *The Demonic*, 97; Wright, *A Theology*, 51, cf. Wright, *The Fair Face*, 40.

Therefore, without entering into the debate regarding the church's traditional understanding of the ontology of evil and a satisfactory theodicy,[36] it is very apparent that if these reached conclusions are juxtaposed with Fiddes' non-Augustinian doctrine of God, then we arrive at a theological impasse. On the one hand we have a doctrine of God which lends itself more naturally to a semi-dualistic, metaphysical understanding of evil and SW, and a definition of evil which primarily appeals to libertarian freedom of all creation (human and spirit beings), which creates the evil that befalls God and continually threatens to reduce creation back to chaos. This strongly contrasts with the non-dualistic, monistic doctrine of God that minimizes the chaotic and malevolent freedom of evil, defines evil in non-personalist terms and upholds an overarching strong sovereignty-control picture of the nature and character of God. Indeed, as Blocher notes, many theologians maintain a critical distance from a theodicy that emphasizes autonomy and independence and paints God as takings "risks," since this all leads to fundamental questions about the sovereignty of God.[37]

Historically in the debate over spiritual conflict and warfare, "theologians seldom consider evil spirits, and 'spiritual warfare' advocates seldom consider philosophical aspects of evil."[38] The Augustinian *privatio boni* model describes evil as non-being or the absence of good and tends to minimize "the biblical portrayal of God's opposition to evil, does not address the anecdotal evidence in 'spiritual warfare' literature, and seems inadequate to explain extreme or dysteleological evil, and demonization."[39] Whereas views of limited dualism are more effective in affirming people's perceived reality of evil by validating people's experience of apparent pointless evil, maintaining the goodness of God, articulating a refined understanding of God's sovereignty and best supporting the biblical and historical-traditional picture of an *ontological over-and-againstness* of evil and the demonic.[40]

---

36. For more, see Blocher, *Evil and the Cross*, 36; cf. Astley, Brown and Loades, *Evil*, 60–78; Hick, *Evil and*, 236–40.

37. Blocher, *Evil and the Cross*, 36–37. Like Fiddes, Yong also defines evil as *privatio boni* but then appeals heavily to process theology to re-articulate the doctrine of God. Yong, *The Spirit of Creation*, 173–225.

38. Warren, *Cleansing*, 59.

39. Warren, *Cleansing*, 60.

40. MacMullen states that in the early church epoch the God of Christianity was known to be at war with many different rivals, which included his angels at war with Satan. MacMullen, *Christianizing the Roman*, 17–18, 27–28.

Therefore, at this juncture it can be safely concluded that Fiddes' *a priori* commitment to a panentheistic and participative doctrine of God, one which naturally imbibes an eschatology of hopeful universalism and doctrine of creation capacious enough for divine suffering,[41] determines an ontology of evil which does not allow a "space" *within* God for personal, autonomous and willful rebellion against God or a "place" that is a punitive destination for all those who come under the judgement and wrath of God as consequence of their defiance and rebellion. Logically, evil as privation is a more congruent fit.

However, I would contend that since Fiddes is a theologian who engages with the biblical text and considers "experience" a valid source for theological formulation,[42] he needs to reconsider the clear *prima facie* biblical witness and contemporary experience of many which validates an understanding of evil grounded in the ontological reality and sentient awareness of diabolical evil. This, I believe, is possible through deeper thinking about ontology and engagement with current, subtle articulations of ontology as naked existence which could encapsulate *privatio boni* while denying *privatio esse*,[43] and create a type of ontology of evil that does not have to deny the panentheistic reality of God. This is addressed in greater detail in chapter five below.

EVIL'S PERSONIFICATIONS: SATAN, TRIUMVIRATE, DEMONS, PRINCIPALITIES AND POWERS

Notwithstanding the previous critical comments, the above-mentioned ambiguity and nothingness of evil continues to be the main controlling framework for Fiddes as he articulates his understanding of metaphorical language used to represent evil, especially language of personification, which helps humanity comprehend regular occurrences of perceived evil. Drawing much from both theology proper and tragic literature, Fiddes offers an all-encompassing representation of evil by reconstructing the

41. See "The Consequence of Evil" (pp.55–58) section below.

42. See "The Place of Experience" (pp.9–13) section above.

43. Much good work on this subject has been done. For more see Warren, *Cleansing*, 260–76; Noble, "The Spirit World," 216–18; Jenson, *Systematic Theology, Vol.1*, 117; Wright, *A Theology*, 81–82. Revelation 13:18 numbering of the beast as 666, the ultimate "falling short" of absolute perfection, could substantiate a reading of Dante's account of Satan casting him as definite privation with necessary existence, a personification of absolute evil which is a form of existence but stripped of all potential "goods." See Alighieri, *The Divine Comedy 1: Hell*, Canto 34, 285–91.

traditional personified manifestations of evil in modern language thereby offering a culturally relevant and acceptable understanding of evil that helps explain modern society's observation and experience of evil.

Significantly, Fiddes redefines and rejects certain parts of Christian tradition regarding evil. Before doing that, however, he acknowledges the New Testament's diverse portrayal of the forces of evil, including Satan and principalities and powers, and also notes that in Christian tradition Satan has indeed become the full representation of evil, the rubric under which to locate all other personifications of evil.[44] In terms of redefinition, Fiddes revises the traditional understanding of the triumvirate of evil, i.e. the flesh, world and devil, as the "sinister triumvirate of *sin, law and death.*"[45] Since that which connects the flesh, world and devil is the potential to tempt and this presupposes the existence of willful sentience or even personhood, it seems likely that Fiddes, following Tillich and Macquarrie, redefines the triptych of evil in a way more congruent with evil as *privatio boni*, since sin, law and death are all perversions of something good and become evil when held up as tyrannical idols to be obeyed.[46]

Regarding what he rejects, Fiddes suggests that the historical understanding of Satan as the totality of evil and akin to the devil is very problematic since it contravenes the root understanding of personhood: "it is not possible to apply the term 'person' to an entity which is absolutely evil and thus capable only of depersonalizing . . . what is surely essential is to recognize the spiritual reality to which the name 'Satan' witnesses."[47] Fiddes jettisons the traditional understanding of Satan as a fully ontological evil being in order to maintain a distinction between personhood and Satan, which also sustains the redeem-ability of every person without extending this to Satan.[48]

A non-ontological Satan, together with evil as *privatio boni* and essentially "nothingness," aligns Fiddes firmly with other modern

---

44. PEPS, 114–25.

45. PEPS, 114.

46. PEPS, 114–18. Similarly, Caird posits that the law, sin and death can be seen as part of the principalities and powers. Caird, *Principalities and Powers*, 43–51.

47. PEPS, 118. It should be noted that Fiddes often uses "personality" and "personhood" as synonymous terms. I will distinguish them and use "personhood" when ontology is the focus and "personality" when the combination of human characteristics and qualities is being discussed.

48. PEPS, 119. This position sets Fiddes at odds with Wink. Wink, *Unmasking*, 39–40.

scholars.[49] He applauds Wright's progressive shift away from viewing Satan as a fallen angel to instead a "projection out of human fallenness" since this idea is more coherent if Satan's character is a non-being nothing.[50] This understanding also, argues Fiddes, helps make sense of ambiguity of "the Satan" and the different remits he is portrayed as having at different points. In agreement with Wink, he notes that a fluid and malleable definition of Satan lends itself to the portrayal of development of Satan in the scriptures, whether that be a servant of Yahweh, an *agent provocateur,* or quintessential malevolent enemy of Christ.[51]

Arriving at the conviction that Satan is a nothingness, a mere projection of human fallenness and the dark side of the good, emboldens Fiddes to increase the metaphorical language concerning "the Satan" from his exploration of literature and theology. From William Blake he suggests viewing Satan as a disturbance of the human psyche, a false state of self-righteous selfhood which is chaotic and divided and can lead into satanic spheres of vice.[52] Moreover, theologically, Blake articulates Satan as the empty shell of God's objective existence, an idea that, claims Fiddes, opens the door to Jung's definition of Satan as the dark side of God,[53] and surprisingly finds congruence with Altizer's definition of Satan as an image of God estranged from the God who is normally delineated as abstract transcendence.[54]

There is certainly no doubt that jettisoning certain understandings of the traditional, especially mediaeval, picture of a personalized Satan as the epitome of evil, frees Fiddes to develop a theology of Satan that, similarly to Wink and others, helps communicate the concept of evil to western modern culture in a more palatable way. However, in so doing it seems to me that he creates other points of contention that will undermine the clarity of

---

49. For instance, Noble, "The Spirit World," 210–18, cf. Cook, "Devils and Manticores," 175–77.

50. Fiddes, "Something will come," 91. Fiddes correctly notes that this shift in thinking which took place between two editions is largely down to the influence of Wink and Noble. However, after noting Wright's new section in the second edition on the devil and evil as projections of fallen human thinking, he suggests that the first edition is still exercising significant influence and presence in the second. Fiddes, "Something will come," 89–93; cf. Wright, *A Theology*, 76–82.

51. PEPS, 118–22; Fiddes, "Charles Williams," 77–81; cf. Wink, *Unmasking*, 9–40.

52. FAL, 92–93; Fiddes, "The Passion Story," 752–55; Fiddes, "Patterns of hope," 41–46.

53. FAL, 93–94.

54. TPE, 248.

definition that he seeks. Essentially, he places too much weight on the "two Satans in scripture" motif, the idea promulgated of a systematic evolution of "the Satan" in scripture. In reality, the picture is more ambiguous. The presence or absence of the article is significant, as well as the etymology and context of the use of the noun *sâṭân*.[55]

Secondly, in depersonalizing Satan to non-ontological status Fiddes places himself firmly at odds with much scripture, tradition and experience. Not only is it questionable that this view of Satan is necessary in order to delineate his panentheistic vision of God, hopeful universalism, and current *zeitgeist*-driven metaphorical language about the nature of evil, but it also significantly contravenes much witness of scripture, especially the life and teaching of Jesus,[56] church historical-traditional accounts of deliverance and exorcism of sentient, volitional evil spirits,[57] and current global experience of the reality of the demonic that testifies to demonic elements of communication, tactics and planning.[58] Return-

---

55. "It is difficult to maintain, as many scholars have, that we see in the Hebrew Bible a developing notion of Satan." Breytenbach and Day, "Satan," 1378. Others have noted that the especial use of the noun *sâṭân* in Numbers 22 to render the action of God as "satanic" certainly precludes any systematic evolution of Satan. Pagels, *The Origin*, 39–41; Beck, *Reviving Old Scratch*, 8–9; Forsyth, *The Old Enemy*, 113.

56. In the Matthean version of the Lord's prayer NT scholars agree that Jesus prays for deliverance from the "evil one" (Matthew 6:13). France, *The Gospel of*, 231, 251–52; Hagner, *Word Biblical*, 151–62; Keener, *A Commentary on*, 223–25.

57. Daunton-Fear robustly demonstrates that exorcism was widely practiced in the first three centuries of church history before becoming a minor ministry in the post-Nicene church. Daunton-Fear, *Healing in the Early*, 67, 110, 131, 151, 158–64.

58. Goodman, in her exorcism accounts, states that ultimately "experience is the most powerful of all persuaders" when it comes to claims of interaction with demons and other spirits. Goodman, *How About Demons?* 124–26. Linn and Linn document accounts of thirty-two persons who were part of a group of two thousand people who all testified to beneficial experiences once deliverance prayer had been done over them. Linn and Linn, *Deliverance Prayer*, 160–63. Boyd informs that many areas of the world hold a cultural paradigm of the reality of evil spirits and demon possession which is supported by numerous *a-posteriori* accounts. This evidence has also challenged western anthropologists and ethnographers' framework of naturalism, Boyd, "The Ground-Level," 143–47. In the Anglican church exorcist John Richards not only suggests speaking directly to evil spirits when exorcising either people or places but also perform a reversal prayer over those who have made a satanic promise to renounce Christ which they made by speaking and praying directly to their "master and Lord Satan." Richards, *Exorcism, Deliverance*, 18–21; cf. Richards, *But Deliver Us*, 82. The lived, experienced knowledge of satanic oppression and the use of authoritative monologue and commands to exorcise evil spirits who can hear and obey is commonplace in sub-Sahara African Christianity. For an extensive, academic account of this global-south normality see Bennett, *I Am Not Afraid*, 1–96. For a fair and even-balanced account of modern-day exorcism and deliverance in the modern western church see Collins, *Exorcism and Deliverance*.

ing to the aforementioned 1993 Lausanne working group report and statement on SW,[59] it strongly states that "the principalities and powers of evil *who are seeking to overthrow* the church and *frustrate* its task of evangelization" (emphasis mine) are to be constantly fought in the spiritual realm by the church.[60]

While, like Fiddes, we may not want to bestow full status of personhood upon "the Satan" since we cannot be sure of his origins,[61] I would argue that it is possible to develop a nascent, hortative definition which reflects his sub-personhood and acknowledges a quasi-ontology capacious enough for sentient existence, willful opposition to God and creation, a certain amount of say-so, and ability for accusation, deception and chameleon-type behavior. God's enemy is aware and knowledgeable about his existence and opposition to God.[62]

Moving on to other personifications of evil under the "Satan" rubric, it is firstly significant to note that Fiddes refuses to list "demons" along with other tyrants of evil, claiming that they are too hard to classify and that they can be associated with the above-mentioned three main groups of tyrants.[63] As already noted, the triumvirate of sin, law and death are ultimately perversions of the good and therefore capable of becoming demonic idols with diabolical consequences. Acquiescing to the idols of sin and the law results in death, the antipathetic demonic result to

---

59. See "Setting the Scene" (pp.xix–xxi) section above.

60. "Lausanne Statement."

61. There is simply no consensus, let alone unanimity, on whether texts such as Isaiah 14:12–21 and Ezekiel 28:1–17 correctly reveal the origin of Satan as a fallen archangel or not. Some adamantly claim that these passages go beyond a natural description of a human king and point to another-worldly enemy of God, Satan. Boyd, *God at War*, 157–62; Green, *I Believe*, 36–42. At the opposite pole, it is asserted that these passages about earthly kings were co-opted into a "legends of the fall," especially the Lucifer myth, which was then made very prominent by Milton's *Paradise Lost*. Pagels, *The Origin*, 47–49; Wray and Mobley, *The Birth of Satan*, 108–12. Between these poles we have the honest agnosticism of Wright who maintains that while the exegetical evidence for these passages supporting the fall of Satan theory is very weak and shaky, there can be good *theological* reasons for moving towards an angelic fall conclusion. Wright, *A Theology*, 70–73.

62. Wright's consistent use of "The Satan" is both helpful and instructive at this point. It demonstrates the sub or quasi-personhood of "The Satan" that we can use to demonstrate his malevolent will that opposes both God and creation without bestowing upon him full personhood of the *imago-dei* of humanity. This nuanced position of sub-personhood also allows for the creation of degrees of non-personhood determined by movement away from the good towards nothingness. Wright, *Evil and*, 45, 108–12.

63. PEPS, 114.

transformative life in Christ.⁶⁴ In fact, claims Fiddes, there is much literature evidence, especially during reformation times, of a movement away from the devil's rights and towards the law of God which portrays the real powers and principalities as the existential triumvirate of sin, law, and death, not legions of devils and Satan.⁶⁵

Regarding specifically powers and principalities and noting that the apostle Paul refers more often to them than Satan,⁶⁶ Fiddes fundamentally holds that any structure, political or otherwise, can become a demonic power when it moves towards becoming an idol, away from its intrinsic goodness and service.⁶⁷ Following Caird, he suggests it is a movement away from the good, a return to nothingness and chaotic creation intermingled with a variety of demonic systems:⁶⁸ the "best systems can become demonic, whether economic, political or ecclesiastical; bureaucracies can add a spirit of legalism to their particular demonic tendencies."⁶⁹ This understanding of potential demonic structures acts as a catalyst for Fiddes to identify potential demonic principalities and powers in various types of literature, be that Lawrence's abandoned love,⁷⁰ Frye's world rejected by desire,⁷¹ or King Lear's temporal whole of nothingness.⁷²

There is certainly no doubt that Fiddes' position concurs with much of the significant research on principalities and powers that emphasizes fallen structures of earthly existence instead of nefarious spiritual beings.⁷³ There is also certainty that this understanding of the principali-

64. PEPS, 114–18.

65. Fiddes, "The Passion," 747–50.

66. Fiddes suggests that the Apostle Paul constructed his understanding of principalities and powers based on a belief of a continuous fall of rebellious angels throughout human history, alluded to in passages such as Genesis 6, Deuteronomy 32:8–9, and Psalm 82:2. These passages are used by territorial spirits advocates who claim that geographical regions can be under the spiritual influence of evil spirits that have a regional mandate and corporate possession. Wright also suggests that there is some overlap between Wink's claim that principalities and powers create "atmospheres" over territory that can be open or closed to God's grace, and territorial spirits over cities and cultures. FAL, 93–94; Wagner, *Spiritual*, 167–69; Wright, *A Theology*, 148–49.

67. PEPS, 122–25; Fiddes, "Something will come," 100–104; Fiddes and Lees, "How are People Healed," 25–27.

68. PEPS, 122–25; cf. Caird, *Principalities*, 51–53.

69. PEPS, 124.

70. FAL, 164–72.

71. TPE, 15–22.

72. TPE, 54–57.

73. To mention a few, Berkhof's claim that the apostle Paul has demythologized the powers of their personal and spiritual nature found in rabbinic and apocalyptic

ties and powers finds a natural place within his panentheistic vision of God and hope-filled universalism. However, I have to posit that Fiddes' position simply reveals only one part of the picture and fails to reflect the fully-orbed nature and reality of principalities and powers congruent to scripture and claimed experience.[74]

Clearly, there is a certain amount of ambiguity when it comes to definitive descriptions of the principalities and powers.[75] In contrast to the highly-schematized gnostic assertions of the spirit world, the New Testament vagueness is probably deliberate and therein lies its genius. However, taking a lead from Wright's work on idolatry and the demonic it is certainly possible to define principalities and powers in a way that does not ignore the potential fallenness of structures and institutions (without *having* to demonize them all) while clearly recognizing the ontological spiritual reality *behind* and *within* them. An idol, states Paul, is nothing in and of itself (1 Corinthians 8). However, when a worshipper offers a sacrifice to that idol then they are offering to a demon (1 Corinthians 10). Therefore, an idol is both nothingness and demonic at the same time.[76]

---

texts, Berkhof, *Christ and the Powers*, 18–24; Wink's bi-polar outward manifestation and inner spirituality of principalities and powers that mainly refer to generic, psychic and social forces confronted in everyday life, Wink, *Unmasking*, 4; Kellermann's liturgical-political confrontation and exorcism of institutional, social, ideological, political systemic powers holding sway in western culture, Kellermann, *Seasons of Faith*, 71–102; Yoder's conclusion that the powers are fallen aspects of God's good creation, triumphed over by Christ though not destroyed, and overcome by cruciform ecclesiology and revolutionary subordination, Yoder, *The Politics of*, 134–92; and Newbigin's principalities and powers, which are spiritually very real but never exist apart from the human agencies they embody. Therefore, spiritual conflict with them is not against human beings but rather against the spiritual power that is behind, within and above human beings, Newbigin, *The Gospel in*, 198–210.

74. Green emphatically argues that the understanding of principalities and powers in both Judaism, the Greco-Roman World and New Testament age was of spiritual forces beyond human power and authority. To suggest that the principalities and powers of the Pauline letters are different and separate from the demons of the gospels is misleading and dangerous. Green, *I Believe*, 78–84. In terms of their nature, Green asserts that the "truth of the matter is that words like principalities, powers and thrones are used of human rulers and of the spiritual forces which lie behind them." He also claims that 1 Corinthians 2:8, Titus 3:1, and Romans 13:1 can be taken either way. Green, *I Believe*, 84–85. Other scholars who claim the same include Boyd, "Powers and Principalities," 611–13; O'Brien, "Principalities and Powers," 1–10; O'Brien, "Principalities and Powers: Opponents," 110–43; Schlier, *Principalities and Powers*, 11–39.

75. McAlpine helpfully summarizes the different understandings of powers and principalities from the reformed, anabaptist, third wave, and social science traditions before offering a parallel reading and possibilities for future research and understanding. McAlpine, *Facing the Powers*.

76. Wright, *Evil and*, 112–13.

This same explanation can be applied to principalities and powers. For example, consider the contrasting delineation of the state between Romans 13 and Revelation 13. If the state remains within the limits of its function then it is the servant of God; if it exceeds that limit and parasitically feeds on power and worship, then it becomes a diabolical power: an instrument of Satan.[77] Conflation of passages such as 1 Corinthians 2:8, Romans 13:1 and Revelation 13 with the tensioned age of the eschaton justifies Cullmann's dialectical definition of the principles and powers as the reality of *both* state government and structure authority *and* angelic-demonic ontological forces behind and within those structured authorities.[78] Indeed, returning to Ephesians 6:10–12, it can be affirmed that there are invisible positive and negative spiritual powers whose outer veneer is the human or state institution.[79]

Finally, in Fiddes' position on the relation of "demons" to Satan he continues the non-ontology of Satan theme. In his dialogue with a medical missionary doctor, Fiddes supports Lees' encouragement and call not to ignore the demonic but rather acknowledge its overwhelming reality.[80] However, in contradistinction to his debating partner's belief in the personhood of the demonic, Fiddes states categorically that it is inconsequential whether or not someone believes in an evil force with or without a personhood of its own, so long as we agree on the very real and objective experience of evil as a hostile dark reservoir opposed to the purposes of God.[81]

Fiddes' propensity to give human experience premier position in theological formulation means that, despite holding the contrary view that demons are non-persons, chaotic and irrational nothings, like Wright he is unwilling to belittle or negate others' experience of the demonic in a personified form so long as experiential claims are not exaggerated or embellished in order to create a pre-occupation with the demonic.[82] Of course,

---

77. Cullmann, *The State*, 50–92.

78. Cullmann, *The State*, 95–114; Cullmann, *Christ and Time*, 191–210.

79. Cullmann, *The State*, 108–9; Cullmann, *Christ and Time*, 104. In discussing how to view theologically the biblical evidence on principalities and powers, Wright sees no reason to not follow a path between Wink and Stott in which structures can produce demonic forces and the demonic can use structures for its own purposes. There is no contradiction between Paul's theology and Jesus' confrontation of the demonic in the gospels. Wright, *A Theology*, 139–45.

80. Fiddes and Lees, "How are People Healed," 22–25.

81. Fiddes and Lees, "How are People Healed," 25–27.

82. Fiddes, "Something will come," 101.

however, this difference of understanding will only remain inconsequential so long as there is no attempt to confront the demonic. Approaches to address the demonic will significantly differ depending upon whether or not there is an ontological reality to a demonic, evil spirit.

DEFEAT OF THE DEMONIC: EVIL AND THE ATONEMENT

Having delineated Fiddes' understanding of the identification and ontology of the various personifications that comprise evil, it is necessary to juxtapose this with his position on the atonement in order to see in what way, if any, Jesus' death and resurrection defeats evil and the demonic, however they are construed. As noted earlier,[83] in Fiddes' key text on the atonement he attempts to tackle a fundamental question regarding the atonement, namely "how can a particular event in the past have an effect upon our experience of salvation today?"[84] The question is critical because salvation is dependent upon both the past crucifixion of Jesus and the work of God in the here and now.[85] So in turning specifically to evil, he similarly asks how exactly does the victory of Jesus two thousand years ago deliver defeat of evil in a modern age which appears to be in the grip of much evil?[86]

To answer this question Fiddes broadens his atonement theology and applies it to his understanding of evil. While holding a nuanced transformative view of Abelard's exemplarist theory,[87] Fiddes recognizes that there is a significant Satanward aspect to the atonement (1 John 3:8). Therefore, he elucidates a subjective stress to the *Christus Victor* theory by stating that the possibility of victory over evil is rooted in our subjective participation with the triune God as we enter into God's objective and historical victory over evil and cooperate with divine purpose: "the victory of Christ at the cross empowers us to enter upon God's victory in the present."[88]

---

83. See "Divine Passibility's Impact" (pp.21–26) section above.
84. PEPS, ix.
85. Fiddes, "Salvation," 178.
86. PEPS, 112–13.
87. See "Divine Passibility's Impact" (pp.21–26) section above.
88. PEPS, 135–39; cf. Fiddes, "Christianity, Atonement," 222. There is no noticeable change or development in Fiddes' atonement theology and evil in the near-thirty years between these two works despite his awareness of a number of different ways to

Part of his arrival at this understanding is via rejection of the traditional understanding and uses of the *Christus Victor* theory, ones with an objective focus and subjective appendix. He jettisons the classic understanding of it because it relies on a personalist ontology of Satan and in its "ransom theory" form bequeaths too many rights to the devil.[89] It also offers an inadequate theodicy.[90] Secondly, he repudiates Aulen's description of *Christus Victor* stating that he relies too much on whom the ransom is given to, whereas the focus should be on "by whom" the ransom is given. Aulen's theory also creates internal conflict between the wrath and love in God, which Fiddes argues is never present in God,[91] and it presents an inferior theodicy which allows evil to continue incessantly and God be excused of any responsibility for evil.[92] Finally, Fiddes also renounces Barth's use of *Christus Victor*. While appreciating Barth's rejection of a penal substitution atonement and casting evil as essentially *Das Nichtige*,[93] he concludes that the account leans too much towards the objective end and makes it very difficult to see *how* someone's actual sin has been killed in another person (i.e. Christ).[94] Overall, while an objective view of *Christus Victor* correctly asserts strongly the decisive nature of the past event of the cross, it does not sufficiently explain "the 'slaying' of sin, or the dealing of a fatal blow to Satan, or the quenching of divine wrath."[95]

Greater potency therefore lies in a subjective stress on *Christus Victor*. This view presents Christ's victory over idols, power and principalities and the demonic as a present event into which we can enter. Enlisting the help of Macquarrie, Fiddes suggests there are four ways in which the victory of Christ over idols et al releases victory in human life in the present: releasing the power of revelation; finding creative power

---

understand the relationship between "objective" and "subjective" poles of the atonement. See Fiddes, "Salvation," 179–80.

89. PEPS, 129–31.

90. Fiddes, "Christianity, Atonement," 219–20.

91. PEPS, 132–33; cf. Fiddes, "Christianity, Atonement," 220.

92. Fiddes, "Christianity, Atonement," 221.

93. In accepting "penal suffering" and "substitution" but rejecting "penal substitution" Fiddes agrees with Barth's "substitution/representative" account while claiming that Barth "rejects any [penal substitution] idea that Christ atones for our sin by bearing a punishment in our place." Rather, "Christ 'caused sin to be taken and killed on the cross in his own person.'" PEPS, 134, cf. *CD* IV/1, §59.2, 253–55.

94. PEPS, 133–34; cf. Fiddes, "Christianity, Atonement," 221–22.

95. Fiddes, "Christianity, Atonement," 222.

in the community of the crucified;[96] the unveiling of God's own self from the past in the present; and empowering Christ's story of suffering which helps makes sense of pointless evil.[97] All four possibilities are creatively plausible because of the subjective stress of the *Christus Victor* theory which renders Abelard's theology of transforming love vital to any understanding of impact on the current situation of evil.[98] Only the love of God revealed in the cross creates the possibility of infusing love into an evil situation and moving human hearts to respond to God.[99] The love shown on the cross breaks idols, especially the idol of the self,[100] and helps "people make the victory of Christ their own."[101]

Entering into the victory of Christ also releases a number of other positive consequences that aid the believer in their salvific progressive transformation into a more perfect image of God.[102] First, since Christ wrought victory *through* death on the cross this means that the embracing of human weakness, instead of strength, will let the power and victory of Christ work through ineptitude (2 Cor 12:8–10).[103] Also, those who believe become justified, not due to some transfer of penalty but rather because Christ demonstrates solidarity, identification and participation in the human experience of being under God's judgement. In turn, this participation causes God to absorb and overcome sin which brings destruction not only to sin but also principalities and powers, demonic structures, etc.[104] Thirdly, and most crucially, the journey of creative transformation needs to run through the conduit of forgiveness. Forgiveness—understood as an emotional and vulnerable winning back into relationship—is at the heart of Christian salvation and, contentiously claims Fiddes, needs a suffering God so that evil can be overcome and

---

96. For an articulation of what this entails see Fiddes, "Atonement in the Life," 195–208.

97. PEPS, 136–38; Fiddes, "Christianity, Atonement," 223–25; cf. Macquarrie, *The Principles*, 324–27.

98. Perhaps without realizing it, Fiddes has closely aligned to the classic anabaptist Christus Victor model which is not only "conflictive" but also "transformative." Finger, *A Contemporary Anabaptist Theology*, 341–43.

99. PEPS, 138–39; Fiddes, "Christianity, Atonement," 225–26.

100. FAL, 103–10.

101. PEPS, 139.

102. This language and insight we get from the Eastern tradition. Fiddes, "Salvation," 176–77.

103. PEPS, 125–29.

104. Fiddes, "Salvation," 186–89; Fiddes, "Atonement in," 199–202.

evildoers transformed.[105] Ultimately, this is best achieved within a corporate community of forgiveness.[106]

To supplement and embellish his case of a subjective stress on *Christus Victor* atonement theology, Fiddes uniquely cites works of literature with this theme.[107] To illustrate, in Blake's literary interface with theology Fiddes extrapolates Blake's lucid and perceptive conclusion that the God of Milton's *Paradise Lost* is actually "Satan" and that the only way to deal with the satanic specter of selfhood which results from tensions, imbalance, shame and jealousy in human life caused by human disintegration is in fact an Abelardian atonement theology that decimates demonic idols, especially the idol of the self through the transformative cruciform love of God.[108]

In totality, Fiddes is delineating a holistic atonement theology that not only addresses the problem and reality of evil but also offers a promised end of hope and final destruction of evil. Poetically, he dares to say that "eternally there is a cross in the heart of God" and this is because "only suffering love has the power to persuade reluctant human wills towards the good and so overcome evil."[109] Because suffering love is through the death of Christ on the cross, it has a tragic quality to it and, claims Fiddes, is without consolation. However, like consolation that follows tragedy, the resurrection brings a consolation that transcends since it is of a completely different order and therefore actually changes the ontological reality of things.[110]

THE PROBLEM OF EVIL (THEODICY)

No construction of a theological understanding of evil is complete without considering the question of theodicy; the vindication of God and his providence in view of apparent malevolent evil. Fiddes is acutely aware of the need of a theological construct which tries to exonerate God while responding to the evidential problem of evil that seems to undermine the existence of a benevolent and omnipotent deity but

---

105. Fiddes, "Salvation," 189–92.
106. Fiddes, "Atonement in," 196–99.
107. Fiddes, "The Passion," 745–47.
108. FAL, 107–9.
109. Fiddes, "Is this the Promised?"
110. Fiddes, "Tragedy," 183–87; Fiddes, "Question."

does aver that it should be accepted that there is no one-hundred percent satisfactory theodicy.[111]

That said, this should not preclude attempts made to construct a theological schema that best answers the theodicy question. Fiddes strongly argues that it is vital to reject all anachronisms and formulate appropriately for the current cultural context. This means that we can and should recognize stalwart historic attempts to make and remake a theoretical theodicy by the likes of Leibniz, et al,[112] but also acknowledge that the current post-Auschwitz milieu means there is little, if any, room for theoretical approaches to theodicy. Instead, a new kind of theodicy is needed, one that recognizes resignation and active suffering and is commodious enough for God to be present and empathetic alongside victims. Indeed, states Fiddes, only divine suffering makes sense of any freewill account of the existence of evil and this can be defended by the Old Testament portrait of Yahweh, as well as a theology of Christ's death which allows for a rupturing to take place within the Trinity.[113]

"In this cultural context theology has taken a predominately practical approach which is characterized both by protest against suffering in the light of future hope, and by assurance of God's presence in suffering."[114] God does not lose all culpability by making a freewill-possible world. In fact, Fiddes believes that freewill is given to the entire creation and so the evil that takes place due to the exercised freewill of creatures means that it is something that befalls God. Therefore, the only plausible justification for God initially making this type of creation is that he participates and suffers in solidarity and empathy with it.[115]

Fiddes' conviction regarding theodicy is buttressed by his understanding of the book of Job. Even though this sacred text does not solve the question of theodicy, it certainly confirms that God never deserts us when suffering in pain.[116] Much of his understanding of Job, especially chapters 38–42, emerges from his interaction with literature on

111. Fiddes, "Christianity, Atonement," 229.
112. Fiddes, "Suffering in Theology," 170–74.
113. Fiddes, "Suffering in Theology," 186–87.
114. Fiddes, "Suffering in Theology," 188.
115. Fiddes, "Something will come," 99–100; Fiddes, "Christianity, Atonement," 217–18. Fiddes offers this argument in response to Hick's claim about evil's place in the divine aim. Fiddes contends that Hick's argument still does not offer a satisfactory answer to Dostoevsky's Ivan Karamazov's moral question about whether or not the universe, as it is, is worth the tears of one tortured child.
116. SWKG, 73.

tragedy, philosophy and theology. Following Levinas, Fiddes agrees that Job is really only concerned with the problem of his own suffering and devotes no time addressing transcendent and ubiquitous evil marked by sheer excessiveness.[117] This, it seems, strongly identifies with liberation theology's understanding of theodicy that responds to the fathomless mysteries of creation by focusing instead on the particularity of a tragic situation without expecting God to change the cosmic and structural diabolic causative factors.[118] However, converging energy and protest on the immanent situation does not mitigate against Williams' proposal, that we should imitate Job and rage against suffering instead of adopting a *laissez-faire* posture towards it.[119]

A practical theodicy answer goes some way towards understanding the problem of evil. Fiddes proposes that there are further theological adaptations to be made, especially in the doctrine of God, in order to gain greater understanding of and answer to the theodicy question. Building on Wright's work in which he distinguishes between evil and the "shadow-side" of creation, Fiddes proposes that behind the shadow lies genuine destructive and pointless evil which permeates the entire creation and has origins in the exercising of total freedom by the whole of creation. The consequence is creation falling away from divine purpose and the ultimate good, resulting in "red tooth and claw" evil. Fortunately, claims Fiddes, both scripture (Genesis 9:8, Psalm 19:1–4, Romans 8:19–22) and process theology describe the world as an organic community that can not only respond to God but also potentially enjoy him.[120] Consequently, imbibing the entire creation with freewill means that any evil resulting from creation's freedom is something that befalls God and for which he is *ultimately* responsible. Hence why God stands in solidarity with creation and also suffers all evil ramifications.[121]

Appealing to process theology insights catalyzes more creative steps towards an understanding of why evil exists alongside God. First, states Fiddes, the "God repented/relented" passages understood from a process perspective aid us to speak of evil as a possible occasion for good so long as we jettison some of the classic views of God's omniscience and irresistible grace in favor of a God who self-limits, changes, suffers and interacts

117. SWKG, 66–73.
118. FAL, 200–201.
119. Fiddes, "Charles Williams," 74.
120. Fiddes, "Something will come," 95–99.
121. Fiddes, "Something will come," 99–100.

in time with creation.¹²² Indeed, as argued by Pannenberg, it is meaningless to talk about freewill and open choice of creation while maintaining the timelessness of God.¹²³

Second, the process vision of God and the universe consisting of openness, possibility, potential, divine-creation response and vice versa, and cosmic cooperation, coheres more effectively to the Shakespearean portrayal of comedy that elicits a line of tension in the lives of his characters. Often they fall into disorientations because of their freedom and thereby need love and healing, which can only come by divine love immersing itself into disorder, chaos and evil.¹²⁴

Third, the emphasis upon process and development of creation and creator can be applied to human persons *post-death* and this could aid in answering the theodicy question by maintaining that those whose lives were tragically and perhaps painfully cut short still have a chance to actualize their full potential beyond death.¹²⁵ Fiddes strongly believes that this belief will mitigate some of the moral objections contained within the theodicy question and also, by developing Lewis, help locate evil and suffering within God's perichoretic dance in which evil that disturbs and thwarts and is caused by creation's freewill is overcome and transformed within the movement of the divine dance. God has the power to incorporate change into the beautiful whole, and this includes transforming evil.¹²⁶

In sum, Fiddes works hard to articulate good answers to the question of theodicy which involves steering a course somewhere mid-spectrum between the poles of evil as a fateful determinism that cannot be avoided, and a perfect answer to the theodicy question which could explain all evil.¹²⁷ There is a *necessity* to evil since everything is an occasion for love and joy, and this includes evil. This does not mean however that evil is a "necessary" part of reality.¹²⁸ God and evil are not comparable realities even though both are uncreated. For only God is self-existent whereas evil is derived existence and strictly nothing, hence why tragic language of evil as *privatio boni* is important and negates any clear and concise

122. Fiddes, "Charles Williams," 76–77.
123. Pannenberg, *Basic Questions*, 107–8.
124. FAL, 66–75.
125. TPE, 133–35.
126. Fiddes, "'For the Dance all Things," 43–46.
127. Fiddes, "Is this the Promised End?"
128. Fiddes, "Charles Williams," 81–83.

definition of evil since it is intrinsically "nothing." Therefore, claims Fiddes, the most satisfactory answer to the theodicy question has to be laced with the rhetoric of tragedy and posits our engagement and participation in God, a God who through the cross contests, absorbs and overcomes evil.[129] In so doing God reciprocates our participation by being divinely present in the midst of all human suffering and pain.[130]

There is much to concur with in Fiddes' exploration for a most satisfactory answer to the theodicy question. While more will be said in the following chapters, suffice it to state briefly that it seems to me that though his case could be modified to generate more explanatory power, there is a substantial flaw that undermines his argument. In terms of helpful modifications, as Fiddes is seeking a most-conducive answer for today's post-Auschwitz situation, he would benefit from greater interaction with science, especially chaos-theory and indeterminism, in order to buttress his case for the apparent randomness and ambiguity of evil; natural evil especially.[131] Secondly, his rejection of a theoretical answer to the theodicy question in favor of a practical and experiential one may significantly reduce the intellectual robustness of his answer, especially now that some philosophers of religion demarcate between intellectual-logical approaches and emotive approaches to the problem of evil.[132]

Notwithstanding these improvements *vis-à-vis* Fiddes' answer to the theodicy question, his firm rejection of an ontology of evil in favor of a *privatio boni* position, in my opinion, significantly damages his attempted explanation of natural evil. As noted, his starting point is the conviction that no completely satisfactory theodicy exists.[133] This certainly seems the case if trying to causally explain the reasons behind natural evil from a *privatio boni* understanding. For, as some scholars argue, it is far more plausible and consistent to understand all types of evil—moral, human

---

129. Fiddes, "Tragedy," 189–92.

130. Fiddes, "Is this the Promised End?"

131. For example, Colwell, "Chaos and Providence," 131–38. After technical definitions, Colwell proceeds to effectively explain God's answering of Elijah's prayer to stop the rain for 3 years (1 Kings 17:1f, cf. James 5:17) from the perspective of chaos theory. This shows the complexity of creation thus helping to explain the ambiguous nature of much evil.

132. In his articulation of the freewill defense to the theodicy question, Davis separates the problem of evil into a logical form and an emotional form. The latter form hinders a strong positive case to be made to *believe* in an omnipotent God who co-exists with evil. Davis, "Free Will and Evil," 69–83.

133. See "Divine Passibility of Suffering" (pp.18–21) section above.

and natural—using a freewill defense argument which insists that all evil finds its origins in the freewill decisions of moral and sentient agents, particularly non-human ones.[134] As Augustine held, Satan (Lucifer) and his minions are the primary cause of natural evil,[135] a belief that catalyzes an option for the church to attempt to counter it through prayer in the Spirit.

THE CONSEQUENCES OF EVIL: DEATH, DARKNESS AND DEVELOPMENT

Fiddes is a thorough-going post-Auschwitz theologian. His predilection for practical, not theoretical, theodicy means taking very seriously the consequences of evil, both in this life and in the one to come. He holds that evil is very real and objectively experienced by many irrespective of whether or not one believes in an ontological evil power with personhood and willful volition.[136] That way all can agree that it is imperative to seek the best understanding of the consequences of evil in order to unearth possible antidotes and responses to its existence.

Fiddes discusses at length the greatest consequence of evil, *death*, especially in relation to its place in literature (biblical and otherwise) and subsequently the implications for Christian doctrine. The central common theme is its sheer ambiguity. He primarily notes that in scripture there is a complex delineation of death, one that is far removed from a simple attribution of "death is the result of the fall and sin." Fiddes notes that a detailed reading of the Old Testament reveals that death is described as a negative force before actual biological death, part of creation with a remit of boundary marking and then enemy to life after the fall,

---

134. Boyd, *Satan and the Problem*, 50–84; Boyd and Eddy, "Evil," 288–89; Hart, *The Doors of*; and Braaten, "Powers in Conflict," 96–98.

135. Plantinga insists that Augustine, rightly, locates natural evil in the free action of non-human spirits. Plantinga, *The Nature of*, 191–95; Plantinga, *God, Freedom*, 57–59. Interestingly, the works of Augustine cited by Plantinga to support his claim make no mention of Satan. It seems that Plantinga takes Augustine's explanation of moral evil caused by human freewill and applies it to explicate how natural evil is caused by non-human freewill. For a robust development of this application see Allen, "St. Augustine's Free Will," 84–90. Contrary to Plantinga, Hasker, while acknowledging that Plantinga does raise the bar to attempt "to prove positively that the existence of God is consistent with that of [all] evil" by demonstrating logical consistency, concludes the attempt as monumentally implausible since science has already identified the causes of many natural destructive phenomena, such as the discipline of plate tectonics to explain earthquakes. Hasker, *The Triumph*, 63–65.

136. See "The Place of Experience" (pp.9–13) section above.

and not permanent in God's creative intent but rather provisional while necessary within an evolutionary framework.[137] Hence why, philosophically speaking, there is an ambivalence to death as it is a sliding scale from neutral non-being to annihilating nothingness that is totally hostile to love and life.[138]

In other literature, death overlaps with tragedy and both are explicitly declared as *waste*. Tragedies contain much waste, expense and regret and often result in death when tragic figures, especially in Shakespeare, fail to affirm positive values and vision once held. This causes much tragedy to be played out against the background of death where the word spoken lives within the grasp of death, a reality exemplified in the tragic story of Christ who fully participated in human loss by the self-giving of his life.[139] Yet, insists Fiddes, precisely because of the crucifixion, cry of dereliction, and resurrection of Jesus Christ, the other side of Easter is the *only* place from which we can see reconciliation and in which our ultimate hope lies.[140] Evil and its consequence of death does not hold the final story and is not the end. In fact, death can be our servant instead of enemy, seen as a good thing spoilt as it forces us to accept it and respond in protest by facing our own immortality as well as affirm fundamental human values such as love and forgiveness, the kind of which death cannot destroy.[141]

The ambivalence of death with respect to human experience of it, together with the potential conquering and use of it on the resurrection side of Easter, creates the need for a re-articulation of the place of death within the triune God, especially since humans and their relationship with death participate within the Trinity. Drawing from Jüngel, Fiddes offers a nuanced definition insisting that God experiences death and dying in the form of perishing and relationlessness without *actual* death.[142] He arrives at this conclusion after rejecting Moltmann's insistence that humans do not experience their own death, only the death of others, and the same applies to the Father and Son.[143] Instead, Fiddes argues that there is good psychological evidence that humans do experience their

137. PIG, 230–35; TPE, 66–71.
138. PIG, 235–36.
139. FAL, 75–82; Fiddes, "Is this the Promised End?"
140. FAL, 82; Fiddes, "Tragedy," 176.
141. Fiddes, "Tragedy," 174–76; Fiddes, "Is this the Promised End?"
142. PIG, 239–42, cf. Jüngel, *God as the Mystery*, 199–219.
143. Moltmann, *The Crucified God*, 207, 217, 243ff.

own impending death and so within a participatory understanding of the panentheistic triune God this means that death is an experience known to God in God's own life. Consequently, therefore, we can refer to God owning death, death belonging to God, his own nothingness and his perishability. God is willing and able to experience his own relationships in a new way in the face of death.[144]

A second, less guaranteed, consequence of evil in lived life and existence is *darkness*. Its reduced inevitability is grounded in the fact that it is a shaded experience extrapolated from the tension created in fallen existence between freedom and limit.[145] Fiddes' critique of literature draws attention to differing modalities of darkness all of which aid the theologian to approach the ambiguities of human life and presence of evil. From Golding, Fiddes identifies a continuum of darkness, from a basic darkness that arises out of the general anxiety of human life through to a darkness that merges with a deeper kind of dark; one permeated with evil. Some of Golding's characters quintessentially demonstrate movement along this spectrum by failing to trust each other, relapsing into the fallen tides of their nature, or bombastically over asserting their pride and neglect. Ironically, in trying to deal with the anxiety that is causing the darkness without turning to grace and its source, the characters are led into deeper, more sinister darkness.[146]

In his analysis of poetry and sonnets, Fiddes uses Hopkins' work to elucidate the need for negative and positive expressions of the sublime and beauty in order to fully and experientially participate in the life of the triune God.[147] In his poetry there are shifting boundaries between positive and negative sublime; between the beauty of the world and the imposing, destructive nature of creation. It is in the negative sublime that arises a sense of dread and horror in the face of vast and significant forces of power and destruction, which in turn creates a *darkness*, one present in the romantic sublime, and one in which, according to Hopkins, Christ is absent and no longer at the center of the world or its universal forms that

---

144. PIG, 236–44. Fiddes' entire argument about death in the triune God is a highly metaphorical attempt to answer the "death of God" theologians and state that while God does indeed endure death, he is not dead.

145. FAL, 207–8.

146. FAL, 208–14.

147. Fiddes, "The Sublime," 148–49.

he calls "inscapes." Fiddes concurs that the darkness is real but contends that God is never absent but hidden.[148]

Finally, and differently to much church tradition, Fiddes holds to a final and complete overcoming of all evil, which he describes as a "hopeful universalism;" a Christian hope in which no one is left outside, alienated or rejected.[149] Instead of a "dogmatic universalism" which Fiddes argues does not deal sufficiently with evil and wickedness, his account of hopeful universalism eradicates evil as it allows people to repent, grow and be sanctified after death and best explains scriptural texts that speak of God wanting "all to be saved" (2 Peter 3:9; 1 Timothy 2:4).[150] Other advantages of this position include an eschatological end that makes room for an optimistic version of conditional immortality that offers the most hope in the face of death and the best theodicy answer since justice is found in post-death growth and development of those whose lives were prematurely cut short.[151]

CONCLUSION

This chapter had two aims to meet: to analyze and discuss Fiddes' theology of evil deciphered from his corpus on literature and theology and the doctrine of God, and to formulate a doctrine of evil that will be used in the following chapters as I seek to locate a theology of SW into a doctrine of God in a theologically coherent way. As demonstrated, Fiddes delineates a portrait of evil which does not fully answer the theodicy question and is not a closed, systematic theology of evil with no room for further deliberations and additions. Just like his doctrine of God, there is openness and a malleable quality to his understanding of evil that can be shaped and adapted.

---

148. Fiddes, "The Sublime," 142–48. According to Fiddes, the idea of "inscapes" came to Hopkins primarily from his reading of scripture: Psalm 18 and 139 to be specific. Fiddes, "G. M. Hopkins," 572.

149. Fiddes, "Question."

150. I say "his account of hopeful universalism" because in drawing from Hebblethwaite, Whitehead and Hartshorne, Fiddes' hopeful universalist version comes with the opportunity for people to repent or not, according to their freewill decision. The inclusion of freewill sets Fiddes at odds with more standard accounts. TPE, 190–96; Fiddes, "Tragedy," 188–89, cf. Balthasar, *Dare We Hope*; Jones, "A Hopeful Universalism," 22–27. For a recent defense of dogmatic universalism, see Hart, *That All Shall*.

151. TPE, 49–52, 133–35.

It has been shown what impact Fiddes' theology of evil has upon different areas of his work. The analyses and discussion on Abelardian atonement theology of transformation and its effect on evil, together with the consequences of evil seen especially in tragic literature, will serve more effectively as foundational concepts on which to build a theology of omnipotence and theology of omnipresence in chapters four and five than use for a particular facet of a theology of evil. Hence the lack of critical engagement in those two sections.

From interlocution of the other three sections in this chapter, i.e. the ontology of evil, evil's personifications, and the problem of evil, it is possible to formulate a fundamental rubric concerning evil that will be used and applied in the forthcoming critical analyses, discussion and delineation of a doctrine of God capable and coherent enough to contain a theology of SW. Concluding from the above, it seems clear that there is no overarching imperative to follow Fiddes' binary thinking and jettison the biblical and experiential witness of ontologically-grounded evil—whether in satanic, demonic, power and principality or triumvirate form—in order to maintain his panentheistic vision of God or avoid rendering "the Satan" personhood and full salvific potential that accompanies it.

Following Fiddes' insistence to formulate a practical theodicy that is coherent in the present milieu, I insist that any theology of evil needs, potentially, to hold explanatory power of both the biblical and traditional picture of ontologically-grounded evil, as well as humanity's experience of situational, moral and natural evil, especially that of a dysteleological kind. Evil, in whatever form, is quasi-personal with intelligence, volition, freewill and awareness.[152] It is also, following Augustine, "hell-bent" on driving humanity towards nothingness and *me on* non-being through continual action of its remit to kill, steal, devour and destroy (John 10:10; 1 Peter 5:8). While ambiguity remains concerning the origin of evil and its personifications, this is not the case regarding its reality in people's lives and the world-at-large.

A heavily nuanced doctrine of evil: one which maintains the ontological over-and-againstness of evil; does not deny its malevolent work towards a destination of non-being; gives space for the potential exercising

---

152. As Noble, following Green and Wright, suggests, Satan can be viewed as a sub-person, an anti-person of sorts, who possesses a malevolent intelligence that wills, acts and knows but is totally without any personal feeling or sympathy. Instead, he is obsessed with self-aggrandizement and feeds parasitically on human wickedness. Noble, "The Spirit World," 217–18.

of diabolical freewill planning and strategy; and recognizes its operative but limited power in light of the cross, has, I believe, significantly more congruence apposed with the doctrine of God held by Fiddes than his definition of evil as primarily *privatio boni*. Therefore, in the following chapters I will critically engage with Fiddes' doctrine of God in order to shape and articulate a doctrine of God which can best make sense of God's nature and character in the midst of evil as defined in this chapter. First, let us address God's omniscient knowledge.

PART TWO

A Doctrine of God

3

Knowledge
God's Omniscience in a Context of Spiritual Warfare

INTRODUCTION

> Then, you've asked the question, does God know what is going to happen in the future and I would say, no, God *does not know* that *in detail*. Now, this is because God wants the world to be free, to make its own decisions, to do new things in cooperation with God, and if God knew the future in detail it would be closed and determined . . . I think *foreknowledge and predetermination belong together* . . . I don't think that we can simply distinguish foreknowledge from predetermination. The one does mean the other. (emphasis mine).[1]

THE UNWILLINGNESS OF FIDDES to advocate exhaustive divine foreknowledge ("EDF" hereafter) is determined collectively by his participation in the triune God vision and a theological understanding of a suffering God who participates in time, interacts with creation, and constantly moves from states of potentiality to actuality. Therefore, his denial of EDF leads to an understanding of divine omniscience which contends God's

---

1. Fiddes, "Is God All-Knowing? Repeated in Fiddes, "Is the Future Open?" cf. TPE, 128.

knowledge to be perfect concerning possibility *and* actuality but not possibility *as* actuality.²

The use of Fiddes for a discussion on divine omniscience is very appropriate. Trying to understand what God knows in the midst of spiritual conflict is a subject matter relevant to a number of theological disciplines and in Fiddes there is an eclecticism which merits inclusion in the conversation. Academically, Fiddes approaches God's omniscience as a theologian, not philosopher. Yet his contributions to the debate are not typical of most theologians. Similarly to his position of holding an Augustinian position in matters concerning the nature of evil but non-Augustinian when relating that to the doctrine of God, it will be shown that unlike the typical theologian who seeks to defend and protect God's sovereignty and usually holds to a form of theological determinism, Fiddes atypically aligns more closely to philosophers by holding a robust conception of libertarian free will and vigorously defending it.³

Overall, Fiddes' commitment to the free will of all creation shapes and undergirds his doctrine of God which offers an attempt at a more nuanced understanding of God's omniscience which may be more congruent to a theology of SW than other historical-traditional doctrines of God.⁴ This is especially the case as we consider the eschatological context of the phenomenon of SW. Eschatological visions of the future often result in either over or under realized understandings of the present. Biblical theology has consistently adopted a "both-and" position by articulating a semi-realized eschatological reality. The current age of tension imbibed with an "already-not yet" nature is rooted in the biblical development of the kingdom of God, best articulated by Christ's statement "the kingdom of God has come near,"⁵ and demonstrated by his example as a first century Palestinian exorcist who, when encountering the existence of malevolent and dysteleological evil, brought spiritual emancipation and deliverance via exercising the truth and power of the kingdom of God.⁶

2. Fiddes, et al, *Baptists and the Communion*, 140. Fiddes' Oxford colleague Bradshaw comments that the seminal open theist text, *The Openness of God*, would have been enhanced if it had included a chapter by Fiddes without any real evangelical-theological incongruence. Bradshaw, Review of *The Openness of God*, 29.

3. Hunt, "If God knows the future."

4. See chapter 1 (pp.3–31) above.

5. Mark 1:15. For substantial discussion and conclusion about the meaning of the tensioned verbs, ἤγγικεν and ἔφθασεν, see Ladd, *The Presence*.

6. Twelftree, *Christ Triumphant*, 20–86.

Therefore, while resting on a guaranteed final full consummation of the kingdom of God,[7] we presently inhabit this continuing realized age of tension which can manifest itself, experientially and phenomenologically, as semi-dualistic in spiritual conflict terms. This is the reason why the didactic material about armor and warfare stated in Ephesians 6:10–20 with regard to our πάλη against authorities,[8] cosmic powers of darkness, and spiritual forces of evil is an important consideration from the Pauline corpus to use analogously. If we logically extrapolate the warfare analogy and its underlying truth value by conflating the idea of "struggle" or "wrestle" against powers, authorities and principalities *with* the scriptural witness, tradition of the early church,[9] and many claimed accounts of possession and exorcism,[10] then we can conclude that the current existence of evil operates within a metaphysical "now and not-yet" reality marked by contingency, openness, ambiguity, non-determinism, and significant say-so in this current age of ongoing SW and conflict.

This therefore leaves much potential for casting a new theological vision of divine omniscience within a SW reality by using Fiddes' contemporary theology as the key primary source. In the rest of this chapter, I will delineate and analyze Fiddes' understanding of divine omniscience, focusing primarily on divine passibility and mutability, God's relationship to time and eternity, implications for divine and human freedom, and the universal hope of the eschaton and its content. From this there will be a brief proposal of some central features of God's omniscience which can bring greater clarity to a theology of SW.

THE PASSIBILITY AND MUTABILITY OF GOD: OUR FELLOW SUFFERER WHO UNDERSTANDS

Despite having written only a small amount specifically about divine omniscience,[11] Fiddes' continual grounding of his corpus of work in the doctrine of God means that he returns to God's knowledge with

---

7. The last chapters of Revelation reveal that all dualism is removed. Richard Bauckham, *The Theology of*, 106–8.
8. Fighting, battling, struggling or wrestling.
9. Daunton-Fear, *Healing in the Early*.
10. Bennett, *I Am Not Afraid*, 1–96.
11. CSG, 77–109.

frequency.¹² While denying EDF, he adamantly states with clear succinctness that God knows everything that has happened in the past and everything that is currently happening; this is a very important part of the notion of God's omniscience.¹³ At this early juncture, however, we encounter the first problem with Fiddes' "presentism." The overlap and synthesis of human future choice and the future of the world means that God has *no* foreknowledge at all, neither the future contingent agency of free moral beings or his own response. Is it not impossible, philosophically, to know the future in outline but not in detail?¹⁴ Second, to defend presentism hermeneutically results in tying oneself in theological knots. While accepting that all language about God is to a greater or lesser extent metaphorical, rejecting the traditional hermeneutical concepts of anthropomorphism and anthropopathism, as Fiddes does in his studies of Hosea and Jeremiah,¹⁵ consequentially presents challenges accepting God's exhaustive knowledge of both the past and the present, as well as the future.¹⁶

That said, as stated above, Fiddes advocates the doctrine of a passible God of suffering love which includes a presentist understanding of divine omniscience because it answers a number of theological challenges.¹⁷ It also has important implications for Christian living, church history (especially within one's own denomination), and the relationship between scripture and theology.¹⁸ On this latter point Fiddes claims innu-

12. To illustrate, Fiddes, "Relational Trinity," 178–82; Fiddes, "Charles Williams," 73–77; SWKG, 373–96.

13. Fiddes, "Is God; Is the Future."

14. "Either God foresees all the future or none of it." Picirilli, "An Arminian Response, 479.

15. Since modern psychology teaches that to love involves suffering with, empathy for, and vulnerability with, the sufferer, God's covenant *hesed* involves suffering with Israel. CSG, 16–25; Fiddes, "The Cross," 176–78.

16. For example, if God had no future knowledge of how Abraham would respond to his test (Gen 22:12), then it seems difficult to escape the conclusions that God did not know the present situation in Sodom (Gen 18:20–21), forgets the past like the sins of his people (Isa 43:25), what the rainbow is for (Gen 9:15–16), or delightfully smells the sacrifice of Noah which delights his "heart." Ware, *God's Lesser Glory*, 76–77; Gray and Sinkinson, *Reconstructing Theology*, x.

17. See "Chapter 1 (pp.3–31) above. cf. PEPS, 207–20; PIG, 62–112.

18. Prayers are petitions in time *in God* who lives in relationship without a hint of coercion or unilateral action, only persuasion. Fiddes, "Introduction: A Theology," 1–16; PIG, 115–51. In literature, there is the offer of possible future worlds, a hope that expects the unexpected. FAL, 1–46; TPE, 110–80; Fiddes, "The Promised End: Response," 191–95. Baptist Daniel Turner debated "Socinian" general Baptists Foster and

merable positive theological benefits including a tenable account of God involved with humans in their suffering;[19] a foundational tenet for any theology of trust;[20] equipping us to elicit more in-depth understanding and appreciation of tragic literature that contains theological themes such as the writings of Blake and Hopkins;[21] transformation of humanity towards God himself;[22] a more robust account of God's involvement in believers' baptism;[23] and a significantly stronger foundational platform from which to develop sermons on forgiveness using a definition of forgiveness as a divine journey of anguish, and targeted movements towards some examples of restorative justice.[24]

While it is beyond doubt that Fiddes has considered and articulated a multifarious defense and advocacy of divine passibility with limited foreknowledge, it is necessary for the purpose of this study to examine the center of this vision in order to establish whether or not they help construct an understanding of omniscience befitting a doctrine of God which is congruent with a SW reality. Therefore, let us consider the historical influences of Baptist and process theology and if divine passibility infers mutability and vice versa.

Fiddes is a Baptist theologian and he recognizes there is a live history of Baptist scholarship on suffering, both divine and human, which has had an impact on his theology.[25] That, together with his increasing openness to "experience" as a source for theology has resulted in Fiddes propounding divine suffering in order to find a satisfactory theodicy in the face of much contemporary human suffering.[26] Divine passibility

---

Bulkley when promoting universal revelation over natural theology. Fiddes, "Daniel Turner and a Theology," 125–27.

19. SWKG, 60–83.

20. Fiddes, et al, *On the Way of Trust*, 11–35.

21. FAL, 85–145.

22. Fiddes, "The Passion," 755–58.

23. Fiddes, *Believing and Being Baptized*, 17–20, 44–45.

24. Fiddes, "Preaching Forgiveness," 11–15; Fiddes, "Memory, Forgetting," 130–33; Fiddes, "Restorative Justice," 5–8.

25. Fiddes concurs with Mason who highlights the Baptist emphases on direct *experience* of God and standing up to powers in dissent has led to the idea of the passibility of God. Fiddes, "Towards a New Millennium," 22, fn.5; Fiddes, "Prophecy, Corporate Personality," 90, cf. H. Wheeler Robinson, *Redemption and Revelation*, 150, fn.1. Fiddes, "Prophecy, Corporate Personality," 94. Mason, "Response to Paul," 95–98.

26. See "The Place of Experience" (pp.9–13) section above.

offers a helpful explanation for the three primary forms of the phenomenon of suffering: theoretical, practical and aesthetic.[27]

Divine passibility is, according to Fiddes, the most satisfying way to present the biblical God who works out his purposes and plans in a world that is a living organism and constantly in a state of flux.[28] If, as he maintains, the world should be conceived as a social, interconnected organism with an intrinsic reality that is always becoming and changing through actual occasions, then we need a doctrine of God that articulates power as persuasion, knowledge as actual *and* potential, and mutability as a result of God being affected by the world.[29] For this Fiddes leans heavily on process theology.[30] However, as previously noted,[31] attentive listening to Fiddes reveals that he does not accept it as a water-tight theological system and is critical of a number of its key tenets, especially its trinitarian deficiencies,[32] and the highly controversial insistence that divine limitation is due to the supreme value and superiority of creation and creativity, not God's freedom and desire.[33]

This reliance on a nuanced version of process theology by Fiddes, which views divine love as suffering and defines creation as consisting of a significant element of co-operation between God and finite beings,[34] causes him to postulate divine change as an integral part of divine passibility. This has to be the case if the reality of divine suffering is taken

---

27. This is primarily because we see the call on the prophet to enter into the divine pathos and into a redeeming transformation of the situation of suffering by entering into the divine forgiveness and thereby being able to start to forgive the perpetrator of the suffering. Fiddes, "The Cross," 176–78, 186–88; Fiddes, "Suffering in Theology," 169–70.

28. Fiddes, "Suffering, Divine," 634.

29. Fiddes, "Process," 472–75.

30. There are, of course, different process theologies. Nash, "Introduction," ix–xii; Oord, *The Uncontrolling Love*, 119–20.

31. See "The Contemporary Need" (pp.4–9) and "The Challenge of Divine" (pp.26–30) sections above.

32. Attempts by theologians to re-formulate process theology in trinitarian terms include Boyd, "The Self-Sufficient Sociality," 73–94; Bracken, "Panentheism from a Process," 95–113. Of Bracken's earlier work, Fiddes claims that he fails to successfully position process theology within the Trinity because he objectifies the Father, Son and Spirit and ends up with tritheism. Fiddes, "The Trinity in Process," 2–5. cf. Bracken, *The Triune Symbol*.

33. See "The Contemporary Need" (pp.4–9) section above. Fiddes also recognizes process theology's limitation for Baptist ecclesiology and mission. Fiddes, "Baptism and Membership," 87–90.

34. Fiddes, "Process Theology."

seriously and God is viewed as existing in an ontological state that includes, as suggested by the Hebrew prophets, waiting, interacting in time, and moving forward into future states of reality in a way different to that of created beings.[35]

Overall, this raises the question whether or not Fiddes needs to embrace a particular version of process theology that results in locating divine mutability into divine suffering in order to continue the recent Baptist writings on divine passibility? To start, despite claims that process theology is bringing a counter-balancing alternative to the heavily-Platonized traditional doctrine of God,[36] ironically the same accusation could be made towards process theology.[37] Not only is this a recapitulation of the ancient debate between different Greek schools of thought that emphasized either "being" (Parmenides and Plato) or "becoming" (Heraclitus and Protagoras),[38] but it is also apparent that Fiddes' application of process thought attempts to integrate theology with today's dominant western philosophical worldview. Since science and chaos-theory has established that the world is complex with an open future consisting of randomness and many possibilities, Fiddes argues that God should be defined as necessarily complex who in *perfect incompleteness* moves with perichoretic delight abounding with freedom, persuasion, love and cooperation.[39] However, despite accepting that evolutionary theory is an established fact which demonstrates that every strata of creation, grows, changes and is ever-becoming,[40] Fiddes' insistence that divine limitation be based upon God's freedom and desire, not ontological superiority of creation, rules out using evolutionary terms to define God as active and involved in the process of evolution, not transcendent over creation.[41]

---

35. CSG, 77–78.

36. See "The Contemporary Need" (pp.4–9) section above.

37. It could be questioned whether Fiddes gives classical theism found in Augustine, Calvin, and Luther any substantial consideration. They certainly do not regularly appear in CSG, Fiddes' key work on divine passibility.

38. Hartshorne and Reese, *Philosophers Speak of God*, 2; Gruenler, *The Inexhaustible God*, 7–8.

39. CSG, 91–98; SWKG, 130–66.

40. Cady, "Extending the boundaries," 15–17.

41. Some process thinkers use evolutionary theory to develop a diverse nature of Christianity by actualizing its infinite potential, creativity and divinity thereby becoming a potential model of multi-religious understanding and harmony. See Faber, "Introduction to Process," 318–21.

Related, we also should consider if it is possible for divine suffering to take place without divine change. It seems that Fiddes has not seriously engaged with the key theologians of western church tradition and so some interlocution with current theologians of the tradition is merited. To begin, as noted above,[42] Weinandy strongly maintains that the impassible God of scripture and tradition is more loving and compassionate than a God who suffers via change.[43] After accurately summarizing the pathos of God movement (which includes Fiddes),[44] Weinandy directly criticizes Fiddes on the need for a creator-creature distinction and argues that holding to a panentheistic understanding of God while maintaining that God is the creator is incoherent, as the creator God is wholly other to the created order. It is metaphysically impossible for him to be ontologically part of the created order while simultaneously its creator.[45]

One wonders, however, whether just like Fiddes, Weinandy lets his philosophical commitments from tradition belie his theology. For it appears that his acceptance of Aquinas' *apatheia* and *actus purus* cause him to unsatisfactorily explain scripture's portrayal of a God who on a *prima facie* reading, appears to be both immutable (Numbers 23:19, Malachi 3:6; James 1:17) and mutable (Genesis 6:6–7; 1 Samuel 15: 11, 35; Jonah 3:10; Amos 7:3).[46] His commitment to divine simplicity rules out a dialectically synthesized understanding—say divine moral immutability and relational mutability—and so he concludes that all change is predicated upon the change in the humans involved, despite the clear statements that God, as subject, *changed, relented, grieved*.[47] Moreover, he philosophically critiques Fiddes' panentheism without exegesis of verses used to supporting panentheism, e.g. Acts 17:28 or Colossians 1:16–17.[48]

Another interlocutor defending the tradition is Frances Young. As a patristic scholar she critiques Fiddes' divine possibility of suffering love on two fronts: first, since the Fathers consistently held the Chalcedonian paradox of Christ as one who suffered without suffering, they would have resisted Fiddes' use of personal language analogously for God's being as too anthropomorphic, and also reacted to any suggestion of change in

---

42. See "The Contemporary Need" (pp.4–9) section above.
43. Weinandy, *Does God Change?*; Weinandy, *Does God Suffer*.
44. Weinandy, *Does God Suffer*, 1–26; Weinandy, "Does God," 35.
45. Weinandy, *Does God Suffer*, 153–57.
46. Weinandy, *Does God Change*, 74–82.
47. Weinandy, "Does God," 37–38.
48. See "The Nature and Character" (pp.13–18) section above.

the divine being.⁴⁹ Second, and more compelling, as a mother to a severely handicapped son she strongly argues that emotions and feelings cannot be trusted and humans are ambivalent in their evaluation of those emotions. Young rightly states that since human experience of tragedy clearly calls for both times of empathetic suffering with the victim and occasions for the helper to be beyond self-involvement and suffering, the same should be predicated of God.⁵⁰ This interesting interchange certainly opens the way for an analysis and exploration into divine omnipotence and whether the use of human power can be analogously used to speak of God. This will be explored further in the next chapter.

The final idea to briefly consider is von Balthasar's thesis that God does not need to change in order to suffer. Fiddes lists the thesis as part of the historical development of divine passibility and an important influence on the debate.⁵¹ Following his critique of Moltmann's capitulation to Whiteheadean metaphysics, von Balthasar convincingly argues that we cannot accept any form of world process that is identified with the eternal and timeless hypostases in God. Rather, all discussion of God's triune life (including suffering) must start from a theology of the cross, rooted in the mystery of the absolute, which will open up the possibility of suffering experience being considered with implications that are trinitarian and Christological, and ultimately grounded in God.⁵² In other words, there is potential for divine suffering *within* God himself and it consists of the reckless giving away of the Father by himself, and the divine recklessness of the Son, in the power of the Spirit, in allowing himself to be crushed.⁵³

IN GOD TIME IS HEALED AND CREATION IS FREE

Fiddes' panentheistic vision of participating in God is the overarching framework of his doctrine of God.⁵⁴ Therefore, the idea that all reality is *in* God has interesting ramifications in how to think about the concept of time and the nature of freedom. Fiddes, like all astute theologians, is

---

49. Young, "*Apathos Epathen*: Patristic," 79–94.

50. Young, *Face to Face*, 237–39. Fiddes acknowledges that this is a very strong challenge to the concept of a suffering God but responds by arguing that divine empathetic suffering does not overwhelm God in the way that it may a human being. PIG, 179–84.

51. Fiddes, "Suffering, Divine," 634.

52. Balthasar, *Theo-Drama*, 321–24.

53. Balthasar, *Theo-Drama*, 328.

54. See "The Nature and Character" (pp.13–18) section above.

very aware of this and seeks to offer a particular understanding of time that remains effective and coherent when articulating creaturely libertarian freedom without undermining his panentheistic model or arriving at some version of causal predetermination *and* foreknowledge, which he sees belonging together. So, to continue to formulate a definition of omniscience that makes sense of SW reality, critical engagement with Fiddes' position on the nature of time and eternity, together with the implications this has for EDF and divine and human freedom, is needed.

Fiddes primarily looks to literature as it raises a number of doctrine of God matters such as divine relations to time and eternity.[55] Literary endings are often left open with both certainty and possibilities, which mirror God's knowledge of the future; *he knows what can be known.* Eternity is not static but rather open and consists of a unity of space and time that implies immensity, eternity, growth and development as time is healed and fully integrated through God's participation in it via perichoresis and eternity's participation in the triune God.[56] Any idea of foreordination or predetermination is foreign to Fiddes' vision of God that consists of co-working with creation to bring about the future, which infers a logical denial of any kind of EDF.

In *The Promised End* Fiddes offers his most substantial discussion on God, time and eternity which he extrapolates from discussion of literary works by T.S Elliot and Virginia Woolf. Their works highlight the problems of time's fragmentation, isolation in time between inner and outer time, timelessness, and eternity as simultaneity.[57] He rejects Elliot's "eternity as simultaneity" position claiming that it is very Augustinian and holding eternity to be timeless does not necessarily lead to the human broken self being healed by an interplay between timelessness and humanity, as claimed by Elliot.[58] Jettisoning other versions of the eternal moment, the absolute presentness of Moltmann,[59] and the eternal presentism of Boethius,[60] Fiddes calls for a return to the way eternity is seen

---

55. See "Chapter 2 Introduction" (pp.32–33) section above. cf. Fiddes, "Concept," 17–22.

56. Fiddes, "Patterns of hope," 31–50; Fiddes, "Dystopia, Utopia," 11–21; Fiddes, "The Promised," 191–95; SWKG, 130–66, 299–323.

57. TPE, 110–47.

58. TPE, 123–24.

59. That "kairotic" moment that is fulfilling and our experience of the eternal moment itself. Moltmann, *The Coming*, 289.

60. That is, the past, present and future are one simultaneous point in the eternity in which God exists.

in scripture and its presentation of the God of the ages living in unending durations. Not only will this accord well with the special relativity of Einstein and current views of time in modern physics, but it will also elicit new possibilities in thinking about participation in time, post-death growth and development in eternal duration, and posit the concept of timelessness as the healing of time, made possible by bringing "love" into the discussion.[61]

While Fiddes correctly understands that "as modern relativity theory tells us, time is characterized by its relations—to space, velocity, to the observer—rather than being something absolute,"[62] it does seem that his concepts of the healing of time in God,[63] and the continual integration of time within God, which makes sense of the image of the "journey,"[64] are difficult to ground in the experience of the observer. Crucially, what does the healing of time and the harmonizing of time with the self actually mean, and how are *humans* to speak of it?[65] There are ways, I believe, in which Fiddes' account of time's healing in God could be clarified and developed.

To begin, it appears that Fiddes has not correctly understood Barth's definition of God's eternity and his charge that Barth's use of Boethius' simultaneity is another form of timelessness is a misunderstanding of the nuanced approach of Barth.[66] Barth goes to great lengths to frame God's eternity as a perfection of his freedom and avoids defining divine eternity with either timelessness or everlastingness concepts.[67] God is lord of time and so his eternity is a positive description of what God *is* in his absolute freedom, and it is this divine freedom—something Fiddes completely acknowledges—which determines the need to differentiate eternity as God's time from fallen human experience of fallen time.[68] As stated, "God's eternity is authentically temporal but it is *authentically*

61. TPE, 124–40.

62. TPE, 140.

63. Fiddes acknowledges taking this term from Barth, but he disagrees that an understanding of the healing of time can be done with a Boethian formula of simultaneity. Instead, a healing of time retains a distinction between the phases of time. TPE, 138–39, cf. *CD* II/1, §31.3, 617–18.

64. Fiddes, "Spirituality as Attentiveness," 55–57.

65. TPE, 139.

66. TPE, 139.

67. *CD* II/1, §31.3, 608–40; cf. Bromiley, *Introduction*, 80–81.

68. "God is the God whom God has determined to be." Fiddes, "Is God." Fiddes, "Is the Future."

temporal: it is our experience of time that is *unauthentic*."[69] Therefore, when it comes to the complex idea of time and eternity Fiddes' concept of the healing of time in God may be a perfect aspect of God's eternity rooted in his freedom but completely impotent when trying to articulate divine eternity from the creaturely experience of human temporality.

Second, as a theologian Fiddes could enhance his understanding of divine eternity by supplementing his discussion with recent scholarship by modern philosophers of religion. As is well known, theistic philosophers generally fall into one of two categories concerning the nature of time: some hold a tensed theory of time in which the past, present and future are objective realities and tensed language reflects that reality, while others, like many physicists, postulate a tenseless theory of time which holds that all moments and events in time are equally real and existent.[70] Fiddes, rooting his discussion in the eternal dance of the Trinity together with salient examples from poetry, claims that there is no theological model of time and space that proves either static or dynamic understanding of time and so theology needs to integrate its discussion of time into the doctrine of God, in which our successive moments of time have their source in God's time.[71]

However, without any philosophical critique of the tenseless view of time, Fiddes' entire understanding of God's omniscience is predicated on a tensed theory of time. Indeed, he assumes a type-A understanding of time without any real examination and critique of the tenseless model because the former fits his doctrine of a suffering God. Only with a tensed view of time can "the now" exist as a privileged temporal location independent of our experience, and in a way different from the past and the future. Moreover, only a tensed view can conclude that God, like humans, is temporal and has to change since he is present in the midst of changing reality. This accords well with Fiddes' view of a passible, mutable God who co-creates the future—a future that does not *actually* exist—by partnering with creation. Without specifically referring to tensed or tenseless understandings of time, Fiddes' account is grounded on a type-A tensed

---

69. Colwell, "The Contemporaneity of the Divine," 150. The temporality of God consists of the Trinity of pre-temporality, supra-temporality, and post-temporality. God shows himself as the one who precedes time, accompanies time and is there after time. Bromiley, *Introduction*, 81.

70. For extensive discussion see Craig, *The Tensed Theory*; Craig, *The Tenseless Theory*; cf. McTaggart, *The Nature of*.

71. TPE, 181–218.

model of time since God in his continuing temporality has, despite its non-existence, exhaustive knowledge of *the past* together with unlimited understanding of the present.[72]

Also, while a clear proponent of God's partial knowledge of the future and divine temporal interaction with creation, Fiddes is less clear on the nature of time and the creation of the universe. When he proposes the healing of time in God does he, like Lane Craig, see God as timeless before creation and temporal since the creation of the universe?[73] This would logically support creation *ex nihilo* and divine interaction with the universe, both attested by scripture and Fiddes.[74] Or does God transcend time since he is more fundamental than time itself and therefore "the freedom of God from ontic determination is the ground of creation's goodness: precisely because creation is uncompelled, unnecessary . . . it can reveal how God is the God he is."[75]

Moreover, is Fiddes correct to coalesce foreknowledge and predetermination and thereby conclude that divine foreknowledge *cannot* co-exist with creaturely freedom?[76] In short, is it imperative to maintain God's absolute knowledge of past and present but only partial knowledge of the future in order to enhance divine and creaturely freedom so as to not undermine Fiddes' panentheistic vision? Fiddes, like relational, openness and process theologians, espouses freedom, both divine and creaturely, solely in libertarian terms and rejects any kind of compatibilism.[77] This commitment to libertarian freedom, so he claims, means that exhaustive predetermination and foreknowledge do not exist, and the nature of the future is potential, not actual, and therefore not fully knowable, even by God. The one exception to this definition of freedom is *ecclesiological* freedom which Fiddes, like historical and orthodox Christian thought,

---

72. "God knows everything that has happened and everything that is happening." Fiddes, "Is God."; Fiddes, "Is the Future."

73. Craig, "Timelessness and Omnitemporality," 129–60; cf. Craig, *God, Time*, 3–42, 134–39.

74. In order to defend God's self-existence without necessary self-sufficiency Fiddes grounds creation *ex nihilo* in divine internality, i.e. God's will, love and good pleasure. CSG, 75. For God's divine interaction and human contribution to God's creation see Fiddes, "Faith, Theology and Imagination," 58–59.

75. Hart, *The Beauty*, 158.

76. See "Chapter 3 Introduction" (pp.63–65) section above.

77. Given his emphasis on the conflation and interweaving of process theology and Barth's theme of God's freedom and desire, Fiddes could aid his claim by critiquing Gunton's claim of metaphysical incongruence between process theology and Barth. A brief footnote does not suffice. Gunton, *Becoming and Being*, 220–24, cf. CSG, 15, fn. 42.

sees not as personal autonomy but life bound up under the rule of Christ and obeying him (John 14:23–24).[78]

Fiddes advocates libertarian freedom, both divine and creaturely, for a number of claimed advantages. Not only does it accurately reflect the paradoxical tension between freedom and limit of the human condition,[79] it also brings understanding to human experience of the sublime,[80] opens humanity up to trust-laden relationships,[81] best articulates *how* God continually creates new things in the world,[82] and brings greater understanding to the divine name revealed to Moses in Exodus 3 as "I am what you will find me to be."[83] Not only that but, as already discussed above, divine and creaturely libertarian freedom is also central to understanding the suffering inherent in creation and this paves the way for the construction of divine suffering, a theology that offers the best answer to the theodicy problem.[84] As Blocher states, this post-renaissance thinking that emphasizes human autonomy and independence as the best explanation of why evil exists, arose due to dissatisfaction with the compatibilist explanations offered by Augustine and Aquinas.[85]

Notwithstanding the pervasiveness of compatibilist theologies of freedom in the tradition, the majority of scholarly work on SW assumes a libertarian understanding of freedom.[86] Fiddes coheres well within this corpus of work. However, a significant problem arises when it is claimed that the only way to have genuine creaturely freedom is through limiting God's foreknowledge and thereby denying his EDF of the future. When we apply this nuanced definition of omniscience to eschatological hope for the future, it ultimately fails to offer the certainty and hope for the eschaton as articulated by both scripture and church tradition.

Therefore, if we could find a robust theological case that maintains divine and creaturely freedom while simultaneously espousing divine EDF (i.e. God sees and knows all reality which from the human

---

78. Fiddes, "A Fourth Strand," 153–59.
79. FAL, 85–115; 173–204.
80. Fiddes, "The Sublime," 128–32.
81. Fiddes, et al, *On the Way*, 17–35.
82. Fiddes, "The Place of Christian," 80–82.
83. Fiddes, *The Escape*, 5–9.
84. See "Divine Passibility of Suffering" (pp.18–21) section above.
85. Blocher, *Evil and the Cross*, 36–37.
86. Yong, for instance, offers five good reasons for the libertarian notion of freedom. Yong, *The Spirit of*, 94–95.

perspective falls into past, present and future categories) then one could articulate a doctrine of divine omniscience that accords well with the scriptural witness of semi-dualistic SW worldview that still guarantees a dynamic sovereignty of God and an assured eschatology. Subsequently, this need to maintain divine EDF negates theological systems under the rubric of relational theism such as process theology and open theism,[87] and the imperative to define freedom and free will in libertarian terms invalidates the different types of compatibilist theologies.[88]

The remaining widely held theological cases, which claim to appose divine EDF and creational libertarian freedom, are Molinism and simple foreknowledge, specifically the nuanced account of David Hunt. Unfortunately Molinism—despite some recent excellent work on Molina's claim that God's omniscience consists in chronological order of *scientia naturalis* (God's knowledge of all possible truths); *scientia media* (God's knowledge of all counterfactual truths); then God's *divine creative decree;* and finally *scientia libera* (God's knowledge of all actual truths)—still undermines genuine creaturely freedom because "God becomes the arch-manipulator, knowing in every case exactly 'which button to push' in order to elicit precisely the desired result from his creatures."[89]

Similarly, simple foreknowledge as articulated by Hunt does not manage to circumvent the Achilles heel of simple foreknowledge—the problem of theological fatalism—and solve the apparent binary problem of divine foreknowledge and creaturely free will, which is an aporetic challenge. Despite insisting that an increase in divine foreknowledge does not diminish human agency since God contemporaneously knows what we freely choose to do,[90] Hunt's account of simple foreknowledge

---

87. Process theology, like Fiddes, rejects any notion of a coercive, interventionist God and so it is very difficult to see how God can guarantee the eschaton. Cobb Jr and Griffin, *Process Theology*, 52–54, cf. Fiddes, "How does God Relate." Slightly differently open theism maintains divine power and knowledge to intervene when God sees fit. However, as Fiddes states, this creates moral problems considering God's apparent arbitrary decision making of when to intervene and when not to. Fiddes, "How does God Relate."

88. "Given that the compatibilist God has control over all 'voluntary' actions performed by moral agents, it would appear, accordingly, that we must consider him responsible for all the gratuitously evil states of affairs." Basinger, "Human Freedom," 493.

89. Pinnock, et al, *The Openness of God*, 145, cf. MacGregor, *A Molinist-Anabaptist*, 38–45.

90. Hunt claims this happens when the focus is on knowledge of *propositional* truth, which sees future contingent truth as a real datum which is omni-temporal with truth conditions for the past, present and future. Hunt, "Two Problems," 273–85.

is only successful when we redefine our understanding of the conditions of human free agency.

Libertarian freedom consists of the condition of alternatives (X could do A or non-A) and the condition of non-compatibilist source-hood (X is the complete source of decision A or decision non-A). Hunt advocates prioritizing source-hood over alternatives as a way to make free agency distinct from causal determinism since God foreknows what a person is going to do *because* she is going to do it, not she does it because God foreknows she is going to do it. In sum, Hunt's definition of free agency maintains source-hood as the deep core of free will thereby concluding that humans are free to make decisions and this is not diminished if a divine fore-knower is added into the frame.[91] Analogously, God looks through a time telescope and sees future truth propositions, which establishes the existence of the future in some sense.[92]

The question about Hunt's proposal is whether or not removing the condition of counter-factual alternatives leaves an adequate definition of freedom? It seems clear to me that it does not since any person could be the primary cause of an action done without any counter-factual option to do otherwise or not do at all; their freedom is illusory. So Hunt's claim that one can satisfactorily hold together EDF and free will, within a tensed definition of time, without having to adapt our doctrine of God by denying complete EDF as Fiddes does, comes at too much cost if the only plausible way to do this is by adapting the definition of human agency.[93] If it is not an option to reduce free will action to only the condition of source-hood or redefine God's omniscience to complete knowledge of past and present but not EDF, then another question comes to the fore. Is there another way to articulate God's EDF and the complete libertarian freedom of all sentient creatures, human and otherwise, which will guarantee an eschatology faithful to the Christian tradition, and uphold any SW account where God is in conflict with malevolent spiritual forces who are exercising their freedom and autonomy to rebel against their creator and oppose his willful actions?

---

91. Hunt builds his argument using Harry Frankfurt's claimed counterexample to the principle of alternative possibilities. Hunt and Shabo, "Frankfurt cases," 599–622.

92. Hunt, "Divine Providence," 394–414.

93. Leftow holds a similar view of simple foreknowledge but specifies that God sees free will action from outside of time. God's sight and knowledge comes when humans do something, and this causes God to be in a cognitive state that registers the information that we do something. Leftow, *Time and Eternity*, 246–66; 279–82.

Kathryn Tanner proffers an account of the Christian faith which is Christocentric and builds upon two key themes: a stress on God as the ultimate giver of gifts and a non-competitive understanding of God's knowledge and power.[94] In brief, Tanner's starting point is that God is creator and creation is not. Therefore, God and creation operate on completely different planes of existence, and this means that divine and human agency also operate on totally different ontological fields and are thereby not in competition at all.[95] Basically, human beings deliberate and act freely while God simultaneously intends, and this is simply non-problematic. Indeed, there is no incompatibility between God's universal, direct creative agency and the creature's own power and efficacy.

The real advantage of this non-competitive view of God's agency, and by inference his knowledge, is that it does not succumb to the usual problem of a trade-off definition of divine sovereignty and human freewill.[96] It avoids the typical conclusion that there is a kind of zero-sum transaction between God's and creaturely agency and so God's power and knowledge to act need to decrease in order to make room for human agency. As we know, Fiddes partakes in this zero-sum game by insisting that God's power is defined in terms of persuasion and non-coercion in order to maintain human libertarian freedom.[97] If he applied Tanner's non-competitive view to his theological vision, then this would significantly help Fiddes offer a better guaranteed active sovereignty of God and more accurately theologically exegete passages of scripture that juxtapose human freedom and divine providence in apparent tension.

UNIVERSAL HOPE AND THE ESCHATON

The imperative to maintain EDF and libertarian freedom is a necessity when considering the eschatological vision of scripture and Christian tradition. Put simply, the promise of the seven "no mores" in Revelation

---

94. Tanner, *Jesus, Humanity*; Tanner, *Christ the Key*.

95. This non-competitive relation between divine agency and human freewill is rooted in God the ultimate gift-giver. For it means all gifts to creation come from the abundance and fullness of God and so he does not need to decrease in order to allow creatures to increase. Tanner, *Jesus, Humanity*, 1–5, 41–46, 90–92. Tanner, *Christ the Key*, 53–55.

96. The same trade-off exists in many analyses of God's transcendence and immanence.

97. See "The Challenge of Divine" (pp.26–30) section above.

20–22 offer hope and encouragement to tenaciously endure all forms of evil and pain common to humanity while believing that one day all wrongs will be righted and full justice actualized.[98] However, Fiddes' close affinity with process theology means that there is significant doubt as to whether a non-interventionist deity who "determines to be the kind of creator in which nothing is ever achieved without the partnering of God with the covenanted creation he is in covenant with,"[99] will be able to actualize the promised eschatological fulfilment.[100]

Fiddes' fundamental understanding of covenant in terms of non-unilateral cooperation and partnership with creation, significantly interweaves itself through all his body of work. There is a universal and certain promise of hope in the eschaton but both its content and timing is an open mystery.[101] So within this ambiguous eschaton Fiddes seeks to understand the open nature of the future and the universal hope contained within that open future.[102] Taking his cue from literature and theology, Fiddes notes that both storytellers and poets are in positions of providence and they delineate visions of the apocalyptic that are open-ended and full of possibilities while still containing a guaranteed promise of final fulfilment.[103] God, as divine author, works in the same way.[104]

This understanding, claims Fiddes, also greatly impacts our understanding of the future of Christian ministry. Not only does God co-labor with all of humanity in a context of openness,[105] but he also genuinely journeys into an unknown-content future with the church as a pilgrim community moving into the future with an openness to the new things which God is doing.[106] One area where this is very evident is in prayer

98. All the "No More's" (Revelation 20:10, 14; 21:4, 25, 27; 22:3). Concerning the debate about how literal or metaphorical to view the language in these chapters, Fiddes sees the chapters as highly metaphorical speech about God and not to be taken literally. Fiddes, personal communication with author. cf. Fiddes, "Law and Divine Mercy," 125–26.

99. Fiddes, personal communication with author.

100. Nash notes that in process theism "no ultimate triumph over evil is possible for God." Nash, "Introduction," 20.

101. Fiddes, Haymes and Kidd, *Baptists and the Communion*, 136–42.

102. Fiddes, "Ambiguities of the Future," 281–98.

103. Fiddes, "Versions of the Wasteland," 29–52.

104. Fiddes, "When Text Becomes Voice," 97–111.

105. Fiddes, "Ecclesiology and Ethnography," 29–35.

106. Fiddes, *Forms of Ministry*, 47–51. Fiddes illustrates this in his account of Gainsborough covenant when churches pilgrimed together with God into an open future. Fiddes, "Walking Together," 47–50.

and prophecy; there is no divine blueprint or prediction but rather a divine promise to partner into the open future with the church.[107]

Therefore, the key question to ask is whether or not Fiddes' "apocalyptic eschatology," which does envisage an end to the cosmos and history because there is still a confidence in God to bring his divine purposes to completion despite the openness of the future, can be framed within an eschatological vision consisting of a non-unilateral, non-interventionist deity who only works by divine fiat if and when the wills of creator and creation coalesce?[108] Can God know the "end" as a certain event when the content leading up to that event is dependent upon the partnership between God and the world?[109] It appears very difficult to offer any assurance of a guaranteed eschatological end when God never coerces or acts unilaterally but only works with a creation, imbibed with irrevocable libertarian free will, through gentle persuasion or influence. If, as has been clearly established, Fiddes only thinks God's providence can be actualized when there is an aligning of human and divine wills, then considering humanity's intrinsic freedom to rebel and exercise autonomy strongly suggests that there may never be that needed alignment, theoretically or actually.[110]

Like Barth, Fiddes holds to a universal hope and not some form of dogmatic universalism.[111] However, the similarity comes to an end in the fact that Barth's theology of hope is rooted in divine freedom and the ability for God to freely intervene or not; a possibility not present in the process eschatology to which Fiddes adheres. Can one indeed have any basis for eschatological hope for the ending of all evil if God is part-reliant on the very creation that manifests evil for his divine action in the open future? The answer from both process thinkers and their interlocutors is clearly negative: "There is not and there will not be an end of evil. . . there is no final end of evil. And that is 'good.' . . . that there will be no termination of evil in the universe is not something that we should regret."[112]

---

107. Fiddes, "Introduction," 11–13.

108. TPE, 23–26.

109. Fiddes, "Facing the End," 203–7.

110. Even his appeal to the universal hope in the power of suffering love does not, admits Fiddes, offer a full guarantee of the overcoming of evil and fulfilment of God's purposes within creation. Fiddes, personal communication with author, cf. Fiddes, "Is God." "Is the Future."

111. See *CD* II/2, §35.3, 417–19; *CD* IV/3.1, §70.3, 461–78; cf. TPE, 49–52.

112. Keller, "The Mystery," 57–58; Peterson, "God and Evil," 133–36.

Notwithstanding Fiddes' non-acceptance of the idea of divine intervention, since it suggests God's absence and also raises teleological and moral problems concerning the why of divine intervention, it appears that the very idea of eschatological hope on a universal level needs to be predicated, in the least, on some form of potential ultra soft-unilateral divine action. This could be grounded in divine freedom as articulated by Barth or in a relational theistic account which maintains creaturely libertarian freedom and divine omnipotence that is generally kenotic but with the caveat that the power of creation to influence God is finite.[113]

FINAL COMMENT: DIVINE OMNISCIENCE IN A SPIRITUAL WARFARE CONTEXT

Let me conclude by returning to the over-arching research question being asked: does Fiddes' contemporary theology, especially his doctrine of God, offer a better theological framework to understand God's nature and character in the context of the reality of SW? While the above analysis and critique highlights some weaknesses, there are a number of strengths in Fiddes' approach that can be used to delineate a theology of SW. There are also several key areas integral to a SW theology and understanding that Fiddes never addresses in his written corpus, such as the libertarian free will of angelic beings, a theological account of the exorcisms in the gospels, or the relationship between the demonic and modern psychiatric conditions.[114]

However, some of his written work can aid an explication of the place of divine omniscience in a theological understanding of SW. His insistence on divine passibility is advantageous when it concerns formulating a satisfactory answer for theodicy. It also reflects scriptural witness.[115] Given the divine gift of irrevocable freedom to creation (including angels

---

113. Boyd, for example, argues that there is finitude of creaturely freedom that stipulates "that *to the extent* that humans or angels are self-determining, to *that* extent their moral responsibility must be irrevocable." Therefore, there is a limit to creations' self-determination, and this explains why God can intervene *sometimes* but not always and also why God can give assurance of winning the eschatological cosmic battle, not immediately but eventually. Boyd, *Satan and the Problem*, 178–206.

114. Boyd, *Satan and the Problem*, 50–84; Boyd, *God at War*, 169–237; For an excellent investigation into exorcism and psychiatry see Instone-Brewer, "Jesus and the Psychiatrists," 133–48.

115. For example, the third hypostasis of the Trinity, i.e. the Holy Spirit, can be grieved (Ephesians 4:30).

and demons), the idea that God is a fellow sufferer who stands in solidarity with the afflicted has much merit. Where it gets problematic, however, is the argument that divine passibility needs to be established upon divine ontological mutability, divine becoming, necessary growth in knowledge, and a denial of simplicity or *actus purus*. To deny anthropomorphic or anthropopathic language and insist that God *actually* grows in his knowledge of the future, especially future spiritual battle strategy, raises a number of obstacles to a satisfactory understanding of God's omniscience, particularly his knowledge of the future. We can accept that it may appear this way phenomenologically and experientially from a human perspective without affirming it *de facto* as actual divine ontology.

As well as the above-mentioned charges that theology should not necessarily take all its cues from science and philosophy, that delineating God as both creator and part of creation is impossible, and that to base divine passibility on a human understanding of emotion and feeling is mistaken,[116] Fiddes' understanding of divine passibility and omniscience also assumes that there cannot be divine suffering without divine change nor divine change without limited divine foreknowledge. Regarding the first assumption, the work of von Balthasar plausibly presents a case of divine suffering without ontological change by locating divine passibility *within* the Trinity, a Trinity that inculcates a theology of the cross into its very being.[117] Therefore, we can advocate divine passibility without holding to ontological change in God, a position which could introduce arbitrariness and undermine God's necessary virtuous nature and character.

Moreover, Fiddes' second assumption that genuine divine change can only happen with limited divine foreknowledge of the future is also in need of nuancing and adaptation of some of the underlying assumptions. Any denial of EDF involves certain convictions about the nature of time and of the future, as well as a specific understanding of freewill which negates exhaustive foreknowing, even on the part of God.

A theology of SW should have a consistent understanding of the nature of time and of the future. If, like Fiddes, one assumes a tensed theory of time in which the "now" exists as the only privileged temporal location, then it has to be held that the past no longer exists except in the divine memory and the future does not exist and thereby is not exhaustively

---

116. See "In God Time is" (pp.71–79) section above.
117. See "In God Time is" (pp.71–79) section above.

knowable. This accords well with most relational theologians whose accounts it is claimed can be sustained by a litany of scriptural examples.[118]

Conversely, a tenseless theory of time not only validates God's perfect knowledge of both the past and present but also removes the very concept of *fore*knowledge and replaces it with simple divine knowledge of that which creation labels "the future." So, if we were to consistently apply a tenseless theory to God's relationship with time then this would still leave open the potential to construct Fiddes' *time is in God*, as well as his concept of the healing of time, within a tenseless understanding. For the idea that time exists within the panentheistic reality of God strongly supports the biblical portrayal of God as the very fundamental ground of being and the eternal, non-created reality at the beginning.[119] Furthermore, by extrapolating Tanner's non-competitive view, the healing of time can only happen in a divine being in whom time is healed without fracture. Indeed, time is already healed in God's tenseless reality despite it not appearing so *vis-à-vis* the perspective of creation.

God, in his tenseless existence which transcends time as we know it, has perfect knowledge of all things, including all future actions of creation, all possible counter-factual realities, all potential alternative worlds, and therefore the direction, content and final outcome of the spiritual battle which is an intrinsic element of the tensioned "now and not yet" we inhabit. Yet this does not have to lead to the problem of theological fatalism as is often claimed. A non-competitive understanding of God's power and knowledge means that human and divine agency are not in a zero-sum knowledge and power struggle since they are operating in completely distinct fields of being.[120]

God's full knowledge is contemporaneous with human and angelic free agency and so guarantees creational freedom without undermining the full sovereignty of God. Contrary to Fiddes,[121] there can be human freewill without predetermination. There is no lack in God's knowledge of all action. This knowledge comes when humans exercise free agency while God is in a different plane of existence and cognitive state that registers that information. This enables both human and angelic freewill to operate and God to have all knowledge that allows him to respond

118. See Basinger, *The Case*, 51; Hasker, *God, Time*, 194; Sanders, *The God Who Risks*, 131–32.

119. As Genesis 1:1 attests *In the Beginning, God*.

120. See "In God Time is" (pp.71–79) section above.

121. See "Chapter 3 Introduction" (pp.63–65) section above.

appropriately according to his understanding and will. Therefore, there is enough freedom for human and angelic beings to have significant "say-so" in terms of the content of the eschaton without the potential to derail the ultimate final destination of the eschaton. This alone offers universal hope to creation in the face of diabolical powers and reinforces that evil will be conquered when the new heavens and new earth are fully inaugurated.

4

Power

God's Omnipotence in the Realm of Spiritual Conflict

INTRODUCTION

> *When the thousand years are over*, Satan will be released from his prison . . . surrounded the camp of God's people, the city he loves. *But fire came down from heaven and devoured them.* (emphasis mine).[1]

THE IMAGE, SCOPE AND description we receive from scripture *vis-à-vis* Satan, the demonic and evil is multifarious and multi-layered.[2] Confirming Pauline language about putting on spiritual armor in order to stand strong in our "struggle" with principalities and powers, the New Testament picture and much experience of exorcism ministry today, strongly suggests that when it comes to the nature of evil, the phenomenological reality is not uniform.

Not only do we have the biblical-theological account of Satan adopting many different personas and roles in relation to God,[3] but a

---

1. Revelation 20:7–9 (New International Version). Bauckham notes that "the destruction of evil at its deepest level is portrayed not as an immediate consequence, but one delayed a thousand years." Bauckham, *The Theology*, 106.

2. Walter Wink gives a strong account of the fluidity of "The Satan" in scripture. Wink, *Unmasking*, 9–40.

3. From God's viceroy (Job 1–2) to His malevolent foe whose diabolical work the

theological reading of the gospels and Acts unearths an unsystematic theology of the demonstration of divine power by God incarnate in Jesus of Nazareth; what is sometimes referred to as "power encounters" with evil.[4] Nowhere in the gospels is there a sense that any evil spiritual opposition to Jesus is disingenuous, or that Jesus is merely humoring Satan when confronted by him. There are incidences of absolute divine authority over the demonic: Jesus not letting the demons speak,[5] exorcising an evil spirit at a distance,[6] authorizing his disciples to exorcise demons,[7] and others using the name of Jesus to drive out demons.[8] Conversely, however, there are instances of a more dualistic reality in which demons resist Jesus' command, trade with him and put in a final request that he acquiesces to,[9] and certain individuals overpowered by a man with an evil spirit and beaten extensively in spite of an attempted exorcism using the name of Jesus.[10]

This, together with modern eye-witness accounts of drawn-out exorcisms, especially in the global south,[11] brings to the fore appropriate questions about the reality of evil spirits, suffering and theodicy proper. Specifically, why, if God is omnipotent as traditionally articulated, does he not simply bring the event of the Parousia forward to the present, thus ending the age of now-and-not-yet tension, and inaugurate the new heavens and new earth? Given that the global church currently testifies to the conquering, but not total destruction, of evil, what does this suggest

---

Son of God comes to destroy (1 John 3:8).

4. Powlison, *Power Encounters*.

5. Mark 1:34 (cf. Luke 4:41).

6. Mark 7:24–30 (cf. Matthew 15:21–28). It is most likely that it was these inimitable demonstrations of divine authority that lead the Pharisees and scribes to conclude that Jesus was possessed by and using the power of Beelzebul, the prince of demons, Satan himself (Mark 3:22–30 cf. Matt 12:22–29; Luke 11:14–20). Twelftree, *Jesus the Exorcist*, 104–6.

7. Mark 6:6b–13 (cf. Matthew 10:1; Luke 9:1–6).

8. Mark 9:38–40 (cf. Luke 9:49–50).

9. Mark 5:1–17 (cf. Matthew 8:28–32; Luke 8:27–39). Contra Wink (see below, p. 174 fn.103), a *prima facie* exegesis suggests supra power that enables the demoniac to break physical iron chains literally and be overtly violent.

10. Acts 19:11–16. Arnold correctly asserts that given the scarcity of other accounts or references to evil spirits by Luke in the rest of Acts, this supports the case that Ephesus was a center of demonic activity. Arnold, *Ephesians: Power*, 30–31. Acts 19:17–20 also supports this thesis.

11. For example, Ferdinando, "Screwtape Revisited," 118–20; Ferdinando, *The Battle is God's*, 17–23.

about God's being and character, as well as the nature and make-up of his operational power?

What follows is a definition of God's omnipotence that helps constitute a doctrine of God suitable to locate a theology of SW within. Fiddes' writings on divine power, especially the power of suffering love which is driven by an ontology of divine kenosis will be central to this account, and also his kenotic understanding of divine interaction with creation, a cruciform nature of power as demonstrated by Jesus on the cross. Also, key will be a nuanced dialectical synthesis of Fiddes' Abelardian atonement of transformation with the *Christus Victor* view in order to better elicit a pertinent definition of omnipotence.

KENOSIS: A DEFINITIVE ONTOLOGY OF OMNIPOTENCE

> But this kind of vulnerability can be combined with the faith that God's love can never fail or be destroyed, and that love is—finally—the strongest power in the universe, able to overcome evil with its resources of persuasion.[12]

To repeat, Fiddes constructs his theology using a redefinition of omnipotence. God's ultimate and most effective power is the power of suffering love, grounded in divine vulnerability and freely chosen self-limitation, centered in the perichoretic dance of the Trinity and operated via persuasion and influence. Granted there is risk involved but this does not, as is often claimed, make God impotent since God's "weak power" of persuasion can be very constraining and if it aligns with the wishes and desires of creation will result in actualizing God's will without the need of any strong intervention or coercion.[13]

As we know Fiddes is influenced by process thought when it comes to defining omnipotence in terms of divine persuasion and influence.[14]

---

12. Fiddes, "A Theological Reconsideration," 326–27.

13. See "Chapter 1 Conclusion" (pp.30–31) section above. Fiddes rejects all worldly ideas of coercive and dominant power when defining divine power. Fiddes, "Is God All-Powerful?"

14. See "The Contemporary Need" (pp.4–9) section above. Where Fiddes diverges from process theology is in his locating God's persuasion and influence within the freedom of God. Defining God's omnipotence as persuasion and influence in the power of suffering love is a central tenet which Fiddes has consistently purported since the beginning of his academic career. For example, see Fiddes, *The Escape*, 18–21; TPE, 166–75;

His embrace of the non-unilateral power of suffering love both aligns him with and sets his face against different Christian scholars.[15] For Fiddes, the conflation of process theology's emphasis on persuasion with no domination and the biblical theme of God's suffering, found especially in the prophets, goes a considerable way to help understand God in the context of a fallen creation which exercises its full access to irrevocable freedom in order to use for good or ill.[16]

This conflation by Fiddes immediately raises two critical questions. First, has Fiddes accepted process theology's non-coercive persuasive position without careful consideration of whether or not this is logically coherent? As Basinger asks, is it necessarily impossible for the process God to intervene or coerce or is it an act of self-limitation? If the former, then this raises the challenge of talking about a necessarily powerless deity without any experiential base to draw from, especially when human experience consistently demonstrates the ability to control other human behavior whether through ultra-soft, soft, mid or hard coercion.[17] If the latter, as held by Fiddes rooted in God's freedom, then the same charge can be brought as made against the classic freewill theist: why does God not freely choose to intervene in cases of dysteleological evil such as the holocaust?[18]

The second question concerns Fiddes' use of the prophets, especially Hosea, and whether he uses these prophetic passages correctly to develop this kenotic-based understanding of divine passibility. As has been pointed out by Young, as well as Hosea's language of the "man-like" God (the one who walks in the garden and woos his lover), other prophets such as Isaiah and Amos describe Yahweh as "wholly other" in contrast to the popular gods of the nations around Israel. Therefore, this leads to the use of *synthesis* (observing the highest and most beautiful things of

---

Fiddes, "The Place," 74–80; Fiddes, "Ecclesiology and Ethnography," 13–17, 29–35; Fiddes, "Ancient and Modern Wisdom," 90–95; Fiddes, "Shakespeare in Church," 210–11; Fiddes, "Covenant and Participation," 129–32.

15. Fiddes rejects Healy's unilateralist position in favor of Hauerwas' human-divine co-operation stance. Fiddes, "Versions of Ecclesiology," 332–42; Fiddes, "Ecclesiology and Ethnography," 29–32. Moreover, Fiddes is highly critical of Aquinas' Thomistic causation theology which views God as the primary cause, arguing instead that it is better to imagine God acting persuasively. Fiddes, "*Ex Opere Operato*," 222–29.

16. See "Divine Passibility of Suffering" (pp.18–21) section above, cf. Fiddes, "Father, Son," 217–19.

17. Basinger, "Divine Power," 203–5.

18. Basinger, "Divine Persuasion," 334–35.

creation), *analysis* (using the technique of abstraction, taking away what we know and arriving at apophatic terms), and *analogy* (creating myths and similes) in order to understand God as both infinite, incomprehensible, beyond human knowledge but, via revelation, accommodating and speaking to us in human language that we understand. Fiddes, she suggests, would do well incorporating a more sophisticated form of anthropomorphism into his theology.[19]

The overarching rubric of Fiddes' position regarding the persuasive power of suffering love is kenosis. He defines God as the one who humbly reveals himself and freely desires to limit himself and be the self-emptying kenotic God.[20] Despite Fiddes' denial of being a social trinitarian,[21] a theology of divine triune society is the best setting for a doctrine of kenosis.[22] That said, however, there is still an imperative to converge our focus on the specific nature of Fiddes' understanding of kenosis in terms of scope and implications.[23]

A synthesis of Fiddes' panentheistic vision and definition of power as persuasion and suffering love results in a capacious definition and scope of kenosis. There are, in the main, three theological meanings of the term "kenosis": Christological, trinitarian and generalized.[24] Similarly, Fiddes writes about three kinds of kenosis which he calls *three kenotic moments*, namely "the eternal kenosis of the Father in the sending out of the Son; the kenosis of creation in which God brings into being something that has reality over against God's self who is himself self-emptying, and the cross, which is the deepest kind of self-emptying."[25] In a reversal of the temporal-chronological order of the three kenotic moments, it is the final "moment," the cross in the heart of God, that Fiddes uses as the foundation for kenotic theological development concerned with trinitarian and generalized meanings of kenosis.[26]

---

19. Young, *Face to Face*, 242–47.

20. Fiddes, "The Making," 14–18; Fiddes, "The Story," 89–94.

21. Fiddes, "Relational Trinity," 159–61.

22. Thompson and Plantinga Jnr, "Trinity and Kenosis," 165–89.

23. Fiddes claims that a kenotic definition of God also affects our understanding of God's omniscience. Fiddes, "Charles Williams," 77.

24. Coakley, "Kenosis: Theological," 192–204.

25. Fiddes, personal communication with author, cf. Fiddes, "Participating in," 379–83; PIG, 34–46; Fiddes, "Creation Out," 167–91; PEPS, 51–58. Of note is that Fiddes here departs from Robinson who held that kenosis of the Spirit is the deepest kind of kenosis. Robinson, *Redemption*, 294–95.

26. At this point, the limitations of temporal language such as "moment" (borrowed

As will be shown, Fiddes presumes God's self-emptying on the cross when exploring the atonement without any serious exegetical work on Philippians 2 and other examples of divine limitation in the biblical account.[27] Consequently, he does not enter some of the kenotic Christology debates such as whether the kenotic state of Christ was for the duration of the incarnation or only between crucifixion and Holy Saturday;[28] the relation between kenosis and glorification;[29] the difference between ontological, functional and kryptic kenosis;[30] or what divine attributes did Christ acquiesce in the incarnation without loss of divinity?[31]

Moreover, Fiddes argues that this idea of kenosis has to be an essential concept from which to construct a doctrine of God for today's world, despite the fact that kenotic theology predicated on divine mutability and passibility is only a recent development with little precedent. Unlike other Kenoticists, Fiddes spills little ink analyzing the development of modern-period Kenoticism from nineteenth-century German theology into Anglophone theology in an attempt to make sense of Christ's incarnation as one person with two natures in light of a newly emerging understanding of personality and self-consciousness.[32] Instead he simply presupposes God's kenotic ontology and from this starting-point differentiates his understanding of God as necessarily kenotic from others and what it means for God to be kenotic in his triune being.

This lack of analysis, together with little serious exegetical work on those scriptural passages which possibly suggest kenosis, weakens Fiddes'

---

from Bulgakov and von Balthasar) become significant. Coakley rightly notes that the majority of essays (including Fiddes' chapter) in *The Work of Love* address the significance of kenosis in regard to God's relation to the world and subsequently only turn to Christological or trinitarian meaning for illustration. Coakley, "Kenosis: Theological," 193.

27. Fee, "The New Testament," 25–44; Wright, "*arpagmos* and the meaning," 321–52; Wuest, "When Jesus," 153–58.

28. Without fully aligning with his Holy Saturday kenosis descent, Fiddes appreciates von Balthasar's theory of atonement based upon the formlessness of the Word and Christ's kenotic obedience to descend into hell. See Fiddes, Review of *The Glory of the Lord*," 349–50.

29. Evans, "Kenotic Christology," 200–202.

30. Crisp, *Divinity and Humanity*, 118–53.

31. James, "The Enduring Appeal," 7–14.

32. For a thorough historical overview of the development of modern Kenoticism spreading from the continent to Scotland and England, see Brown, *Divine Humanity*, 36–171. Other historical analyses of modern kenosis development include Dawe, "A Fresh Look," 337–49; Dawe, *The Form of a Servant*," 47–176; Loofs, "Kenosis," 680–87; McCormack, "Kenoticism in Modern," 444–57.

account. Feenstra, for instance, argues for a kenotic Christology that is faithful to scripture and Chalcedon by adopting a "omni-unless-freely-and-temporarily choosing to be otherwise for the purpose of incarnation and reconciliation" definition. Moreover, in order to avoid the common objections of traditional theologians, he concludes that all discussion of kenosis and divine attributes *has to* start with testimony of Jesus of Nazareth, not the doctrine of God.[33] This indeed raises a number of interesting possibilities about God's power and logical limitation: if God can bring into being a pregnant virgin then can he also create a married bachelor or make two plus two equal five? Also, there is a broad critique of kenotic Christology by Weinandy who argues that we should define personhood ontologically instead of psychologically. If done, then kenotic problems disappear, such as postulating the incarnation in compositional ways which inevitably reduce divinity.[34]

Notwithstanding these potential criticisms, God *is* necessarily kenotic, according to Fiddes, but not because of any necessity imposed on him by an external force.[35] Rather his kenosis is rooted in an "internal necessity" caused by his eternal desire and divine will.[36] God chooses kenosis but not in the sense of choosing between option A and option B.[37] God's forming of covenant with creation means he becomes necessarily kenotic and this is perfectly demonstrated when there is a convergence of creation's responsiveness and the desire of God. This accounts for miracles which can often happen if there is complete alignment between God's will and desire and free acts of creation.[38]

Exploring what God's kenotic ontology infers for his triune being is the second kenotic moment that Fiddes often considers. Because the heart of kenosis power is suffering love, not just of the Son but of

33. Feenstra, "A Kenotic Christological," 150–64.

34. Weinandy, *Does God Change*, 118–23.

35. As widely known, Process theology postulates that God has always had a universe somewhere and has always known limitation because of free acts of creatures. Hartshorne, *The Divine Relativity*, 29–30; Griffin, *God, Power*, 279–80.

36. *CD* II/1, §28, 257–321.

37. Fiddes believes that words such as "choose" "desire" and "will" all have their place and so this slightly sets him apart from other necessary Kenoticists such as Oord who believes that God's kenosis is involuntary because it derives from God's eternal and unchanging nature of love. Fiddes, personal communication with author. cf. Oord, *The Uncontrolling*, 94–95.

38. The resurrection is the unique and quintessential great miracle that comes from the perfect response of Jesus and the desire of the Father. Fiddes, personal communication with author.

the Trinity, this removes any notion of monarchical hierarchy from the Trinity and eradicates all concepts of submissive power-over. Any trinitarian theology of dominance, claims Fiddes, leads to oppression and coercion in human relations whether by the state, men or pastors. In the past, the dominance of the state was intertwined with the authority of the church,[39] and since the church was by-and-large patriarchal for most of its history, its authority naturally resulted in the oppression of women.[40] This implicated the pastorate, a servant-leader, shepherd calling that too-often-than-not exercised authority through dominance and oppression, and has been of late undergirded by a charismatic theology which emphasizes spiritual hierarchy and a ministerial pecking order.[41] What makes this emphasis on authority within the charismatic renewal especially egregious is the central role the Holy Spirit plays but with little understanding of his kenotic nature.[42]

KENOTIC RELATIONS WITH CREATION

Paradoxically both Christological and trinitarian kenosis only makes sense when situated within an understanding of a generalized, unprecedented kenosis of creation which intrinsically implicates soteriological and ecclesial kenotic movements. This is Fiddes' third kenotic moment, one that aligns well with Brunner's kenotic definition of creation, a thorough articulation that needs quoted at length:

> God does not wish to occupy the whole of Space Himself, but that He wills to make room for other forms of existence. In so doing He limits himself... The maximum of the divine self-limitation is equally the maximum of actual "over-againstness"—the free position of that being who is "over against" God and is therefore able to answer the Word of the Creator in freedom... Now we begin to see what a large measure of self-limitation He has imposed upon

---

39. PIG, 96–101.

40. Fiddes, "The Status of Women," 138–55; PIG, 101–4; Fiddes, *A Unicorn Dies*, 3, 20–21.

41. Fiddes, *Charismatic*, 24–30; Fiddes, "The Theology of," 32–38; PIG, 62–71; Fiddes, personal communication with author.

42. Despite departing somewhat from Robinson on the depth of the kenosis of the Spirit, Fiddes is still influenced by Robinson's and later Moltmann's kenosis of the Spirit. Fiddes, "Pentecost. The Rhythm," 204–10; SWKG, 381–87; cf. H. Wheeler Robinson, *The Christian Experience of the Holy Spirit* (London: Nisbet, 1928), 83–87; Fiddes, "A Review of *God*," 262–65.

Himself, and how far He has emptied Himself, in order to realize this aim, to achieve it, indeed, in a creature which has misused its creaturely freedom to such an extent as to defy God. *The kenosis, which reaches its paradoxical climax in the Cross of Christ, began with the creation of the world.* (emphasis mine).[43]

God's self-limitation in order to create potential for other types of creaturely existence is for Fiddes a reality that explicates itself in many different manifestations within creation. Crucially, humanity is given space and freedom to participate in, with and through God via intercessory prayer, advancing medical science, literature (despite novels often failing to catch divine kenosis), and non-coercive attitudes and behavior in politics and other public spheres.[44] Since creation is an act of divine kenosis, reliant upon wide movements of the Spirit of God, then creation has to look for these manifestations because God's self-limitation results in divine concealment and ambiguous recognition of his Spirit.[45]

Like Brunner, Fiddes earths his understanding of God's kenotic self-limitation in the freedom and desire of God, not process theology's external necessity.[46] Before the foundation of the world there was the self-limitation of God. This was freely chosen and catalyzed by divine love. All creational kenosis language should be "God's-will-as-desire" speech, not essential nature vernacular, as desire speech mirrors exactly the triune movements of relational love in God's nature and character.[47]

Similar to previous weaknesses, Fiddes' chronological emphasis on kenosis as the basic, freely chosen, self-structure of the Trinity which *then* perfectly manifests itself on the cross of Christ could potentially place too much emphasis upon ontological otherness and thereby render kenosis meaningless to humans' existence and experience. As Macquarrie, with the help of Thomasius, reminds us, there needs to be a differentiation between *logos ensarkos* and *logos asarkos* since the former leads to greater

---

43. Brunner, *Dogmatics. Vol.2*, 20.

44. Fiddes concludes that general Baptists do not go far enough with regard to freewill. Fiddes, "Foreword," ix–xiv; Fiddes, "Attending to the Sublime," 83–85; Fiddes, "Introduction," 11–16, cf. Fiddes, et al, *Baptists and the Communion*, 81–84; Fiddes and Lees, "How are People Healed," 16–22; Fiddes, "Introduction: The Novel," 3–8, cf. FAL, 39–46; PEPS, 190–206.

45. Robinson, *Redemption*, 294–97.

46. "At this point process thought differs from most versions of kenotic theology by claiming that the limitations of divine power are the product of metaphysical necessity rather than voluntary self-limitation." Barbour, "God's Power," 6.

47. Fiddes, "Creation Out," 178–84, cf. *CD* II/1, §28.1, 271–72.

meaning and relevance for creation by grounding kenosis theology in the humiliation of Christ and self-abasement of Jesus of Nazareth on the cross.[48] Moreover, a third alternative to the ontological or ethical view is that the Christological subject is the divine person acting by means of the acts performed by the man Jesus. In short, the man Jesus acts and suffers and the Logos receives suffering up into his own being: "the receptivity of the Logos simply *is* his self-emptying."[49] Perhaps applying these insights would help prevent potential loss of Fiddes' kenosis account to the incommunicable reality of an ontology of complete otherness.

That said, Fiddes' articulation and defense of creation as a kenotic act implies soteriological and ecclesial kenotic movements since God brings into being something contingent that is given *de-facto* over-againstness towards God and his self-emptying being. This emphasizes the humility of God because creation is no longer its original design, and this has inevitably led to arising malevolence and evil which have significant say-so over and against God in his humble and kenotic state. Indeed, the achievement of creation as kenosis is the creation of creatures free to misuse their creaturely freedom to such an extent as to resist God and thwart his will and desires for creation. Hence, kenotic movements of soteriology and ecclesiology.

For Fiddes, salvation is a very wide and deep concept since it is descriptive of the way God is actually working in the world. The atonement is narrower but nonetheless imperative to any understanding of salvation. Since salvation is possible through the healing of relationships, the world-wide and cosmic activity of salvation is bound up and dependent upon the particular self-giving love and sacrifice which brought total relational healing through the life of Jesus of Nazareth; a particular life at a specific historical moment.[50] Because of this historical particularism all soteriological movements of kenosis are, according to Fiddes, movements of the kind of omnipotence manifest in the divine power of cruciform suffering love. As stated above, theories of atonement have been formed by the prevalent culture at the time and so an atonement defined by suffering love is the most effective explanation for today's culture

48. Macquarrie, "Kenoticism Reconsidered," 122–24.

49. McCormack, "Kenoticism in Modern," 455–56. Elsewhere, McCormack claims that kenosis takes the genus of humility and applies it to God the Son thereby communicating human attributes to the divine instead of the usual vice-versa. McCormack, "Karl Barth's Christology," 246–47.

50. Fiddes, "Immortality and Personal Consciousness?"

personality and relational fragmentation.[51] Much of the effectiveness of locating the cross of Christ and divine suffering in the epicenter of God's being lies in the explanatory power it gives to explaining theologically three current key issues in western culture: sacrifice, justice and evil.[52]

The overall impact the divine passibility of suffering love has on salvation and the atonement is to accentuate the process of transformation, i.e. the becoming of salvation. This understanding of salvation is best served by a transformative, subjective view of the atonement which focusses on the objective event of the cross.[53] The atonement's potential to transform has to be framed within an egalitarian participation in the relations and movements of the triune God since this is what redefines authority and power and allows creation to move *through* the objective victory of the cross and participate in today's subjective victories of Christ against current diabolical manifestations of evil. Indeed, "though atonement has been achieved potentially in the event of Christ, it only becomes *actual* in the present, as people make the victory of Christ their own," which is completed by moving the main thrust of the *Christus Victor* motif more towards the subjective than the objective.[54]

There can be no separation of the atonement and the Trinity as this identifies the Logos with the human condition and enables God to enter into the mess of the human predicament, offer forgiveness and reconcile

---

51. See "The Contemporary Need" (pp.4–9) section above.

52. See "Divine Passibility's Impact" (pp.21–26) section above.

53. See "Divine Passibility's Impact" (pp.21–26) section above. Fiddes is correct to ground his subjective view with objective focus atonement theory in a cogent reappraisal of Abelard. He aligns himself with current thinking on the medieval philosopher that seeks to remove the reductionist label of "the exemplarist" that became especially prominent in England at the turn of the twentieth century. Due to the efforts of critics such as Hastings Rashdall, Abelard was appealed to which *reduced* the cross and its meaning to simply a demonstration of the love of God. However, Abelard is more complex than this. Aulen, *Christus*, 47–55; McGrath, *Christian Theology*, 425–30. Despite the continuous existence of the reductionist caricature of Abelard, Fiddes and others engage with Abelard's main writings, especially his commentary on Romans arguing that there can only be a subjective transformation *if* there is an objective transaction. It is rightly purported that Abelard extracted two meta-themes in Romans: an exaltation of divine grace at the expense of human merit, and humans serving God from a well of love, not fear. Eddy and Beilby, "The Atonement," 18–19; Evans, *Anselm and*, 161–62, cf. Fiddes, PEPS, 140–61; Williams, "Sin, grace and redemption," 258–78; Weingart, *The Logic of Divine Love*, 139–44; Clanchy, *Abelard*, 285–87; Marenbon, *Abelard in Four*, 100–101. Of course, the former is objective, a transaction from God to humanity because humanity is dominated by sin. Sin is both objective (i.e. punishment and damnation), and subjective (i.e. concupiscence). Williams, "Sin, grace," 260–69.

54. Fiddes, PEPS, 135–39.

us to each other. Within atonement as participation, divine omnipotence is that of suffering forgiveness and our participation in the divine relations means when we suffer we do so because we are participating in the divine forsakenness between the Father and Son on the cross.[55] Framing the atonement and divine omnipotence as suffering also means that sacrifice is at the epicenter of salvation,[56] and this manifests itself solely through divine persuasion and wooing, not the traditionally held irresistible grace. Grace is prevenient, not unavoidable, since it respectfully treats human freewill as it woos and persuades people into salvation,[57] as well as baptism and body of Christ membership.[58]

Moreover, according to Fiddes, the manifestation of actualized freewill also determines a kenotic ecclesiology built upon genuine *diakonia* and self-emptying. Indeed, the church needs to be a community of worship, justice, forgiveness and sacrifice.[59] Not only does this give greater understanding to the role and experience of intercessory prayer, it also redefines church leadership in kenotic terms of humble service instead of dominance and monarchical demonstrations of worldly power.[60]

For Fiddes, as a Baptist thinker, a kenotically defined ecclesiology and leadership structure sits well with an historic Baptist doctrine of the church. Concepts of power and authority are intrinsically connected to a vision of God.[61] Church authority resides *de facto* in the community congregation,[62] not leadership team,[63] and the *nature* of that authority is necessarily grounded in the doctrine of our kenotic, self-sacrificing triune God.[64] Therefore, given that a passible God dwells in a broken and

55. Fiddes, "The Atonement," 111–17.
56. Fiddes, "Sacrifice," 63–66.
57. Fiddes, "The Understanding of Salvation," 25–31.
58. Fiddes, "Believer's Baptism," 8–13; Fiddes, "Baptism and Membership," 91–93.
59. Fiddes, "Atonement in," 195–208.
60. See "The Nature and Character" (pp.13–18) section above.
61. Fiddes, "Authority in," 59–61.
62. This is why, as argued by Kierkegaard, Christianity should be governed by a life of kenotic discipleship which includes suffering and offense, so that when congregations come together their expression of authority is genuinely kenotic. Law, *Kierkegaard's Kenotic*, 243–47.
63. It appears less plausible to work out the implications of kenosis for church leadership and governance in an *episkopos*-structured denomination that operates hierarchically. See less-than-convincing attempts by Anglican Archdeacon Herrick, *Limits of Vulnerability*; Herrick and Mann, *Jesus Wept*; and Anglican Priest Herbert, *Kenosis and Priesthood*.
64. Fiddes, *A Leading Question*, 7–11, 47–71, cf. Fiddes, et al *Something to Declare*,

imperfect church as an expression of the humility of God,[65] this leaves no room for dominating power but only persuasive, servant *dunamis* demonstrated by vulnerable leadership in mutual relations of absolute trust.[66] Indeed, this is the necessary ecclesiology for the broken body of the undivided Christ.[67]

Having now assessed Fiddes' theological description and discussion on divine power of suffering love that is undergirded by a broad and all-encompassing ontology of divine kenosis, it is now incumbent upon me to construct a kenotic understanding of omnipotence that necessitates a particular type of divine interaction with creation. My intention is to define God's omnipotence within a doctrine of God which can help explain the various scriptural and phenomenological accounts inside a systematic theology of SW.

OMNIPOTENCE'S KENOTIC WARFARE WITH EVIL: ITS NATURE AND SCOPE

Before defining God's omnipotence, some critical comments on Fiddes' propositions need to be made. First, is the definition of power as "suffering love" the only way God exercises power? If no, then what other facets of power sit comfortably with a non-coercive, softly-persuasive idea of the power of suffering love? As we will see, the classic (and especially reformed) paradigm of biblical warfare theology is predicated upon a strong definition of sovereign and providential divine power, which seems unlikely to be consistent with power as suffering love.[68]

A corollary, which is also related to the above discussion on omniscience,[69] is that it is not obvious how a divine being who operates power only by persuasion can actualize the Parousia in a way faithful to

---

12–16.

65. Fiddes, "Christian Doctrine," 202–7.

66. Fiddes, "Authority in Pastor-People," 61–63; Fiddes, et al, *On the Way*, 11–16, 28–35; cf. Fiddes, *Forms of Ministry*, 26; Fiddes, "The Root of Religious," 177–80.

67. Fiddes, "An Ecclesiology of an Undivided," 200–216. James claims that genuinely authentic relationships are self-emptying since Christ calls all his followers to be self-emptying as he was. James, "The Enduring Appeal," 11–13.

68. Even the slightly more dualistic classic paradigm of the early church still believed in and practiced *ekballistic* ministry that used the command-control mode, somewhat antithetical to soft-persuasion through suffering love.

69. See "Chapter 3" (pp.63–85) above.

scripture if he does not know the *kairos* time, or if he does can only bring it about in co-operation with creation in a non-unilateral way. Finally, given that Fiddes focuses the majority of his account of omnipotence of suffering love on soteriological matters, it is unclear whether or not non-coercive suffering love will overcome and finally eradicate diabolical evil, especially if evil has no ontological status but is rather *privatio boni* ambiguously expressed as *nihil*.[70]

Moreover, some of Fiddes' early ecclesiological work unambiguously claims that God can and does *overcome* hostile forces including powers and principalities. Conflict is represented by the symbol of chaotic water and so the exodus and baptism are understood as overcoming the hostile powers that oppress human beings.[71] However, these powers are not demonic but rather political and this-worldly which means that divine creative power is not battling it out with Satan *per se* but rather emancipating the people of God by leading them out of exilic despair and disillusionment back to Canaan in order to rebuild Zion.[72] Therefore, does this suggest that God *can* act unilaterally when he has to or has intervention-causal power evolved into the power of suffering love as part of the theological drama of God's people, especially this side of Golgotha? Fiddes unquestionably takes the latter option. The problem of evil and suffering can *only* be satisfactorily explained by divine mutability and vulnerability. Whatever the type of theodicy—consolation, story, protest, or freewill—it has to be addressed by the full passibility of the divine and the reality that evil, whether moral or natural, which is totally alien to God, does actually befall him.[73]

However, the question remains unanswered if we view theodicy and SW as realities that are both caused by diabolical spiritual entities with volition and being. For if this is the case, then it needs to be conceded that Fiddes does not examine this in his corpus since he does not view Satan and demons as ontological realities but as a mystery caught somewhere between personhood and human sin.[74] In fact, it is the denial of an objective reality of Satan that helps drive the subjective stress on the nuanced Abelardian atonement theory of transformation through

---

70. See "What is Evil?" (pp.34–39) section above.
71. Fiddes, "Baptism and Creation," 53–55.
72. Fiddes, *The Escape*, 32–36.
73. PIG, 152–79.
74. PEPS, 118–22.

the redemptive power of suffering love.⁷⁵ This, I believe, leaves Fiddes' definition of omnipotence lacking and so it is imperative to broaden and deepen it in order to better understand the reality of divine omnipotence in the midst of a world marred by malevolence and dysteleological evil.

Fiddes defines omnipotence as suffering love on the ground of cruciform and trinitarian kenosis, which is situated within a *generalized* kenosis. This is certainly an appropriate way to define omnipotence for two significant reasons. First, methodologically, theodicy is a theological concept that can be extrapolated from experience, which is an important source of theological method when dealing with theodicy and human suffering.⁷⁶ Take Levinas, for instance, who wrote philosophy as someone who survived incarceration in Auschwitz.⁷⁷ Of course, not all agree and some see great danger in rooting any aspect of the doctrine of God in experience which may lead to over-anthropomorphizing.⁷⁸ However, as we will see in chapter six the lack of biblical detail and historical-theological material on the spirit world legitimately invites human experience to help form our knowledge base.⁷⁹

Second, kenosis helps to explain perceived divine hiddenness amidst evil and suffering before and after the incarnation of Christ. Those who posit kenosis in the Hebrew Bible without any Christological considerations, relate God's omnipotence to humility. The kenosis of God is realized while retaining transcendence when God manifests himself in

---

75. PEPS, 129–50.

76. See "The Place of Experience" (pp.9–13) section above.

77. Van Riessen, *Man as a Place*, 101–30. Similarly, Wolterstoff starts his philosophy of divine passibility not from philosophy but from experience after the premature death of his son. Fiddes had the same tragic experience. See Clark, "Hold Not Thy Peace," 167–68.

78. Cook believes that titles like *The Human Face of God* and *The Crucified God* use language that reflects weakness in human experience without necessarily differentiating between weakness caused by sin, weakness affected by circumstances, and weakness through an inability to cope. Such an account may well give too much power and significance to circumstances, sin or the power of the evil one, and we need to avoid this. Cook, "Weak Church, Weak God," 69–92.

79. Clark suggests that *sola scriptura* will not produce the full answer needed due to an "under-determination" of scripture. This can happen when scripture rightly interpreted may not settle the issue as it may not address the issue at all; when scripture rightly interpreted could settle the issue, but the right rules of interpretation may not be discernable; and there may be no such thing as the "right" interpretation of scripture. There may be competing explanations of the text all of which are compatible with the text. Clark, "Hold Not Thy Peace," 176–77.

humility alongside the defeated, the poor and the expelled via a gentle whisper (1 Kings 19:12).[80]

Moreover, receding further into the past we note that kenosis helps explain continuous creation and divine action as the two sides of the same coin. Creation is evolutionary and ongoing, governed by a somewhat chaotic orderly disorder, and so generalized kenosis maintains a self-effacing theological position; a kind of kenotic paradoxical theology that enables us to accept both divine hiddenness and the providential work of God.[81] Overall, once we view the activity of God in creation as vulnerable and an act of self-emptying love,[82] then we can think of kenosis in trinitarian terms thereby presupposing kenosis as *the* selfless act of the persons in the inner-trinitarian life of love and placing the kenotic heavenly sacrifice of the lamb at the intersecting point where God and the world are mutually joined.[83]

The consistent challenge in any delineation of kenosis, whether that be Christological, trinitarian or generalized, is on the matter of power and whether or not there are limitations on divine omnipotence or different definitions of power which are greater than sheer semantics. Is it unreasonable to posit that God can choose to self-limit himself at time (T) only to rescind that decision at time (T+1) or does his omniscience make this impossible? Does divine omnipotence include the ability to limit one's omnipotence or is that akin to the logical challenges of the stone paradox? As philosophers agree, there are limitations on omnipotence which create a need to categorize various impossibilities; those limitations which do not negate an omnipotent being from being omnipotent.[84] Following classical thinkers, we should discern between logical (God cannot create a married bachelor) and moral (God cannot lie) impossibilities for God.[85] Other categories include virtuous behavior and non-embodiment;

---

80. Van Riessen, *Man as a Place*, 173–87.

81. Polkinghorne, "Kenotic Creation," 90–106.

82. Vanstone, *Love's Endeavour*, 66–67.

83. Balthasar, *Mysterium Paschale*, 24–36; cf. Forsyth, *The Person*, 271.

84. Wierenga lists certain conditions on omnipotence which include God not needing to be able to do the logically impossible in order to be omnipotent and doing any immoral thing that is incompatible with the essential properties that God has. Wierenga, *The Nature of God*, 14–18.

85. Anselm claimed moral impossibilities for God such as making himself corrupt or telling lies. This would be a sign of impotence, not power, as these corruptible things would have power over him. Anselm, *Proslogion*, 123–25. Similarly, Aquinas listed many illogical things God cannot do such as making himself not to be and making the

does it impinge on divine omnipotence if God cannot act courageously or because he is everywhere (Psalm 139:7–8) is unable to be closer to the train station than the post office?[86] These various kinds of impossibilities are coterminous under the rubric definition of omnipotence offered by Swinburne and others as the ability to bring about all states of affairs so long as those states are not impossible for that being to bring about, and the making of these states of affairs is not incompatible with that which has already happened and is viewed on balance as a good thing and significantly better than restraining from doing it.[87]

It is beyond the scope of this thesis to fully investigate the philosophical detail of this question. Suffice to say, taking our cue from Swinburne, the paradox of the stone demonstrates that God cannot do that which is logically impossible, and yet this does not necessarily invalidate his omnipotence.[88] One simply has to note the logical challenge a synoptic reading of Jesus' return to Nazareth gives to witness the multi-voiced reasoning given for the lack of miracles performed.[89] Furthermore, the sheer ambiguity of the New Testament data especially in the pertinent gospel texts that display some form of self-limitation of divine prerogatives in the life of Jesus of Nazareth,[90] suggests that there can be limitations placed on God by creation that thwart the divine plan; God is not simply deciding to accede or not to a prayer petition or cry for deliverance.

As I am arguing that there are good reasons for using the concept of kenosis to form an instructive framework to define divine omnipotence within a theology of SW, it is critical to construct a concept of omnipotence using a nuanced version of kenosis: one that shows congruence with the current reality of evil and spiritual conflict and the full eradication of it at the final consummation of the eschaton. Following Fiddes' three kenotic moments,[91] which extrapolate trinitarian and general kenosis from a deep kenotic Christology rooted in the deepest expression

---

past not to have been. Aquinas, *Summa Contra Gentiles*, 73–76.

86. Rundle, *Why there is Something*, 83–84.

87. Swinburne, *The Coherence*, 149–61; Davis, *Logic*, 68–85.

88. Swinburne, *The Coherence*, 152–58.

89. Mark 6:5–6 cf. Matthew 13:58. Commentators go to great lengths to avoid the natural conclusion that the lack of faith seemed to have limited Jesus' ability to display *dunamis* in Nazareth. See France, *The Gospel*, 550 and Morris, *The Gospel According*, 367.

90. See Fee, "The New Testament," 37–44 for an insightful discussion into these passages.

91. See "Kenosis: A Definitive" (pp.88–93) section above.

of divine self-emptying on the cross, a case will be constructed using Philippians 2:5–11 as the quintessential model of kenotic power with the assumption that the cross at the heart of kenotic Christology is also at the epicenter of the triune God and God's relationship with creation. Moreover, the use of a kenotic theology of the cross better serves a subjective, transformative *Christus Victor* authoritative atonement theology with much potential for divine omnipotence.

To construct this kenotic power model I propose using the Christology of Hans Lassen Martensen.[92] Specific to our purposes, he embraced and promulgated a Lutheran theology of divine kenosis, a condescension of God in solidarity with humanity which revealed the capacious nature of divine love.[93] Uniquely, he suggested that the Son had two centers of consciousness: one in heaven and one on earth. Christ grew in his divine consciousness while incarnated on earth and this climaxed during the passion. The major impact was his idea that this two-fold actuality of the Son was "not divine and human as on the two-natures model but rather one divine nature simultaneously in full power and kenotic."[94] Omnipotence is dialectic, a synthesis of full and varying kenotic power:

> In the place of world creating omnipotence enters the world-vanquishing and world-completing power, the infinite power and fullness of love and holiness in virtue of which the God-man was able to testify "all power is given to me in heaven and earth" (Matthew 28:18).[95]

Martensen's articulation of kenosis holds much explanatory capacity for God's omnipotence within a battle-worn creation. The idea of two lateral strands within the life of God, one permanently in the triune life and one kenotically in the incarnation and after coheres well with the

---

92. A Danish social critic trained in philosophy and theology, who has in recent centuries received greater attention for his own writings instead of simply being the object of Kierkegaard's antipathy. Since the first translation of his work into English in the 1860s [Martensen, *Christian Dogmatics*] there has been a gradual growth in English translations of his work. The first was completed in 1969 but only published recently as Horn, *Positivity and Dialectic*. Intellectually, Martensen stands between Hegel and Kierkegaard and was part-responsible for introducing the former to the Danish intellectual world of the latter. Godlove, *Between Hegel and Kierkegaard*, 1–4.

93. "We follow, therefore, the apostle Paul, who represented to himself the incarnation of God as a self-emptying (ἐκένωσεν) of the divine logos, manifesting itself primarily as self-abasement . . . (Phil 2:6,7)." Martensen, *Christian Dogmatics*, §133, 265.

94. Brown, *Divine Humanity*, 61.

95. Martensen, *Christian Dogmatics*, §135, 267.

Christ hymn of Philippians 2. Not only does the story of Jesus function as a tale of God's assumption of finitude but it also narrates the ascendancy of humanity, a humanity originally formed to be the temple of the divine. Consequentially, "Jesus' human nature is eternally receptive to divinity and in Jesus human nature is perfected and reaches its true idea."[96] Overall, therefore, the kenotic Christ cannot remain unchanged: not only is there an internalizing of new experiences for the first time but also after Christ's exaltation a continuation through the Spirit's ministry of drawing people to himself.

This narrative movement maps effortlessly onto the Christ hymn's self-emptying descent, death, and exaltation of the Son. The Son descends to earth through *kenosis* in the heart of God, gives up dominant and full creative power for persuasive influence and is filled with the Spirit of God which manifests in love, compassion and miraculous signs (Philippians 2:6–7).[97] Upon his crucifixion and death, the ultimate *moral kenosis* of suffering love is exemplified by a fatal rupture in the body-ness of the incarnation and alienating forsakenness within the Trinity (Philippians 2:8).[98] God's self-emptying is followed by the exaltation of Christ at his resurrection, a *plerosis* state of the Son's self-realization, which establishes our redemption (Philippians 2:9).[99]

Collectively, the crucifixion, death and resurrection of Jesus Christ allows us to theologically describe the now and not-yet milieu we currently inhabit as a continuum that moves between the poles of kenotic emptiness and the fullness of plerosis. As scripture, tradition and experience reiterate, this current time between Pentecost and the full Parousia of Christ consists of moments of healings and death, forgiveness and resentment, deliverance and torment; all evidence of full power, underused power, and no available power.[100] Finally, when the full eschatologi-

---

96. Barrett, "Martensen as Systematic Theologian," 89, cf. Martensen, *Christian Dogmatics*, §137, 270–73.

97. Brown, *Divine Humanity*, 259–61; Ward, "Cosmos and Kenosis," 161–64.

98. PIG, 224–50; Balthasar, *Mysterium Paschale*, 23–36; Vanstone, *Love's Endeavour*, 55–74. Torrance argues, following Rahner, that since the imminent Trinity is the economic Trinity then only Christ can speak into the stark meaninglessness as the one God enters into and takes into himself all aspects of earthly pain and suffering. Torrance, "Does God Suffer? 364–68.

99. The plerosis establishes both the humanward movement to God and the Godward movement to humankind. Forsyth, *The Person*, 321–57.

100. "The attempt to follow Christ in this world should not always take the kenotic path. Sometimes [unilateral] power is the right instrument to use." Brown, *Divine Humanity*, 264–66.

cal consummation happens, as described in Philippians 2:10–11, it is the sublime and supreme *henotic* moment, an intimate uniting of infinite and finite personhood resulting in the divine and many creaturely persons becoming one,[101] which concludes with *theosis*, that complete unity with the triune God and sharing in the divine life (2 Peter 1:4), which, according to Ward, is the final telos of God for creation.[102]

Because the death and resurrection of the Son signifies an immemorial cross in the being of God, the kenotic journey of Christ is foundational for trinitarian and generalized kenotic sojourns. What is true of kenotic Christology is true of kenotic Trinitarianism and kenotic cosmology.[103] Therefore, to better understand the kenotic reality that conflicts with spiritual powers of evil, extrapolation from the life of Jesus is needed.

First, Jesus, empowered by the Holy Spirit, often operates with full power through authoritative usage of his being and instruction (Luke 4:1; 10:21; Mark 4:39; 5:7; etc.).[104] Second, after his death, he plunges the depths of hell in a radical descent of kenosis to have solidarity with the dead and identify with the complete godforsaken-ness and outright evil he wants to defeat and rescue humanity from (Ephesians 4:7–9; 1 Peter 3:19; 4:5–6).[105] Third, following the precedent established by Jesus empowering his disciples over the demonic (Mark 6:7, 13), after his ascension his name was authoritatively used by his apostles to command demonic powers to leave (Acts 16:18).[106] Finally, at the final consummation of the eschaton, there will be, as part-cited above,[107] the full eradication of all evil—Satan, demons, the beast, false prophet—initiated by the Son appearing in full glory and power (Revelation 19:11–21) and completed by the great judge on the almighty throne (Revelation 20:7–15).

Theologically, spiritually and phenomenologically, our current epoch is one which fluctuates between kenosis and plerosis. The reason for the coming of the Son incarnate was to destroy the works of the demonic (1 John 3:8) yet the total eradication of evil is still to happen. In

---

101. Galatians 2:20.
102. Keith Ward, *The Christian Idea*, 191–203.
103. Ward, "Cosmos and," 152–66.
104. Fee, "The New Testament," 37–39.
105. Oakes, "The Internal Logic," 188–93.
106. Conversely, we can also see the fluctuation within the kenosis-plerosis continuum as Jesus' name is used without authority with powerless and disastrous results (Acts 19:13–16).
107. See "Chapter 4 Introduction" (pp.86–88) section above.

the meantime, we see and experience proleptic divine events of emancipation from the diabolical, fueled by the plerosis of the triune God. Unfortunately, we also see moments of kenotic servitude when humanity and creation remain enslaved to the free-but-always-evil decisions of the demonic. So, because of the nature of enslaved freedom of Satan and hordes, for which they will be held morally responsible,[108] the power of suffering love will never persuade or influence them to change, thereby only leaving one apocalyptic option: the exhaustive eternal destruction of all evil in the all-consuming *henotic* and *theosic* power of the triune God.

CONCLUSION

I have sought to formulate a definition and understanding of an incommunicable attribute of God, divine omnipotence, in order to help explain God's interaction with creation. This current creation endures a now-and-not-yet spiritual warzone reality between the kingdom of God and the realm of darkness, and continues to groan in labor pains longing for the day of redemption and renewal (Romans 8:20–23). As articulated, a theology of divine power has to consist of the spiritual concept of kenosis in order to have congruence with much of the witness of scripture and experience of real life. For, I would proffer, the doctrine of omnipotence, as historically understood as unlimited power, when conflated with the absolute goodness of God is the main impediment to belief in the God of scripture. Many ask the original question of this chapter; why does the biblically good and all-powerful God not just usher in the consummation and bring an end to all evil and spiritual darkness that plagues creation and humankind in particular?

A kenotic definition of omnipotence, based in large measure on Fiddes' theology of suffering love, partially answers this question both in terms of the being of God and his interaction with creation. While it insists that God *could* bring about the end of suffering and an answer to the theodicy question, it does not suggest *when* he will do it, or indeed *why* he has not already done it. As argued, there is simply no complete solution to the problem and reality of evil in the here and now and any

---

108. For a helpful account of the philosophy and theology of Jonathan Edwards concerning the type of freedom a person (or spiritual being) needs to have to be morally culpable, see Holmes, "Edwards on the Will," 273–85.

attempt to fully explain it is flawed, since the tragic is mysterious and remains without adequate explanation.[109]

Notwithstanding this limitation, the alternative definition of kenosis as suggested by Martensen and used to supplement and develop Fiddes' definition of omnipotence as suffering love, holds much potential for further understanding of God's power in the midst of a reality of SW. First and foremost, it coheres well with the descent and glorification of Christ as described in Philippians 2 and this forms a satisfactory *Christian* theology based on the life and death of Jesus of Nazareth, which according to the gospels and letters of Paul, was rooted in human weakness (1 Corinthians 1; 2 Corinthians 12). Hence, therefore, this offers a theological account of variable demonstrations of power in the gospels but without concluding, as in process theology, necessary kenosis since this does not account for answered prayer and the consummation of the Parousia.

Second, the use of Martensen's account helps negate a couple of the weaknesses of Fiddes' account. It allows us to articulate how kenosis can be extrapolated from Christology to a trinitarian and generalized concept. The juxtaposition of full and varying kenotic power permits the idea of suffering love to be one *mode* of divine omnipotence, not omnipotence *en esse*. Second, Martensen's dialectic of kenotic power offers a way to advance Fiddes' nuanced Abelardian atonement theology by maintaining an emphasis upon subjective experience, but this experience includes genuine events of exorcism and deliverance when full kenotic power is at work; this is all a proleptic foretaste of the ultimate end of all evil.

Overall, this definition of omnipotence goes a considerable way to maintain a traditional understanding of divine power in the now-and-not-yet milieu of the contemporary reality while helping to address some of the perennial questions of theodicy. It also forms the beginnings of an understanding upon which to delineate and articulate the other divine attributes since, as Swinburne correctly claims, omnipotence is central because all the other divine characteristics flow from it.[110]

---

109. Brown, *Divine Humanity*, 120–25.
110. Swinburne, "Is God All-powerful?"

5

Panentheism
The Spiritual Combat Situation Within the Omnipresence of God

INTRODUCTION

PANENTHEISM IS "THE BELIEF that the Being of God includes and penetrates the whole universe, so that every part of it exists in Him, but (as against Pantheism) that His being is more than, and is not exhausted by, the universe."[1] Fiddes is a self-identifying panentheist:[2] "My own proposal is that 'pan-entheism' as the participating of everything in God is a sharing in interweaving movements of relational love."[3] As worked out in CSG, he claims that a panentheistic participative doctrine of God is superior to both the classic and pantheistic doctrines of God in order to account for existence, being and non-being in God and creation, and how moral and natural evil affect a passible God of suffering love.[4]

Fiddes' central theological tenet of participation in God is very much the underlying structure of his articulated panentheism. Not only does it help explain divine agency in a world of flux and decay,[5] it also

---

1. Cross, and Livingstone, *Oxford Dictionary*, 1213.
2. It is claimed that panentheism is popular among philosophical theologians but not systematic or biblical theologians. Clayton, "Panentheism in Metaphysical," 74.
3. PIG, 292.
4. See "The Challenge of Divine" (pp.26–30) section above.
5. See "The Contemporary Need" (pp.4–9) section above.

describes God's ontology in ways which undermine historical abuses of power and hierarchy. Moreover, the concept of participation helps humanity in its relationships through forgiveness, as well as intercessory prayer and the use and application of love in creative ways. Paradoxically, participation through perichoresis can also be used to explain moments of perceived bodily healing as well as apparent divine hiddenness.[6]

In relation to the main thesis of this work, any account of God's omnipresence that articulates God's panentheistic reality is confronted by a significant challenge: *how* does evil exist within God without making God the primary cause of evil and *where* does this evil reside in God's omnipresent holiness and goodness? As discussed above, Fiddes rejects Barth and Moltmann's descriptions of the nature and location of evil and instead takes Augustine's *privatio boni* and juxtaposes it with Heideggerian being and non-being in order to develop an understanding of evil as a slipping into nothingness.[7] From these conclusions of the nature and location of evil, Fiddes subsequently arrives at a number of outcomes regarding the consequences of evil.[8]

The aim of this chapter is to construct a doctrine of divine omnipresence that has room for, and helps make sense of, those things that must be real for SW to be real. Building upon the above account of the nature and ontology of evil, I intend to take Fiddes' panentheistic vision of God's participative triune nature and reconstruct it in order to help explain the presence of personal, ontological evil within the omnipresence of God. This aim will naturally involve discussion of evil's impact upon God's passible nature and, in light of scripture's strongly suggested eradication of all evil and suffering, the eschatological and teleological implications of this account.

In order to reconstruct Fiddes' panentheistic vision and make room for ontological evil, his articulation of panentheism will have to be critically analyzed. This will involve understanding the covenant theology of panentheism he proffers, defining and critiquing his espoused form of panentheism by examining his trinitarian theology of participation as "persons as relations," and succinctly investigating his claim of divine presence and hiddenness. From this a reconstruction of a panentheistic doctrine of God will be done, one which allows for the presence of ontological evil and forms a didactic theological schema that takes seriously

---

6. See "The Nature and Character" (pp.13–18) section above.
7. See "What is Evil?" (pp.34–39) section above.
8. See "The Consequences of Evil" (pp.55–58) section above.

claimed experiences and stories of evil and classical theology's assertion of the future eradication of all evil.

COVENANT THEOLOGY OF PANENTHEISM

As a theologian within the Baptist tradition, Fiddes seeks to undergird his philosophical and theological ideas primarily with sound biblical exegesis. While he accepts that God can and does speak to creation through non-Christian texts and sources, known as the word (small "w") of God,[9] the canon of scripture has a sufficiency because of its openness to meet with and participate in God.[10] The covenantal nature of panentheism is, for Fiddes, fundamentally rooted in the earliest biblical covenant expressed in scripture. Creation shares in the divine perichoresis from the moment God makes a post-flood covenant with all living creation (Genesis 9:8–17),[11] which in turn participates in God to greater or lesser degrees.[12]

As this covenant is never reversed then there is a natural building on this foundational principle explicated by other key biblical texts. The psalmist declares there is nowhere in all of creation where God's Spirit is not (Psalm 139:7–12),[13] and the prophets unequivocally announce that God makes other covenants with creation and has relations with other peoples while maintaining a particular covenant with Israel (Hosea 2:18, Amos 9:7, Isaiah 45:1–4).[14] Meanwhile, Jesus prays that all believers will be *in* the triune God just as the Father and Son are *in* each other (John 17:20–23).[15] Paul, appropriating a philosophical idea from Cretan philosophy, states that all humanity lives, moves and has its being in God

---

9. Fiddes, "A Review of 'Persuade us to Rejoice,'" 110–11.

10. Fiddes, "The Canon as Space," 128–32, 142–45.

11. Perichoresis, claims Fiddes, is a theological conviction he sourced, not from Moltmann, but from C.S. Lewis. Fiddes, "'For the Dance," 37–41. For an in-depth study of perichoretic co-inherence in the writings and friendships of C.S Lewis see Fiddes, *Charles Williams and C.S. Lewis*.

12. Fiddes, "Participating in," 388–90; Fiddes, "Preface," 1–4.

13. Fiddes agrees with Hopkins that this Psalm shows God indwelling all the ubiquitous inscapes of the world. Fiddes, "G. M. Hopkins," 572–73.

14. Fiddes, "Preface," 2–3; Fiddes, "Covenant and Participation," 127–28. For agreement among scholars on the "sandal of particularity" see Brueggemann, *Isaiah 40–66*, 74–76; Hubbard, *Joel and Amos*, 247; J. Dearman, *The Book of Hosea*, 125–26.

15. Fiddes takes issue with Volf's comment that humans cannot indwell the person of the Spirit, but only his ambience. PIG, 46–48, cf. Volf, *After Our Likeness*, 211.

(Acts 17:28),[16] and most central for participation as relations, the Petrine school spiritually encourages their readers by promising that the calling and election of Christian believers results in their participation in the divine nature of God (2 Peter 1:4).[17]

Consequently, establishing a biblical-theological foundation for God's universal and panentheistic omnipresence justifies further application into Fiddes' other two academic disciplines. Regarding the relationship between literature and theology, since God can speak through non-Christian literature, wisdom can be identified and received not just through observation and mediation but through participation in the world which is participating in God.[18] Fiddes defines this as the *fear of the Lord* and it is categorized by an open pluralism and boundless knowledge of the world,[19] a world which has holistic unity since God in his panentheistic glory relates to each part of it within himself.[20]

Concerning ecclesiology, a covenant theology of panentheism comprises of the covenant ecclesiology of the body of Christ, which is a vertical and horizontal covenant through which God uses the local church as the center point in order to interact and partner with creation.[21] Despite the future eschatological vision of a hope-filled unified and fully operant body of Christ, the *de facto* reality is that the church is a fractured body with missing parts and much inequality. The reason for this, states Fiddes, is the inherent tension created by the vertical and horizontal covenants: tension between the rule of the congregation and church leadership, and between the local church community and wider church body.[22] The needed antidote is a re-establishment of covenant freedom, defined not as personal autonomy but as living under the ubiquitous rule of Christ; churches need to make covenantal room for this rule.[23]

Notwithstanding this continual falling short, these covenants of the panentheistic God are the spiritual blueprint for God's relationship

---

16. Fiddes, "Covenant and Participation," 128–29; Fiddes, "Ecclesiology and Ethnography," 32.

17. Fiddes, "Participating in," 375.

18. SWKG, 203–12.

19. Fiddes, "Where Shall Wisdom," 186–90.

20. Fiddes, "Old Testament Principles," 36–38.

21. Fiddes, "An Ecclesiology," 212–14; Fiddes, "Covenant and the Inheritance," 69–72.

22. Fiddes, "Baptist Concepts of the Church," 293–300.

23. Fiddes, "A Fourth Strand," 157; Fiddes, "Baptist Concepts," 310–12.

with the church and creation. God indeed opens up his triune self for creation and the church in order that all of creation currently shares in the life of God, the very life that God determines for himself.[24] Revealing himself to all creation enables God to make different covenants that go beyond the church;[25] a covenant with the world and an inimitable type of covenant with Christians.[26] This "Christian-type" covenant is one of the three vertical covenants God enters into with his people: a covenant of grace with human beings for their salvation in Christ, a divine covenant between the Persons of the Triune God, and a covenantal agreement God makes corporately with a church or a group of churches.[27]

As I will demonstrate below, Fiddes takes this covenant theology of panentheism and uses it to propose a commodious participatory doctrine of God; one that undergirds all claims of a passible God of suffering love. While the biblical basis for a covenant theology of panentheism is plausible, this does not establish what form of panentheistic notion Fiddes is espousing, since there are various accounts of panentheism being suggested, especially in dialogue between theologians and scientists.[28] To this ambiguity we now turn.

PANENTHEISM DEFINED: "PERSONS AS RELATIONS" PARTICIPATION

While claiming that all God-speech is metaphorical, Fiddes holds that human beings can know and speak of God and, in a limited way, say who God is without resorting only to literalism or apophatic language.[29] Ontologically, God is love and has loving relations within his triune self and so the optimal way to describe this is via the language of participation. Humans exist within a universe of participation with relationships

---

24. Fiddes, *Believing and*, 19, 44; Fiddes, "Christianity, Culture and Education," 9–10; Fiddes gives full credit to Barth for the grace-filled and free basis of God's covenant with creation. Fiddes, "'Walking Together,'" 58–63; cf. *CD* II/2, §33.2, 161–94.

25. Fiddes, "Baptists and Theological Education," 188–92.

26. Fiddes, "Christian Doctrine," 216–19.

27. It is the second type of vertical covenant, a divine transactional covenant between the persons of the Trinity which is the basis for "persons as relations" participatory panentheistic theology. Fiddes, "Theology of Covenant," 124–26; Fiddes, "Church and Sect," 43–50.

28. Powell, Review of *In Whom We Live*, 107–8.

29. Fiddes, Review of *Karl Barth*, 696–99.

at the center, all of which is experienced within the very being of God. The entire universe is engaging in God like this and so we should place all other asked existential questions into this experienced framework.[30]

"An 'event of relationships' is a participatory concept that makes sense only in actual life events. This does not replace revelation with human experience, but locates the self-disclosure of God where God wants to be."[31] In debate with Holmes, Molnar and McCall, Fiddes succinctly depicts his panentheistic and participatory doctrine of the Trinity as "persons as relations."[32] He claims that not only is this the most appropriate language that we have to speak of the persons of the Trinity but that it is also methodologically sound,[33] uses the majority of theological sources, and was the approach of the early Church fathers who defined hypostasis relationally, not objectively.[34] Moreover, relations language offers the best analogy for God-speech and it also helps us understand Rahner's rule by finding a concept of the divine that expresses the relational experience of persons and helps us understand our participation in the triune God.[35]

By his own admission, Fiddes believes that his *unique* contribution to trinitarian theology is defining the Trinity as "persons as relations,"[36] which ungirds his panentheistic vision of God. As discussed,[37] his panentheistic doctrine of participating in God using a persons-as-relations

30. Fiddes, "What is God [parts 1&2]?"
31. Fiddes, "Relational Trinity," 185.
32. Fiddes, "Relational Trinity," 159–206.

33. McCall is critical of Fiddes' notion of relationality without involving language of persons. It jettisons classic Christology and embraces degree Christology. McCall, "Response to Paul, 197–203. Fiddes' rejoinder is that all human language falls short and that our own human experiences of living in relations with others can be seen to reflect and participate in the relations in God. Fiddes, "Rejoinder Comments and Clarification," 205–6. On degree Christology, Fiddes remains ambiguous. Fiddes, Review of *Christology in Conflict*, 700–703.

34. Holmes disagrees, claiming that the Eastern Fathers were committed to divine simplicity more than Fiddes acknowledges and that the concept of "relations" does not connect to the idea of personhood, as claimed by Fiddes. Holmes, "Response," 188–90. For a sustained defense of his first rebuttal point, see Holmes, *The Holy Trinity*, 97–120.

35. PIG, 34–46, cf. Karl Rahner, *The Trinity*, 22.

36. Fiddes, personal communication with author. Of course, Fiddes is aware that this language comes from Augustine and Aquinas. His claim of uniqueness lies in taking an extra step beyond "subsistent relations" and using radical language that talks about the "event of relationships," which is the best language of participation. Fiddes, "Participating in," 379–83.

37. See "The Nature and Character" (pp.13–18) section above.

trinitarian definition permeates the entire substantial corpus of his work in systematic theology, theological insights from literature, and Baptist and ecumenical ecclesiology.[38] Consequently, however, this exclusive claim creates a challenge when attempting to situate him on the continuum of panentheistic understanding which some suggest currently exists.[39] On this continuum between the poles of pantheism and classic theism Gregersen helpfully suggests that there are, generally, three varieties of panentheism.[40] Despite the differences, however, for our current purposes it is vital to note that there is the challenging but important ontology of bilateral relations between God and the world in which "the world is *somehow* 'contained in God' and there will be *some* 'return' of the world into the life of God." (emphasis mine)[41] This generic ontology commonly runs through all three varieties and affects every attempt to define the "somehow" and the "some."

Gregersen examines the nature of the bilateral relations in order to differentiate. Within the above-mentioned generic ontology, he discovers two different bilateral relationships. The first he labels *strong* (or *strict*) which holds that there is a *necessary* interdependence between God and the world. In its dipolar form it asserts that God cannot exist without the world, and that there is a necessary bilateral relationship between God and world.[42] The second Gregersen names is *qualified* panentheism and argues that it is a form of *Christian* panentheism because,[43] in contrast to

---

38. A selection of his work in the three areas of research where this is the case includes Fiddes, "Participating in," 375–91; Fiddes, "Father, Son, and Holy Spirit," 207–10; Fiddes, personal communication with author; Fiddes, "Concept," 22–23; Fiddes, "The Late-Modern Reversal," 124–30; Fiddes, "Not Anarchy but Covenant," 147–55; Fiddes, "Attending to," 83–85; Fiddes, "The Church and Salvation," 143–48; Fiddes, "The Church Local and Universal," 97–108; Fiddes, "Koinonia Ecclesiology," 250–53, 262–65.

39. That Fiddes is situated somewhere on the continuum is reflected in the attempts he makes to differentiate his position from both pantheism and classical theism. Fiddes, "Response to Paul D," 104–8.

40. *Soteriological* panentheism (similar to *eschatological* panentheism espoused by Polkinghorne and Ward), *revelational* (or *expressivist*) panentheism, and *di-polar* panentheism (also known as Whiteheadian panentheism). Gregersen, "Three Varieties," 20–34.

41. Gregersen, "Three Varieties," 20.

42. Gregersen, "Three Varieties," 22–23.

43. Olson concurs and argues that this Christian panentheism, which is a qualified view, is now a serious option for all orthodox Christians and it is located via media between modern (strong/strict) panentheism and classical theism. Olson, "A Postconservative," 337.

the strong bilateral relationship, qualified panentheism holds that while the world cannot exist without God, God is self-existent and does not need the world to exist. Any co-determining that happens in this kind of panentheism is an act of divine grace and freedom in which God freely desires temporal events to influence him and creatures to share in the life of the triune God.[44]

Before we attempt to situate Fiddes on this continuum of panentheism, a qualification is in order. Fiddes is a sophisticated theologian whose theology cannot be reduced to a certain kind.[45] While Gregersen's varieties of panentheism is a helpful heuristic guide, it would be erroneous to subject Fiddes' theology to an over-simplification in order to make it fit one of Gregersen's categories. The main problem it seems with the varieties on the continuum used in this debate, as Olson suggests, is that the term "panentheism" is overstretched and is now used to cover too much.[46]

To illustrate, we can observe debate concerning the placement of other apparent panentheists on a spectrum. Cooper argues that Pannenberg is indeed a panentheist despite Pannenberg forcefully stating that he is not.[47] Similarly, Edwards joins Cooper to label Moltmann and his trinitarian-perichoretic panentheism as modern (i.e. strong/strict) by grouping him alongside process thinkers such as Griffin,[48] and claims that his philosophical framework comes from neo-platonic dialectical ontology found in Hegel and Schelling.[49] In contrast, Olson states that Moltmann comes approximately from the same theological stable as Pannenberg and definitely advocates a soteriological panentheism which

---

44. Gregersen, "Three Varieties," 23–24.

45. Fiddes' claim of drawing from and going beyond Augustine and Aquinas is prominent in his ecclesiology work and serves to theologically analyze different ecclesial and spiritual practices. Fiddes and Ward, "Affirming Faith at a Service," 61–65; Fiddes, "Ecclesiology and Ethnography," 24–29; Fiddes, et al, *Baptists and the Communion*, 78–80. His source claim comes from a certain reading of Augustine and Aquinas concerning God's subsistent relations which suggests that the relations in God are as ontologically real as anything that is created or uncreated. CSG, 49–57 cf. Fiddes, "Relational Trinity," 167–69. One can conclude that Fiddes is correct in this assertion given than none of his interlocutors challenge this point and Holmes even concurs with it. Holmes, "Response," 186–90; Molnar, "Response," 191–96; McCall, "Response," 197–203.

46. Olson, "A Postconservative," 328, 336–37.

47. Cooper, *Panentheism*, 259–81, cf. Pannenberg, *Introduction*, 45. Fiddes sees Pannenberg as a theological bed fellow. Fiddes, "Response to Paul," 104.

48. Edwards, "A Relational and Evolving," 202.

49. Cooper, *Panentheism*, 257–58.

affirms God's freedom and the voluntarist nature of his chosen dependence upon the world.[50]

One probable reason for the variety of opinion when attempting to situate any theologian on this continuum is the number of complex factors and variables involved in the definition of panentheism. I suggest, therefore, that to elicit as much understanding as possible about where in relation to other panentheist thinkers Fiddes sits, we need to reduce the number of variables to a single dependent one on this continuum: *the degree to which God's perfection is influenced and affected by the world and creation.*

This focus on the God-world bilateral relations helps to identify what Fiddes does not mean in describing panentheism as a sharing in interweaving movements of relational love. As well as distancing himself from any hyper-weak panentheistic model where, due to his absolute aseity and transcendence, God is not affected at all by the world, Fiddes also refuses to endorse any Hegelian statement of a dependent, bilateral collapse of God and the world,[51] or any process theological statement denying divine self-existence by insisting on a non-contingent, necessary universe as part of the being of God.[52] That said, it is considerably easier to state what Fiddes does not believe, rather than what he does. However, upon closer inspection, one can identify a number of claims by Fiddes which can be used to build a constructive understanding of the nature of his panentheism that will help to form a panentheistic definition of divine omnipresence within which it will be possible to locate a theological understanding of SW.

To begin, Fiddes does not believe that the theological tradition of the church should never be either challenged or departed from and

---

50. Olson, "Trinity and Eschatology," 213–27; Grenz and Olson, *20th-Century Theology*, 170–99. Boyd agrees stating, "While Moltmann sometimes uses panentheistic-sounding language, he clearly differentiates himself from process panentheism by affirming God's freedom in relation to creation as well as by affirming creatio ex nihilo." Boyd, *Crucifixion of the Warrior God*, 477 fn.37. Both scholars rightly base their conclusions on a number of Moltmann's writings in which he explicitly commits himself to God's intrinsic freedom, divine voluntary self-limitation, and *creatio ex nihilo*. See Moltmann, "The Trinitarian History," 643–46; Moltmann, *God in Creation*, 72–93; Moltmann, *The Trinity*, 105–11.

51. "Without a world God is not God." Hegel, *Lectures on the Philosophy*, 308 fn.97. On what Hegel meant by the statement see Shanks, *Hegel's Political Theology*, 87–89.

52. See "The Contemporary Need" (pp.4–9) section above. cf. Whitehead, *Process and Reality*, 348. Decades later Hartshorne and Reese theologically develop and nuance Whitehead's position. Hartshorne and Reese, *Philosophers Speak*, 22.

is increasingly open to *experience* as a legitimate source of theological formulation.[53] One painful experience Fiddes personally went through which has influenced his thinking with regard to *where* God is in mentally alternate worlds, was the premature and tragic death of his son Benjamin, to whom he dedicates *PE*. Juxtaposing this experience with Bonhoeffer's Christology has brought Fiddes to the conclusion that God through Christ was not only incarnated in this world but also in all *other* alternate worlds people mentally inhabit in their mind.[54] This has, in turn, led him to promulgate what he terms "everyday theology," which contra Coakley's narrow definition, is a participating in God in a wide and boundless panentheistic reality and if applied to the church and the sacraments can lead to creative and capacious sacramental and Eucharistic theology.[55]

One implication of sacramental theology that pushes the boundaries leads Fiddes to consider the world as the "body of God." The term is suggested by Fiddes as the best metaphor to help understand sacramental and divine presence, especially within an online age and physical bodiless communication.[56] In a reality of bilateral relations with the divine, how is it possible to encounter a bodiless God especially at the Eucharistic table with elements that claim to be the blood and body of Christ?[57] Largely in keeping with McFague's thesis, Fiddes insists on holding the incarnation of Christ as the key to understanding the world as God's body, asserting that we work from the particular to the universal so that the "yes" of the Son is inseparable from the "yes" of Jesus of Nazareth. This, he claims, helps avoid pantheism and certain unsatisfactory forms of panentheism. It also guarantees a participating of everything within

---

53. See "The Contemporary Need" (pp.4–9) and "The Place of Experience (pp.9–13) sections above. One could tentatively identify Fiddes as a theologian who utilizes a post-conservative approach to theological construction, which is open to using both reason and experience (especially phenomenological-empirical evidence). "The great theologians of each generation have realized that merely repeating particular formulations inherited from the previous generations would only preserve the gospel by petrifying it." Shults, *Reforming the Doctrine*, 201.

54. Fiddes, personal communication with author.

55. Fiddes, Review of *God, Sexuality and the Self*, 142–46. Examples can be found in Fiddes, Review of *Material Eucharist*, 387–92; Fiddes, "Sacraments in a Virtual World?" Fiddes, "*Ex Opere Operato*," 222–29; Fiddes, et al, *Baptists and the Communion*, 163–84.

56. From McFague, *The Body*.

57. PIG, 278–85.

the life of the triune God alongside all the diversity and otherness that accompanies it.[58]

This assertion does find common ground with a number of other panentheists but not complete assent. Not all panentheists concur that the world is the body of God as it creates other theological complications. Two in particular are salient when discussing Fiddes. First, as Fiddes is a proponent of radical, irrevocable freewill,[59] some claim that the body of God metaphor is not compatible with any concept of libertarian freewill and only works with a compatibilist understanding. Ward, for instance, argues that early proponents of this type of thinking sought to uphold human individuality and causality in the history of the universe. If God is the head and he wants the body to operate holistically as a body, then where does this leave individual freedom and genuine human determinative say-so?[60]

Secondly, in aligning himself closely to McFague's delineation of the body of God metaphor, Fiddes situates himself very close to elements of process panentheism he distinguishes himself from in other works.[61] His "persons as relations" work is thoroughly trinitarian and personal whereas McFague's theology has aspects of non-personal constructs of the divine and non-trinitarian assertions of God.[62] Moreover, given Fiddes' ambivalence to degree Christology, it would be prudent to maintain

---

58. PIG, 285–94, cf. McFague, *The Body*, 131–95.

59. See "Divine Passibility of Suffering" (pp.18–21) and "The Problem of Evil (pp.50–55) sections above.

60. Ward, "The World as the Body," 64–67. A third way through the impasse of this perennial debate could be Page's concept of "Pansyntheism." Focusing on prepositional change, she suggests that to get beyond the divine sovereignty-freewill debate that remains problematic if everything is *in* God, we reframe it as God is *with* everything and everyone. That way divine and creaturely freedom is preserved and the connection comes through divine love seeking a response. Page, *God and the Web*, 40–52. For global-ecological implications see Page, "Panentheism and Pansyntheism," 222–32.

61. Of course there are many similarities including non-patriarchal models of God, divine passibility, and language of bilateral intertwining of God and the world. Hence Fiddes and McFague have been located in the same panentheism-promoting group of theologians. See Brierley, "Naming a Quiet Revolution," 3, 8, 11.

62. While critiquing the monarchical model of God, McFague states everything in the world can become God's saving presence, and it should not be limited only to the "word" of God. This part of her thinking prompts a suggestion from fellow feminist theologian Ruether that her theology has a strong Neo-Platonist similarities found in both Plato and Plotinus. McFague, *Models of*, 63–69, 200 fn.9; McFague, *The Body*, 193–94.

critical distance from McFague who fully endorses a panentheistic, evolutionary understanding of Christ.[63]

Another feature of Fiddes' persons-as-relations panentheism which resists easy categorization is his work on panentheism, forgiveness and reconciliation. It is with this consideration that his understanding and advocacy of nuanced bilateral relations involving God and the world helps to place him on the single variable continuum consisting of degree differences in relation to God's perfection and to what extent it is influenced by the entire creation. Forgiveness is, attests Fiddes, a two-stage journey: a journey of discovery and a journey of endurance and anguish, both of which are journeys into God himself since Christ modelled them in his declaration of forgiveness from the cross (Luke 23:34) and subsequent death.[64] In this act, Christ teaches that there is a difference between divine perfection and divine completion; the latter is grounded in God's sovereign desire to relate to creation without any loss or addition of perfection.[65]

Further, locating the journey of forgiveness and reconciliation in the participatory relations of the triune God means that when we forgive, we are actually partaking in the divine rhythms of the forgiveness of God. Also these movements of forgiving which participate in the divine dance of forgiveness obligate us, like Jesus, to pronounce and release unconditional forgiveness on people who have not apologized or repented in order to unlock hatred and hopefully bring them back into full relationship through reconciliation.[66] If this does not work, suggests Fiddes following Derrida and Riceour, then with God's enabling grace, radical forgetting or memory locking will be appropriate.[67]

These unique elements included in Fiddes' panentheistic definition and vision defy reductionism and, in contrast to some claims, preclude his general inclusion in a group of panentheistic thinkers on the continuum

---

63. "Jesus is not ontologically different from other paradigmatic figures either in our tradition or in other religious traditions who manifest in word and deed the love of God for the world." McFague, *Models of*, 136.

64. PIG, 191–210.

65. PIG, 211–15.

66. PIG, 215–20.

67. Fiddes, "Memory, Forgetting," 130–33. Fiddes has embarked upon further original work locating the Mennonite practice of "restorative justice," which is currently sometimes used in the British criminal justice system, within the panentheistic movements of participation in the divine. See Fiddes, "Restorative Justice," 1–12.

somewhere between deism and pantheism.⁶⁸ Collectively, together with his "persons as relations" definition of panentheistic, divine participation, these factors allow us to arrive at a panentheistic definition of divine omnipresence that can didactically be used as part of a systematic theology of SW. For it seems entirely plausible and appropriate that when we consider all aspects of Fiddes' theological construction of panentheism we are justified to place him on the continuum of Christian (qualified) panentheism; that qualified view that stands via media between classical theism and traditional panentheism and states that God necessarily exists without any creation, that the creation cannot exist without God, and that God willingly opens up his self-sufficiency to contingent creation in order to have a genuine, bi-lateral relationship with creation.⁶⁹

Moreover, Fiddes' belief in post-death development and progressive possibilities also aligns him with *soteriological* panentheism which frames God "all-in-all" talk in eschatological terms recognizing the future consummation of all things dwelling in God in the eschaton.⁷⁰ This naturally implies that in the now-and-not-yet milieu we currently inhabit a complete panentheistic reality does not exist. It should be clear that this is an understanding of God's omnipresence that is fully congruent with the thus far explicated theology of SW. The rest of this chapter will articulate an understanding of panentheism that makes room for the presence of the demonic and SW. However, before that, a brief excursus is needed to consider a corollary of the non-fully realized panentheism of the here and now and how Fiddes explains it by focusing on the hiddenness and presence of God.

---

68. Brierley is careful and correctly identifies a number of nuanced differences held by Fiddes that set him apart from other panentheists, Brierley, "Naming a Quiet," 3, 8–11. Conversely, Molnar is off mark by pronouncing that Fiddes' panentheism is closer to Ted Peters and Catherine LaCugna, which can only be concluded if there is a misunderstanding of Fiddes' subtle distinction between self-existence and perfection, and self-sufficiency and completion, the latter of which God freely desires to be influenced by creation. Molnar, "Response," 194–96.

69. My suggestion in order to help Fiddes clarify his position would be to use as one of his defending scriptures Acts 17:24–28, not v.28 alone, as the five verses clearly establish both God's self-existent ontology and panentheistic reality.

70. See "The Consequence of Evil" (pp.55–58) section above. Fiddes, "The Making," 12–14; Fiddes, "Acceptance and Resistance," 228–36.

DIVINE HIDDENNESS AND PRESENCE

> "Hey God... where do you go to get away...away?"[71]

Rea claims that theological exploration into the question of divine hiddenness became a significant focus of academic theology in the second half of the twentieth century.[72] An overview of the Fiddes corpus regarding divine hiddenness and presence supports this assertion. In his early work the "death of God" movement generates implications for divine hiddenness and presence that Fiddes addresses with explorations into kenotic metamorphosis and the "death of the living God" where he posits that since God through Christ enters into the realms of death, it is in God experiencing death that we know he is hidden, not absent or dead.[73] These critical reflections have evolved over the decades to the point that the subject of God's presence and hiddenness is a substantial element of his panentheistic vision of participation. Most recently Fiddes has constructed a theology of presence and place in which he draws from diverse sources: the biblical text (Job 28), the *khora* of Plato and other philosophers, and the contemporary challenge of culture against language of domination and hierarchy—which collectively reveal that the presence of God is a hidden presence and that, in his triune nature, there are relational non-places that create space within God.[74]

Fiddes contributes to our current focus on divine hiddenness and its relevance for understanding the incomplete, pre-eschaton panentheistic reality which currently exists. Using literature as a starting point, he observes from Huxley and Le Guin the myth of a present, full utopia. By confusing the eternal present with the eternal presence, the post-modernist posits that only the present, not past or future, is real. In the present there is no real presence but just traces of it. Fiddes, using Heidegger, claims these traces of presence lead to Being itself which is only found in its hidden presence situated in the *khora*—a place that is a no-place, which is where wisdom is found.[75]

---

71. King's X, *Get Away*, from *Ogre Tones*.

72. Rea, *The Hiddenness*, 6. Rea lists a number of texts that came out in the last 30 years of the previous century by Terrien, Morris, and others, including Schellenberg whose main thesis Rae critically interacts with in his text.

73. CSG, 174–206.

74. SWKG, 218–65.

75. TPE, 228–43; Fiddes, "Millennium," 7–22; cf. Fiddes, "The quest for a place," 35–42.

If the fullness of wisdom is hidden and found in the place which is a no-place, then the heart of present reality is hiddenness, specifically the hiddenness of God. Fiddes notes that a number of attempts to identify these no-places have been made, such as the *zimsum* of the Jewish Kabbalah, the apophatic tradition of mutual indwelling of God and cosmos in individual persons, and the subject-object participating in many places as espoused by Barth. However, Fiddes' radical proposal is that no-places are found in the spaces between the relational movements of God; no-places found in God's presence can house the "nothing" of the *khora*, apophatic theology's "empty place," and both Barth's and Levinas' "hiddenness as encounter" theology.[76]

Therefore, asserts Fiddes, in the current semi-realized eschaton, both divine presence and hiddenness are realities that we experience in the world around us: in culture,[77] in literature,[78] and ecclesiastical structures.[79] Yet using soteriological panentheistic-sounding language, our current desire for fuller presence unveils the millennial, especially post-millennial, inclination that has permeated much of church history.[80] Whether it is labelled "limited utopia" or "millennial hope," it is in these expressions which defy a dominating presence, resist associating "presence" with "present" and set faces to the open future, that a future millennial hope situated in the Trinity emerges. Seeing the eternal God not as a dominating subject but a humble divine being who operates kenotically, a millennial hope looks towards the future and hopes for the final coming of God in all his panentheistic fullness.[81]

---

76. Fiddes, "The quest for a place," 43–55; TPE, 250–58. Notwithstanding the alleged affiliation, Fiddes joins Bentley-Hart to criticize Levinas' use of Kabbalah in which God retreats in order to make nothingness, arguing that God does not need to withdraw to create space for "no-place" and the sublime does not need to be demarcated from the beautiful to preserve the hiddenness of God. Fiddes, "Attending to," 78–80; cf. Hart, *The Beauty*, 75–93.

77. Fiddes, "The Story," 80–83.

78. Fiddes claims that the coming and going of Aslan between Narnia and other worlds helps us theologically understand the hiddenness of God. Fiddes, "C. S. Lewis the Myth," 144–49. God's hiddenness is also explored in classic literature. FAL, 138–44, 224–33.

79. When Baptist believers gather and baptize members of the covenant community, divine presence is realized in the presence of the triune God who intersects human and divine love in the triune perichoretic relations. Fiddes, "Baptists and the Leuenberg," 189–90.

80. TPE, 221–28, 259–61.

81. Fiddes, "Millennium," 23–25.

ONTOLOGICAL EVIL AND THE PANENTHEISTIC REALITY OF GOD

Clayton claims that most panentheisms, following Augustine, subscribe to a privative view of evil in which the goodness of God works in and through the cosmos to eliminate evil. In contrast, panentheisms that do not take the privative view offer no helpful theodicy since God remains responsible for evil, just as he does in much classical theology.[82] Having delineated Fiddes' panentheism, I will now, in counterpoint to Clayton's assertion, outline a panentheistic doctrine of God which accounts for the presence and phenomenon of ontological evil, near-jettisons God's responsibility for evil, and strongly aligns with the scriptural witness of the final eradication of all evil in the eschaton.

In the above discussion concerning Fiddes' understanding of what evil is and whether it has ontology, it was recognized that his *a-priori* commitment to a panentheistic-participatory doctrine of God leads to the conclusion that evil as non-ontological *privatio boni* is more coherent, thereby corroborating Clayton's assertion.[83] However, as already mentioned, there is a case to be made for the existence of ontological evil within the panentheistic reality of God if there is engagement with contemporary definitions of "naked existence" ontology; existence which maintains ontological *privatio boni* without a reductionistic *privatio esse*.[84] I will argue that this constructed framework better reflects both a *prima facie* understanding of the biblical witness regarding the evil realm, and personal experience of SW as a valid source for theological formulation.

As established, Fiddes jettisons Moltmann's concept of *zimsum* arguing that it implies that evil is a necessity of creation.[85] Instead he adopts a nuanced, dialectical understanding of Barth's *das Nichtige*

---

82. Clayton, "The Panentheistic Turn," 293.

83. See "What is Evil?" (pp.34–39) section above.

84. See "What is Evil?" (pp.34–39) section above.

85. See "What is Evil?" (pp.34–39) and "Chapter 5 Introduction" (pp.108–110) sections above. In this conclusion Fiddes agrees with Wright that the necessary result of creation is not evil, but rather than evil is a distinct possibility of creation and so is to be viewed as a threat to creation. "Something will come," 93–95; cf. Wright, *A Theology*, 77. Both Wright and Fiddes' analysis of Moltmann's *zimsum* is accurate given that Moltmann states that the *nihil* created by God's withdrawn presence in which he creates his creation, is non-avoidable God-forsakenness, hell, and absolute death. It is this forsakenness, i.e. nothingness, that God on the cross enters into, overcomes, and makes part of the eternality of God. *This* is his omnipresence, as reflected by the Psalmist in Psalm 139:8. Moltmann, *God in*, 86–93.

account suggesting that on one hand it points towards evil as a necessary, non-contingent part of the creation while on the other offers the greatest definition of hostile and alienating non-being of the fallen world that represents the foreign nature of suffering which arises from a free creation. This non-being, asserts Fiddes, is that which befalls the sovereign God as he exposes himself to it and suffers from it.[86]

If evil is simply a negation of the good, then what has been discussed would progress things when answering the *how* and *where* of evil's co-existence alongside God's omnipresent holiness and goodness. However, to make a constructive-theological case of God's panentheistic nature which accommodates a personalist-ontological account of evil, Fiddes' panentheistic doctrine needs to be developed by taking some influences on Fiddes in a different direction. While acknowledging that there are forms of *privatio boni* which hold a robust account of The Satan,[87] a Barthian account of the nothingness that well captures the ambiguous and chaotic nature of the demonic,[88] and some panentheistic accounts that do hold to an ontological Satan and demons with volition and sentience,[89] I

---

86. See "The Challenge of Divine" (pp.26-30) and "Chapter 5 Introduction" (pp.108-110) sections above. Of course, claims Fiddes, the consequence of the death of the living God on the cross is the allowance of death and non-being within God himself. CSG, 193–200. Significantly, Fiddes' dialectical approach to Barth reflects well the tension in Barth's articulation of "nothingness" which strongly asserts an inevitability of the ontic reality of nothingness alongside creation but the emphatic denial that neither God nor creation is the author of nothingness since "nothingness is neither as the Creator or creature is." *CD* III/3, §50.4, 349–68.

87. Dante's description of Satan is both ontological and parasitical. He is described as "that creature who had once appeared so fair," a reference to Lucifer, one of the sons of light, who has now become a parasitical figure and exists as a "negative image of ultimate truth." This is specifically illustrated by his three faces parodying as the ultimate negative of the Holy Trinity—hatred, ignorance, impotence. Alighieri, *The Divine Comedy*, Canto 34, 154–58, 533–35.

88. Barth asserts that the nothingness, that which is not willed by God, has "real evil and real death as well as real sin . . . there is also a real devil with his legions, and a real hell." *CD* III/3, §50.3, 310. That there is a real ontic reality of the nothingness despite not being what the Creator or creature is, captures well the chaotic and ambiguous nature of the demonic accounts in scripture that synthesize single and plural pronouns of an evil spirit with no apparent contradiction. See for instance Mark 5:1–20 and Luke 4:31–37.

89. Jonathan Edwards is a salient example. Strong and persuasive cases have been made that his doctrine of God is both neo-platonic and panentheistic; a "qualified (Christian)" panentheism, to use Gregersen's terminology. For a convincing case that Edwards' God is a simple and free being and creation is a necessary output of God's creative nature and like an emanation from God see Crisp, *Jonathan Edwards on God*, 138–63. Within his panentheistic doctrine of God Edwards holds to a personalist-ontological account of the Satan which he proffers in his works. See Edwards, *The Works*

propose that the greatest potential for this construction lies in Fiddes' use of von Balthasar's theology of the Trinity in which there is room within the "yes" between the Father and Son for creation to rebel by stating an emphatic and rebellious "no" within the triune relations of God.

Fiddes' appeal to von Balthasar's "yes" and "no" in the relations between the Father and Son has become a persistent and permeating idea in his more recent work.[90] Within von Balthasar's corpus, Fiddes repeatedly draws from his work on dramatic soteriology found in the "Theo-drama" volumes of his trilogy, ones that address "the good" within systematic theology.[91] In these volumes von Balthasar explores the initiating of the incarnated Son into the divine life of the Trinity and the central role played by libertarian freedom. With significant echoes of Barth,[92] von Balthasar delineates the drama of the Trinity, a drama of kenosis couched in divine and creaturely freedom. The creation of the world is the first and most significant of three acts of kenosis. It is also a freely given divine act of kenosis that brings forth the Son and posits an absolute and infinite distance which can contain all other distances, including that of sin.[93]

This first act of kenosis gives the creature freedom over and against themselves and their creator, a freedom located within the relations of the

---

of Jonathan, 589–99.

90. In my research on Fiddes, it first appears in 2006 in Fiddes, "Participating in," 388–90, and since then has reappeared with much regularity, especially within his corpus of work on ecclesiology. See Fiddes, "The Place," 82–86; Fiddes, "Christianity, Culture," 15–16; Fiddes, "Dual Citizenship," 133–36; Fiddes, "Preface," in *Tradition*, xi–xviii; Fiddes, "Ecclesiology and Ethnography," 24–29; Fiddes, "A Conversation in Context," 19–21; SWKG, 368; Fiddes, et al, *Baptists and the Communion*, 95–101; Fiddes, "'Koinonia*: The Church," 41–44; Fiddes, "Ecclesiology and Ethnography: one," 23–29; Fiddes, "Pentecost," 199–204; Fiddes, "The Trinity, Modern Art," 96; Fiddes, "'Is this the Promised," 223–26, 238–40. As Fiddes said to me in person, "there is only one place that anyone can say 'no' to God and this is in the 'yes' of the Son to the Father." Fiddes, personal communication with author.

91. Specifically, volume 4 called "The Action" in which von Balthasar sets the scene of how God reveals himself to the world by focusing upon spiritual conflict and the need for the armor of God: "*Revelation is a battlefield*. Those who do battle on it can only be believers and theologians, provided they have equipped themselves with the whole armour of God (Eph 6:11)" (emphasis mine). Balthasar, *Theo-Drama. Vol. IV*, 12.

92. Barth and von Balthasar influence on Fiddes is shown in his use of them and his identification of overlapping themes. For example, both are adamant that God has complete freedom which is his natural self-expression. There is no process theology external contingent pressure to create. In this freedom God creates reality and being. Beyond being is the *nihil*, nothingness that is not willed by God but real nonetheless. CD III/3, §50.1–4, 289–335, cf. Balthasar, *Epilogue*, 77–86.

93. Balthasar, *Theo-Drama. Vol. IV*, 319–28.

Father and the Son. To quote von Balthasar, "the Father's self-surrender to the Son and their relationship in the Spirit (which grounds everything)—human freedom participates in the divine autonomy, both when it says Yes and when it says No."[94] When creation rebels and says "no," a twisted knot in the Son's pouring out of himself within the relation with the Father is realized, which is a situation made possible because it is only within the Son's *eucharistia* to the Father that human freedom and perversion is exercised.[95]

When defining the demonic and evil realm in terms of personalist ontology, von Balthasar offers threads of enquiry and development not easily discernable in Barth or Fiddes. Von Balthasar postulates a kenotic theology of covenant, one that avoids internal suffering in the Trinity while grounding all experiences of suffering in God. Because of the boundless distance between Father and Son when the Son is freely brought forth in an act of divine kenosis, there is a resultant incomprehensible separation of God from himself in which exists the darkest, malevolent and more bitter forms of separation. This includes the possibility of hell given the voluntary disjunction of the Father and Son.[96]

Von Balthasar, like Barth and Fiddes, at no time defines evil in ontological terms. However, conversely, he does not proffer *privatio boni* or nothingness as the total *esse* of evil. Rather, when juxtaposing God's all-powerful love which contains powerlessness and the genuine freedom bestowed upon any creature made in God's image, this results in a freedom that is perfectly sovereign but still externally influenced by alien freedoms and rebellion; rebellious freedoms that may seem impregnable but are not if countered with the correct weaponry such as intercessory prayer (2 Cor 10:4–5).[97] The use of this weaponry is made efficacious by the kenotic power of the cross; an event that enables Jesus to "psychologically" exhaust evil of its potency and also empower creatures to take evil captive in its intrinsic essence every time we refuse to resist it.[98]

---

94. Balthasar, *Theo-Drama. Vol. IV*, 328.

95. Fiddes borrows the language of a "twisted knot" from von Balthasar. It is not clear what the difference, theologically or otherwise, between a "knot" and a "twisted knot" is. Balthasar, *Theo-Drama. Vol. IV*, 328–32; Balthasar, *Mysterium*, ix, cf. Fiddes, "Participating in," 389; Fiddes, "Sacrifice," 61–62.

96. Balthasar, *Theo-Drama. Vol. IV*, 319–28.

97. Balthasar, *Theo-Drama. Vol. IV*, 330–32; Balthasar, *Epilogue*, 69–74.

98. Balthasar, *Epilogue*, 74–76. These claims of von Balthasar demonstrate that while he is not restricting evil to only *privatio boni* he is also not willing to embrace the scriptural witness of the ontology of evil. Talk of "psychological" exhaustion of evil

In order to adapt von Balthasar's theological construct to allow the rebellious "no" of ontological evil located within the "yes" of the Son to the Father, various degrees of God's omnipresence need to be explored alongside consideration of the origin and freewill of evil sentient beings who have volition and self-awareness. If, von Balthasar argues, because of the freely desired distancing of the Father and Son, there is an interminable and incomprehensible distance which contains all other distances, sin and wicked forms of separation including hell, then arguably this distance is not static and closed but rather resistant to definition, mutable and malleable, which could include the containment of personal-ontological evil.[99]

Fiddes asks, how can there be any rejection within the panentheistic presence of God? He acknowledges that in Barth, Rahner and von Balthasar rejection is a distinct possibility whereas he argues for hopeful universalism via an omni-reconciliation of all beings.[100] Yet, Fiddes' panentheism is a qualified Christian soteriological panentheism in which the current semi-realized panentheistic reality is still waiting for the full consummation of all things.[101] At present, however, creaturely and spiritual rebellion exists within God's omnipresence. Delineation of the current non-fully consummated panentheism allows for the exercising of creaturely freedom in positive and negative ways, intensifications of the presence of God's Holy Spirit, and degrees of divine presence and hiddenness. Focusing specifically on the Spirit, enables an application of Christ's Spirit who is metaphorically described as a divine wind, and who drives and dispels evil wherever there is an increased gradation and intensification of the divine panentheistic presence.[102]

Therefore, if the Spirit of Christ is present and moves in the relations between the Son and the Father,[103] relations in which exist the measureless distance of sin and the incomprehensible separation within God

---

aligns well to Wink's psychological-neurotic interpretation of the Gerasene demoniac, Wink, *Unmasking*, 43–50, and the notion of taking evil captive each time we refuse to resist contradicts James' imperative to "resist the Devil, and he will flee from you" (James 4:7).

99. It is the malleable nature of the relations within the triune God that Fiddes claims grounds human experience such as a sequence of thought in science within the dynamic flow of God's triune life. Fiddes, "Relational Trinity," 178.

100. SWKG, 365–69.

101. See "Panentheism Defined" (pp.112–120) section above.

102. Warren, *Cleansing*, 260–69.

103. PIG, 251–77.

himself that houses darkness, malevolence, hell, and the twisted knot of creation's rebellion against its origins, then it seems consistent to argue that within the yes of the Son to the Father, the Spirit of Christ is continually and actively dispersing evil; evil which is generated by the quintessential ontological and sentient being of rebellion, one created as part of creation who now exercises disproportionate maniacal power as the one who is the *ultimate* denier of his own creaturely origin.

Popular eschatology holds that the metaphorical-theological idea, common to futurist and spiritual perspectives on the book of Revelation, behind the number of the beast, i.e. 666, is the ultimate falling short of divine perfection which is symbolized by the number 7.[104] Therefore, I want to suggest, the rebellion of the creation unwilling to acknowledge its origin as created by God which exercises a "no" within the "yes" between the Father and the Son could be extrapolated to demonstrate the ultimate expression of rebellion if applied to the biblical-mythical account of the angelic fall and the existence of Lucifer, otherwise known as the devil or The Satan.[105] Without repeating the above,[106] the angelic fall account holds that Lucifer was created as an archangel who later rebelled against God, and so his rebellion should be viewed as the ultimate disavowal of his origins. Therefore, as a created being currently in a state of ultimate rebellion, Lucifer (now The Satan) can be located within the relations of the Trinity, specifically in the twisted "no" knot found in the "yes" between the Son and the Father.

In contradistinction to Fiddes' claim that because the world is God's there is no room for Satan but only internal and external structures of evil,[107] I maintain that it is theologically plausible to locate all evil, including personified evil, in God, specifically in the rebellious "no" within the infinite distance of the "yes" between the Father and Son. For this to be theologically coherent one needs to articulate an understanding of the Satan and his minions which sits somewhere between the demythologized, non-personalist position of Fiddes and the fully personal and

---

104. Gregg, *Revelation: Four Views*, 302–7.

105. I use the term "biblical-mythical" not to suggest an untrue account but rather to better reflect the mystery and ambiguity of Isaiah 14:12–21 and Ezekiel 28:1–17, which while not offering a strong exegetical case could be used, as argued by Wright, to justify good theological reasons for reaching an angelic fall account of the origin of the demonic. Wright, *A Theology*, 70–73.

106. See "Evil's Personifications" (pp.39–47) section above.

107. Fiddes, "Internal and External Powers," 324.

autonomous view of many popular SW advocates.[108] The best place to start for this definition is with Boethius' minimalist definition of a person as "the individual substance of a rational nature,"[109] since this could be used to assert the Satan and demons' ontological particularity.

Wink outlines the scriptural revelation of a changing Satan: he who evolves from a divine viceroy residing in God's presence (Job 1–2) to the antithetical malevolent enemy of God who will ultimately meet his end before the full consummation of the new heavens and new earth (Rev 20:7–10).[110] This understanding can be used to define The Satan and demons as "semi-real" with ontology but without-full-personhood. Indeed, Wink argues that the lake of burning sulphuric fire and brimstone into which the Satan will be cast is the same lake found in very presence of the angels and the lamb in Rev 14:10.[111] Presuming this lake is synonymous with hell, we can advance the case, contra Fiddes,[112] that the current location of the hell of evil is found in the panentheistic presence of God, within the extreme depths of the "no" found in the "yes" between the Father and Son. Moreover, hell will remain so until evil is finally *eradicated* when the present part-realized panentheistic eschatological reality arrives at its full consummation, and the fullness of God's omnipresent reality is inaugurated, and all things will peacefully and harmoniously dwell "in" God.[113]

Following Fiddes' rejection of Satan's full personhood without assenting to Fiddes' non-ontological conclusion leaves room for an account of the Satan and the demonic which still endorses evil's quasi-ontology,

---

108. See for example Anglican minister David Watson, Watson, *God's Freedom*, 50–67.

109. Boethius, "A Treatise Against Eutyches," 85, cf. Boethius, *The Consolation*, xxviii–xxix.

110. Wink, *Unmasking*, 9–40.

111. Wink, *Unmasking*, 39–40.

112. Fiddes, "Do Heaven and Hell Really Exist?"

113. The use of "eradicated" in reference to evil is deliberate. While acknowledging the highly symbolic and mysterious nature of the book of Revelation, the hermeneutical dilemma needs solved by interpreting the highly symbolic language through the lens of the plain language. Therefore, mentions of the beast, false prophet and Satan being thrown into the lake of Sulphur in order to be forever tormented (Rev 19:20; 20:10) should be interpreted in light that the lake of Sulphur *is* the second death (Rev 20:14, 15; 21:8), and the previous declaration of the beast going to his destruction (Rev 17:8). For the most compelling conditional immortality case that the lake of Sulphur fire is a consuming fire, and all evil and wicked beings (both physical and spiritual) will be ultimately consumed see Fudge, *The Fire That Consumes*, 234–52.

volition, semi-autonomy and say-so. This, I suggest, best explains the biblical narrative accounts of the Satan and demons found in the gospels and the myriad of accounts of apparently personal demons coming from practitioners, especially in the global south.[114] Indeed, argues Warren, defining the demonic as semi-autonomous helps explain the common phenomenon of a synergy between sin and demonic affliction that operates inside malleable boundaries which adapt according to the individual or structural level of the demonic power.[115]

In sum, therefore, it can be concluded that all origins and expressions of evil can be located within the near-realized soteriological panentheism of God without God being the sole author and originator of evil. Ontological evil is located in the extreme twisted "no" within the "yes" between the Father and Son, an extreme knot in the relations of the Trinity. The reason for its presence is the irrevocable autonomy given to creation, both physical and spiritual, which has manifested itself in choices of extreme rebellion as well as adherence. Therefore, as claimed by Fiddes, God is not free of all responsibility for evil since he created a world of freewill possibilities for good or ill, hence why he participates and suffers in solidarity with creation.[116]

CONCLUSION

In this chapter Fiddes' central theological tenet of God's panentheistic omnipresence via creation's participation in the triune nature of God has been developed in order to construct a theology of panentheism capacious enough to include the reality of demonic personal-ontological spiritual beings. This has involved examining Fiddes' covenantal form of panentheism organized around "persons as relations" participation, placing it tentatively on a typological continuum of various panentheisms, and arguing that the current non-fully realized panentheism of

---

114. In adding to the earlier discussion on the place of experience in Fiddes theology (See "The Place of Experience" (pp.9–13) section above.), it seems clear that despite Fiddes' desire to use story, experience, participation as genuine sources of theology (for example PIG, 3–10; Fiddes, "God and Story," 5–22; Fiddes, "Spirituality as Attentiveness, 38–42), when it comes to personalist-experiential accounts of demonization, Fiddes fails to seriously consider them or wrestle with the implications for his participatory doctrine of panentheism.

115. Warren, *Cleansing*, 274–76.

116. See "The Problem of Evil" (pp.50–55) section above.

God means that divine hiddenness and presence are possible within the non-places in the relations of God.

Taking Fiddes' use of von Balthasar's "no" of rebellion, sin and evil within the "yes" of the Father to the Son has enabled a case to be made in order to establish the location of all beings and expressions of ontological evil within the panentheistic realm of God. Crucial to the construction of this case is using and developing von Balthasar's dramatic soteriology into the theological realm of spiritual beings' autonomy, volition, self-awareness and, following Boethius, a minimal definition of quasi-being and personhood.

Indeed, there seems no conclusive and good reason, despite being argued by Fiddes and other modern panentheists, to restrict an understanding of divine panentheism, which has to account for the existence of evil, to only a *privatio boni* understanding of evil. It is surely plausible to hold a similar view for spiritual beings, especially in light of supporting biblical data regarding the creation of humankind including origins and freewill ability; a biblical demonology does not equal a speculative philosophy of demons.[117] However, regrettably, in adopting certain other themes from both Barth and von Balthasar, Fiddes has limited his definition of panentheism in a way that does not allow for serious exegetical engagement with biblical texts on the demonic nor phenomenological investigation of modern-day accounts of deliverance ministry.[118] Potentially he is vulnerable to the same well-known judgement aimed at Barth, who was criticized for his rejection of the idea of an angelic fall without serious exegesis of the salient passages which are historically held to describe what Augustine called the "angelic catastrophe."[119]

As we proceed to the next chapter in which a Baptist-charismatic unified theology of SW will be constructed, this nuanced panentheistic

117. Barth pleaded that we do not allow theology to become philosophy: an angelology should not be confused with a philosophy of angels. *CD* III/3, §51.1, 410–12.

118. As attested to in UK Baptist life by the Baptist Deliverance Study Group.

119. Barth's denial that demons are fallen angels is primarily based upon two major concerns: First, it conflicts with his argument that, contrary to common misconception, demons belong to intrinsic evil known as the nothingness not the negative side of creation, and second, in light of how little is known about the nature of human freedom, it is far too speculative to postulate about angelic spiritual freedom that, it is claimed, led to the rebellion of Lucifer and one-third of the angels. *CD* III/3, §51.3, 530–31. Barth's strong stance against any notion of an angelic fall has, notes Bromiley, seriously undermined Barth's excellent work on making angels a subject of theological investigation and left him vulnerable to the charge of marginalizing the demonic and whether he is indeed "obeying scripture as the criterion of dogmatic purity and truth?" Bromiley, *Introduction*, 155.

articulation of God's omnipresence will be integrated into the broader theological construct. Via engagement with other scholars it will be argued that Fiddes' "persons as relations" panentheism with certain qualifications is congruent with a unified SW theology which accounts for situations and experiences of ontological evil while maintaining that "the earth is the Lord's and everything in it; in God we live, move, and have our being; and we may participate in the divine nature" (Psalm 24:1; Acts 17:28; 2 Peter 1:4).

PART THREE

Theological Construction

6

Theological Construction
A Doctrine of God for Spiritual Warfare Theology

INTRODUCTION

> Some think spiritual warfare is only deliverance. Others emphasize pulling down strongholds in the heavenlies. Still others say spiritual warfare is doing the works of Jesus—preaching, teaching, and living the truth. Yet another group claims all this is impractical. They claim we should focus on feeding the hungry, resisting racism, and speaking out against social injustice. *I believe we have to do it all.* (emphasis mine).[1]

DESPITE THE ABSENCE OF academic rigor, Sherman's characterization of the different emphases within SW perfectly captures the various paradigms that exist within the literature, albeit across various sub-disciplines of theology. Therefore, in this final chapter the objective is to take the content of the previous five chapters and use it to form the underlying doctrinal premises concerning God's ontology and character upon which to construct a systematic theology of SW. In short, create a dialectical theology, one which takes Fiddes' theology and interacts with various interlocutors, both similar and dissimilar to Fiddes, in order to harmonize the differences and work towards creating a capacious theology of SW that is operant in two spheres: the individual and the corporate.

---

1. Sherman, *Spiritual Warfare*, 187.

To formulate a dialectally unified theology of SW, transcendent and imminent dimensions need to be considered in order to explicate what Hiebert has termed the "excluded middle"; that realm of reality revealed by scripture which consists of spiritual beings and forces operating on this earth but not perceivable by rational assumptions or the scientific method.[2] In order to explore these dimensions effectively, a theology needs constructed which looks at the spirit world through the lens of the individual and the corporate while concurrently assessing the *a priori* assumptions and *a posteriori* conclusions about God's nature and character, focusing specifically on his omniscience, omnipotence and omnipresence. The need to divide the individual from the corporate, primarily for clarity, should not be seen as a denial of the interweaving nature of evil in both the individual and corporate spheres, which afflict human beings. As claimed, there is a definite reality to social evil, an evil with both human and supernatural origins that can with relative ease dominate the lives of human beings when on their own and in a social group setting.[3] However, before turning our attention to the substantive theological-constructive content of this chapter, some comments about the methodological challenges first need to be offered.

METHODOLOGY—CHALLENGES AND SOLUTIONS

Overall, little systematic theological work has been done on SW.[4] While there is a substantial corpus of biblical scholarship on the subject,[5] systematic theology has largely ignored the evil spiritual realm when postulating its doctrine of God, as quintessentially demonstrated by Barth.[6] This lack of scholarly production within systematics and dogmatics means there is a very limited *body* of systematic theology literature to interact with and so, very much in the spirit of Fiddes, a construction of a dialectical theology of SW will necessarily be both connectional and inter-disciplinary within the theological sub-disciplines.

2. Hiebert, "The Flaw," 35–47.

3. Mott, *Biblical Ethics*, 3–21.

4. See "Introduction: This Study" (pp.xxvi–xxvii) section above.

5. A few of the better known ones include Arnold, *Ephesians*; Berkhof, *Christ and*; Caird, *Principalities*; Carr, *Angels and principalities*; Schlier, *Principalities*; Twelftree, *Jesus the Exorcist*.

6. Of course, since in Barth's view demons belong to the nothingness they received indirect consideration when he developed his doctrine of nothingness. *CD* III/3, §50.1–4, 289–368.

Recently, a number of theological works have summarized and in some cases analyzed the limited contemporary theological literature on all matters relating to SW. Warren briefly notes academic literature and authors from various disciplines including NT scholarship, biblical theology, history, Pauline scholarship, interdisciplinary studies, psychology, practical theology, and even what she coins "speculative theology."[7] In more depth, Smith spends a considerable portion of his charismatic-Anglican theology of SW analyzing and critiquing three significant theological thinkers of the subject matter: Nigel Wright, Amos Yong, and Gregory Boyd.[8]

Slightly more dated, missiologist McAlpine elucidates various traditions within scholarship on the powers and principalities, an area of research which has received renewed interest since the horrors of Nazism and publication of Berkhof's seminal text *Christ and the Powers*. He discerns four streams that vary in their definition and understanding of powers and principalities. First, the reformed tradition in which thinkers such as Wink and Kellermann argue that all powers and principalities will be transformed and reconciled to God. Then, with the Lohfink brothers and Yoder, an anabaptist tradition that calls for non-violent and radical over-againstness in order to counter the powers and principalities. Third, a third-wave tradition, illustrated in the writings of Wagner and Dawson, which places far greater emphasis on the ontological nature of all powers and principalities and engagement via "supernatural" means. Finally, McAlpine claims that in the works of Kelsey, Hiebert and Shuster, there is the social-scientific tradition that engages the powers and principalities using the intersectionality of psychology and anthropology.[9]

Finally, Beilby and Eddy highlight four different models currently used in scholarship that have both convergence and divergence across

7. Warren, *Cosmic Cleansing*, 14–17.

8. Smith, *The Church Militant*, 124–82. This author notes that while the historic Anglican SW thinkers analyzed by Smith and the church congregation used as a case study both held a strong sovereignty of God theology, none of the three chosen thinkers do so and there lacks a theological undergirding of what is historically and practically believed in Anglican churches who do SW. Cuthbert, Review of *Church Militant*, 580–82. Löfstedt goes further in his critique. Löfstedt, Review of *Church Militant*, 111–12.

9. McAlpine, *Facing*. There is a difficulty differentiating scholars into different categories. For instance, McAlpine places Wink in the reformed tradition alongside Berkhof, Kellermann, and Green. There are certainly areas of overlap with these thinkers but to then exclude such a significant thinker as Wink from both the anabaptist and social scientific traditions is a major oversight, especially given his emphasis upon non-violent protest and Jungian depth psychology and archetypes.

the different aspects of SW theology.[10] In the text key proponents of each of the four models set out the distinctives of their view and points of convergence and divergence from the other views. Familiar names author three out of the four essays:[11] Wink proffers a social-scientific and Jungian understanding entitled the "World Systems Model"; Boyd delineates a model best suited for exorcism and deliverance of individual persons called the "Ground-Level Deliverance Model"; and Wagner offers an updated third-wave model which focuses specifically on territorially active evil spirits and is entitled the "strategic-level deliverance model."

Overall, a number of theologians who have written extensively on the doctrine of God, evil, and divine conflict have come to the fore in the last quarter of a century. Together with biblical scholars and missiologists there now exists a limited body of literature from different disciplines of the theological encyclopedia that will be appealed to in order to support or counter the overall thesis and help ensure that this dialectical and unified theology of spiritual warfare is as inter-disciplinary as it is systematic.[12]

The final comment to be made is to acknowledge two potential lacunae with respect to the above-mentioned scholars from various disciplines. With the exception of Wright,[13] none have written or dialogued with Fiddes, and second, the obvious lack of non-protestant, non-western, global south, and female voices.[14] The first lacuna is not particularly self-evident, and the rest of this chapter will bring Fiddes into dialogue with these other scholars. The second omission reflects the scope of this constructive theology: a baptistic-Pentecostal systematic theology of SW which draws from scholars, like Fiddes, situated within the western protestant-baptistic tradition.[15]

---

10. Beilby and Eddy, *Understanding*. A significant SW text according to Bradnick. Bradnick, Review of *Understanding Spiritual Warfare*, 240.

11. Powlison, whose work does not appear in much of the literature is whose essay, claims to be the traditional voice of spiritual warfare, one that retains a strong sovereignty of God concept at its core and focus on internal spiritual struggle with the fallen nature. His work is discussed below. Powlison, "The Classical Model," 89–111. Perhaps Smith should have engaged with Powlison's work instead of Wright or Yong.

12. There is some disparity of academic rigor in the literature with more facile intellectual engagement. Warren, Review of *Understanding Spiritual Warfare*, 168.

13. Fiddes has directly critiqued the theology of Wright. See Fiddes, "Something will come."

14. Amos Yong, while originally from Malaysia, has spent his entire academic career in the USA. A number of female authors will be cited in this chapter, but they are a minority of voices.

15. As demonstrated above (See "Introduction: Systematic Theology" (pp.xxii–xxvi)

PART A: THE EVIL TRIPTYCH—SPIRITUAL WARFARE THEOLOGY FOR THE INDIVIDUAL

> As for you, you were dead in your transgressions and sins, in which you used to live when you followed the ways of *this world* and of *the ruler of the kingdom of the air, the spirit* who is now at work in those who are disobedient. All of us also lived among them at one time, gratifying the *cravings of our flesh* and following its desires and thoughts. Like the rest, we were by nature deserving of wrath. (emphasis mine).[16]

SW literature generally defines evil which afflicts the individual as the flesh, the world and the devil.[17] Indeed, recognizing that the life of every Christian is beset with a lifelong struggle with evil, the Anglican prayer book catechism identifies the flesh, the world and the devil as the sources of personal temptation and sin which need countered daily with Christian discipline practices.[18] In so doing, however, this in no way amounts to a denial or preclusion of the continuum that exists between the individual and societal spheres,[19] or the fact that the individual often leads to the corporate.[20] Nor does it offer an erroneous reductionism for the complexity of defining evil, a definition that continues to defy theologians.[21]

Yet, notwithstanding these caveats, in order to create a capacious SW theology pertaining to Christian discipleship that cogently deals with

---

section above), Fiddes is an ecumenical thinker whose sources of theology draw from all traditions and historical epochs. Therefore, despite the lack of diversity among his interlocutors, the use of Fiddes' theology as a primary source guarantees a more diverse and theologically rich account than would be gained from other protestant-baptistic thinkers.

16. Ephesians 2:1–3 (NIV); cf. James 3:15 and 1 John 2:14b–16. The author of Ephesians makes it clear that the past living death, which was characterized by trespasses and sins, was brought about and tied up in the forces of the world, the devil and the flesh. Lincoln, *Word Biblical Commentary*, 117.

17. Beilby and Eddy, *Understanding*, 32. Beilby and Eddy use this triumvirate as the pedagogical basis to arrange their four views text on SW.

18. Working Party. *A Time to Heal*, 178–79.

19. Ediger, "Strategic-Level Spiritual Warfare," 126–27; Friesen, "Equipping Principles," 145–51.

20. Wright, "Charismatic Interpretations," 149–51. For a thorough account of the psychology of collective groups and national evil see Peck, *People of the Lie*, 212–53.

21. McFarland highlights exactly the quintessential problem when the term "evil" is used as a catch-all term given the significant differences, for starters, between moral evil, natural evil, physical evil and metaphysical evil. Therefore, we need to completely rethink the language of good and evil in common and academic discourse. McFarland, "The Problem," 321–39.

the influence of evil in the life of each Christian believer, we need a balanced understanding of evil, the nature of which has the flesh, world and devil as its kernel.[22] Therefore, in this thesis SW theology in the sphere of the individual will maintain the *flesh* (internal human desire towards evil), the *world* (the unhealthy cultural and social environment in which we live) and the *devil* (a powerful and intelligent malevolent spirit-being) as the main definition of evil.

This leads us to consider the synergistic potential of the evil triptych with Fiddes' understanding of evil. Due to his definition of evil-without-ontology,[23] Fiddes redefines the traditional understanding of evil's triumvirate with another biblical triumvirate: sin, law and death.[24] The reason for this redefinition is to align with his proffered understanding of evil as *privatio boni*, since sin, law and death are each perversions of something good and the diabolical result when goods are worshipped as ultimate whose tyranny is to be obeyed. However, as concluded above, there is no convincing reason to situate our depiction of the evil which befalls the individual Christian only within Fiddes' somewhat binary *privatio boni*-only conclusion to the exclusion of much experiential witness and biblical tradition regarding ontologically grounded evil with much over-againstness, volition and some kind of sub-personhood.[25]

Moreover, having explicated in the previous chapter a nuanced understanding of divine panentheism with much room for ontologically based evil,[26] it really is no longer the case that the only understanding of evil congruent with God's panentheistic omnipresence is *privatio-boni*. Rather, a refined doctrine of evil as set out in chapter two, one that maintains the ontological over-and-againstness of evil, is, I maintain, congruent with the critiqued and developed Fiddesian doctrine of God as elucidated in the previous three chapters. With this in mind, let us turn our attention to theology proper and consider the understanding of God's omniscience within a SW theology operant in the realm of the individual.

---

22. Arnold, *3 Crucial*, 32–37. Powlison defines "moral evil" as a three-stranded braid of the world, flesh and devil, which is different to, and needs an alternative approach to, "situational evil." See Powlison, *Power Encounters*, 109–12.

23. See "Evil Personifications" (pp.39–47) section above.

24. PEPS, 114–18.

25. See "Chapter 2 Conclusion" (pp.58–60) section above.

26. See "Ontological Evil and" (pp.123–130) section above.

Two Realms Warfare Theology: The Necessary Prescience of God

As demonstrated in chapter three, Fiddes' account of God's omniscience offers some theological insight that can help undergird a theology of SW. Specifically, his definition of libertarian freedom, both divine and human, aligns well with most of the theological work on the subject. Secondly, his account of divine passibility goes a long way towards offering a satisfactory solution to the challenge of theodicy in modern culture. However, his denial of EDF, insistence on divine ontological mutability, advocacy of a non-unilateral and non-interventionist deity, and a tensed understanding of time, all combine to challenge the over-arching teleological SW narrative: despite the contingent realities created by both angelic and human freedom, scripture and Christian tradition point to an end of all evil and suffering, of which the sole author will be Yahweh.[27] Therefore, as I maintain in chapter three, there is an account of divine omniscience that maintains complete divine knowledge of past, present and future *and* full earthly and heavenly creaturely libertarian freedom, which thereby grounds the divine-dynamic sovereignty of God and assured eschatology that reflects scripture. So, what implications do these hold for a theology of SW in the sphere of the individual?

Interestingly, a number of theologians writing on SW in the life of an individual are scholars who operate in ministerial contexts either as a pastor, doctor or counsellor. Due to dealing with persons as individuals this drives their focus on the ways in which evil afflicts individuals, both believers and non-believers.[28] Of the various thinkers mentioned previously Boyd and Powlison have produced a substantial body of work between them on SW and the impact of the evil triptych on the life of an individual Christian.[29] Boyd's theology of SW centers on the development of a "warfare worldview" which he has developed in two works of theology: biblical and systematic.[30] From a copious body of work that relates counselling approaches and techniques to the Christian faith, Powlison's key text for this thesis sets out a polemical vision to recapture what

27. As perfectly illustrated in Revelation 20:7–10.

28. One scholar, Warren, a medical doctor and theologian approaches her work on SW from a medical perspective and is especially interested in other metaphors that could be used since the term "warfare" does not translate well in counselling situations of abuse, especially occurrences of satanic ritual abuse. Warren, *Cleansing*, 1–3.

29. See "Chapter 6 Methodology" (pp.136–138) section above.

30. Boyd, *God at War*; Boyd, *Satan and the Problem*. See "Introduction: This Study" section above.

he calls the "classic mode" of SW as a corrective to an area of Christian ministry that has, he claims, significantly veered away from the biblical understanding of SW and into dangerous territory.[31]

Concerning the omniscience of God within a SW reality for the individual, any juxtaposition of Fiddes' doctrine of non-detail divine prescience with either Boyd or Powlison and buttressed with other thinkers exacerbates the weakness and limitations of Fiddes' omniscience position and reinforces the need for the nuanced account of a two realms theology delineated at the end of chapter three. Boyd, for instance, mirrors Fiddes' thinking with regard to defining freedom in libertarian, irrevocable terms and rejecting the traditional-Augustinian notion of divine impassibility in favor of the suffering of God.[32] However, when it comes to those weaker elements of Fiddes' omniscience doctrine such as denial of EDF or a complex process mutability of God, Boyd offers an alternative position, but one that still runs into similar difficulties.

Like other theologians, Boyd posits that any hortative explanation for the existence of evil has to consider that God has actualized a "risky creation," the reason being that libertarian freedom is genuine and "love must be chosen" and so this freedom implies necessary risk which is sown into the very metaphysical fabric of creation.[33] Talk of "risk" however raises the same obvious question that Fiddes fails to answer sufficiently: how can God guarantee his future return for his bride, the church and full eschatological consummation? Boyd answers this charge by stating that God can guarantee his future return because the corporate church (not the individuals in it) was predestined before the foundations of the

---

31. Powlison, *Power Encounters*. An abridged version of this text published seventeen years later which shows little change or development in his overarching view of SW is Powlison, "The Classical," 89–122. He claims his book was needed because of the growing number of Christian ministries teaching and practicing "deliverance" in the quest to cast out demons from unbelievers and believers alike. Powlison, *Power Encounters*, 11–25.

32. Boyd, *Satan and the Problem*, 178–206. To repeat, Fiddes' motivation for divine passibility comes from his perception that there is a contemporary need for a passible God in order to help understand the new cultural conceptions of love and provide a defense against matters of theodicy, whereas Boyd is one of those passibilists who base their arguments in "divine repentance" type texts such as 1 Samuel 15. Boyd, *God of the Possible*.

33. Boyd, *Satan and the Problem*, 50–115. Like Boyd, Allen situates the exercise of freewill as the direct cause not just of moral evil among human beings but also natural evil as caused by the exercise of freewill of Satan and his cohorts. Allen, "St. Augustine's Free," 84–90, cf. Boyd, *Satan and the Problem*, 293–318.

earth (Ephesians 1) and also God has perfect knowledge of his *own character* and *ability* to intervene.[34]

It is at this point that Boyd and Fiddes part company. Fiddes' participatory panentheistic doctrine of God which only allows God to operate by persuasion and influence precludes any form of interventionism by God.[35] Fiddes suggests that open theism's intervention doctrine creates as many problems as solutions. He states, "This is the problem with open theism since they have room for final intervention—God limits himself for a period and then ceases to limit himself in order to put everything right at the end. In fact, God could intervene at any moment if God really wanted to; why not at Auschwitz?"[36] Boyd partly answers this challenge with two more theses of his warfare worldview: that despite there being risk in genuine love "This Risk Entails Moral Responsibility" and "Moral Responsibility is Proportionate to the Potential to Influence Others." In other words, there cannot be a conceivable potential to love someone without a commensurate potential to harm or hurt that person, hence why the freedom to love demands the risk of moral responsibility. In God's wisdom he *aims high* in creation which determines God to wager potential for great harm so that the possibility of a Mother Theresa is counter-potentiated by the possibility of a Hitler; this wager is irrevocable and not something God can arbitrarily interfere with.[37]

The intrinsic necessity of "risk" common to both Fiddes and Boyd's theologies of non-EDF presents a substantial problem when applied to the ongoing spiritual battle in the life of any individual Christian. Boyd calls for practical application of his warfare worldview theology to the flesh, world and devil. He gives a clarion call to every Christian to awaken to the reality of the spiritual war and become a spiritual soldier.[38] He also grounds his developed warfare worldview in everyday theodicy realities such as physical suffering, unanswered prayer and natural evil.[39] However, like Fiddes, he cannot give a guaranteed assurance that the

---

34. Boyd, *Satan and the Problem of Evil*, 155–58.
35. See "Contemporary Need" (pp.4–9) section above.
36. Fiddes, personal communication with author.
37. Boyd, *Satan and the Problem of Evil*, 163–77.
38. Boyd, "The Ground-Level," 151–57.
39. Boyd, *Satan and the Problem of Evil*, 209–357. For his popular treatment see Gregory A. Boyd, *Is God to Blame?*

eschatological hope of the Christian faith will eventually appear, whether in this life or the one to come.[40]

In chapter three it was concluded that Tanner's non-competitive model of divine sovereignty avoids the theological pitfalls common to all forms of relational theism, including that of Fiddes.[41] It is able to espouse full divine knowledge of past, present and future whilst defining creaturely freedom, both human and spiritual, in libertarian terms. That God (an uncreated, necessary being) and creation (a created, contingent reality) exist and operate on completely different ontological planes without the playing of any zero-sum game or God's agency having to decrease in order to make room for human agency, goes a considerable length to ensure a doctrine of divine omniscience that accords well with the realities of spiritual warfare in the lives of individual Christians.

Tanner's theology offers a solution whether it is battling the devil by living out a "Jesus-lifestyle deliverance" paradigm,[42] engaging in warfare against the world and its mores by transferring allegiance from the values and god of this world to Jesus and the kingdom of God,[43] or focusing on confronting those sins and temptations that arise from our fleshly nature by practicing the classic disciplines of Bible study, prayer and worship.[44] Her ultimate gift giver and non-competitive model will theologically explain the global phenomenon of SW experience, and the scriptural witness of a semi-dualistic SW worldview during the age of tension. Concurrently, the model sustains a dynamic sovereignty of God and eschatology which guarantees God's full consummation of the new heavens and new earth as described in Revelation chapters 20–22.

---

40. Boyd's defense of openness theology and formulation of a nuanced definition of God's sovereignty that does not consist of divine omni-control and a non-thwartable will is what receives most criticism. Anderson, Review of *God at War*, 128; Holt, Review of *God at War*, 130; Pyne, Review of *God at War*, 235–36. Smith adds that Boyd is still left with the problem of unanswered prayer for the eradication of evil in the here and now. Smith, *The Church Militant*, 178–81.

41. See "In God Time is" (pp.71–79) section above.

42. Eddy and Beilby, "Introduction," 35–37; cf. Boyd, *God at War*, 192–214.

43. Boyd, "The Ground-Level," 151–54; cf. Boyd, *The Myth*. Boyd's ethics situate him in mainstream anabaptist thinking. See Yoder, *The Politics*, 147–55.

44. Powlison, *Power Encounters*, 137–52; Powlison, "The Classical," 98–111.

Dual-Power Warfare Theology: The Kenotic Power of God

The use of Tanner's non-competitive model allows for a definition of divine omniscience that holds together the libertarian freewill of human and spiritual creatures and God's full exhaustive knowledge of the past, present and future. Not only, therefore, does this lead to divergence away from Fiddes and Boyd's differently articulated divine nescience positions, but it also sidelines Powlison's hard sovereignty of God stance that defines creaturely freedom in compatibilist terms.[45] However, when it comes to the matter of God's omnipotence, chapter four's development of Fiddes' three kenotic moments creates room for hard and soft accounts of God's sovereign power, a doctrine that best reflects both the narrative truth of scripture regarding the demonic and claimed experience of individuals' spiritual battle with the flesh, world and devil.

To recap briefly, the developed account of Fiddes' omnipotence of suffering love uses Martensen's concept of divine omnipotence, one that mapped persuasively onto the kenotic hymn of Philippians 2:5–11. It was argued that while Fiddes' three kenotic moments are true, especially the kenosis on the cross which inserts a cross into the very heart and being of God, these moments only part-answer some of the questions surrounding God's omnipotence in an age with evil forces. It may suggest that God possibly *could* bring suffering to an end but certainly offers few answers to the *when* or *why* questions.[46]

Martensen's doctrine offers a mutable kenotic Christology that helps make sense of kenotic Trinitarianism and cosmology thus giving a better explanation of the now-and-not-yet tension that each individual believer currently inhabits and also advances the refined Abelardian atonement theology of Fiddes towards *Christus Victor*. It does this by grounding real events of subjective and transformative deliverance and SW in the light of the atonement's objective transaction; genuine happenings when God's kenotic power is fully at work and the individual person receives a foretaste of the final consummation of all things.[47] Therefore, when we consider SW for an individual person, what foundational help does this theology of kenotic warfare with evil offer in order to understand the

---

45. Boyd accuses Powlison of advocating an over-domesticated spiritual warfare model. Boyd, "Response to David," 119–22.

46. See "Kenosis: A Definitive" (pp.88–93) and "Kenotic Relations" (pp.93–98) sections above.

47. See "Omnipotence's Kenotic Warfare" (pp.98–106) section above.

nature and character of God better in the midst of occurrences of evil of many different kinds?

Let us consider one subject that appears with regular frequency as the example *par excellence* of this matter regarding the power differential between God and the demonic: the demonization of Christians. Much heat is often generated when Christians and scholars debate if believing Christians can be demonized or worse still, demon possessed.[48] Boyd and Powlison are representative of the two centrist camps which oppose each other but avoid the extremes. As already noted, Powlison's main objective in promoting his "classic" view of spiritual warfare is to critique current "deliverance" ministries which he labels *ekballistic* mode of ministry (EMM hereafter),[49] since they all practice casting demons out of both believers and unbelievers. Despite disparity over secondary matters, all streams of EMM agree on the primary issue of the need for Christian discipleship and exorcisms.[50]

Moreover, states Powlison, the claimed demonization of Christian individuals produces two propositions that are adopted *a posteriori* and advanced in deliverance ministry. First, there is the tendency to define moral sin as demonic, ignoring the fact that in the gospels we see both "situational" evil through people's suffering and "moral" evil because of sin, and Jesus' exorcisms were performed for people suffering from situational, not moral evil.[51] Powlison's dichotomizing evil into situational and moral is in order to counteract the claimed common practice within the EMM movement of demonizing sinful behavior which allows for potential "the devil made me do it" type excuses.[52] Second, there is the

---

48. It is irrefutable that the debate has moved from the academy into the pews and politics with the appearance of popular articles and political reports on the subject. For example, see Tennant, "Many Christians Say," 46–56, and the charity-political report, Molina, "The Invention of Child Witches."

49. From ἐκβάλλω meaning "I cast out." Powlison holds to the traditional ontology of demons by stating at the outset that he is not addressing any SW vision that capitulates to psychological or sociological projections. Powlison, *Power Encounters*, 27.

50. Powlison describes 4 streams: charismatic, dispensational, Fuller third-wave, and broadly evangelical. Powlison, *Power Encounters*, 32–34. Arnold agrees. Arnold, *3 Crucial*, 139–40.

51. Powlison, *Power Encounters*, 63–76. Stafford notes that demonizing moral sin is Powlison's over-arching issue to take to task. See Stafford, Review of *Power Encounters*, 48.

52. Powlison illustrates his point by citing Anderson and his suggestions of demonic control of the saints. Powlison, *Power Encounters*, 75, cf. Anderson, *The Bondage*, 174–78.

continuing use of the command-control mode of Jesus as described in the gospels instead of a mode shift to Christian discipleship as demonstrated in Acts and the rest of the New Testament.[53]

Many theologians (including Boyd) fully accept that believing Christians can be demonized to greater or lesser degrees.[54] Where the discussion reaches an impasse, especially within a western context, is differentiating between genuine demonization and cases of mental illness.[55] Those like Boyd who accept the demonization of Christians have the challenge of distinguishing between paranoid schizophrenia and bona fide cases of demonic oppression or even possession.[56] Boyd suggests an adoption of a "shoot in both directions" approach concerning demonization and mental illness. In the discipleship process there needs to be both warfare prayer *and* sessions of counselling, irrespective of what the Christian disciple believes they need.[57] In this both-and approach the three evils of the unholy triptych—the flesh, world and devil—are engaged and battled against whether that involves growing in spiritual disciplines that mortify the flesh, militant adherence to the kingdom of God or deliverance prayer ministry in order to excise demonic oppression.

SW at the level of the individual has often been described as a "power encounter." It is an encounter that often brings both salvation and greater suffering and persecution.[58] Both in scripture and modern phenomenological assertions, there are varying degrees of divine omnipotence at work in situations of spiritual conflict. As some have commented, the

---

53. This shift in mode away from command-control to holistic Christian discipleship fulfils, Powlison claims, the prophetic statement of Jesus that future generations of disciples will do "greater things" than what Jesus and the Father have been doing (John 14:12). Powlison, *Power Encounters*, 77–92. However, he fails to properly address those passages that describe the apostles *and* disciples of Jesus operating in a command-control mode which results in deliverance and spiritual fruit such as Luke 9:1–6; 10:1–24 and Acts 16:16–40.

54. A small sample includes Arnold, *3 Crucial*, 73–141; Boyd, "The Ground-Level," 151–56; Burkholder, "The Theological Foundations," 38–68; Wright, *A Theology*, 105–30; Theron, "A Critical Overview," 79–92.

55. On the difficulties identifying, assessing, explaining and treating mental illness from genuine cases of demonization, see Southard and Southard, "Demonizing and Mental Illness," 173–88; Southard, "Demonizing and Mental Illness (II)," 264–87; Southard and Southard, "Demonizing and Mental Illness (III)," 132–51.

56. Virkler proposes the use of both symptom analysis and the gift of "discerning the spirits." Virkler, "Demonic Involvement," 101.

57. Boyd, "The Ground-Level," 155.

58. Hiebert, "Spiritual Warfare," 118–22.

range of belief, practice and experience in situations of demonology and deliverance is a combination of worldview lenses, explicit adherence to the demonic in a particular culture, and the extent to which God and his sovereignty is brought into the situation.[59] Some argue that because God's sovereign power is infinitely greater than the demonic, all SW should be a quiet, no-fuss affair whereas others conclude that depending upon the severity of someone's demonic infestation determines the people, time and spiritual authority needed to carry out deliverance.[60]

God's omnipotence as a theology of kenotic warfare goes a long way to theologically account for the varying levels and experience of the demonstration of divine power in SW situations involving individuals. In a similar way to Tanner's two-realm approach to God's omniscience, to situate all power encounters in SW onto the kenotic journey of Christ—from divine pre-existence to humiliation to exaltation—in which the divine nature is simultaneously on full power and kenotic power, is to present divine omnipotence as dialectical; a synthesizing of full and varying kenotic power within God's imminent dealings with creation, both physical and spiritual. Theologically, this underwrites Jesus' lesson about the strongman (Matthew 12:43–45; Luke 11:21–26) and the acute awareness needed to walk out the Christian faith consciously with a shrewd sense that it is distinctly possible, just like Judas Iscariot, to give personal territory back to the devil (Ephesians 4:26–27) which could ultimately lead to allowing evil to return and reign in one's life (Romans 6:12).[61]

Participatory Warfare Theology: The Panentheistic Presence of God

Fiddes' participating in God panentheistic vision is the central aspect of his doctrine of God,[62] and his "persons as relations" trinitarian definition, which is the foundation to his panentheistic vision is, by his own

---

59. Ferdinando, "Screwtape Revisited," 103–32; Hiebert, "The Flaw," 43–47; Hiebert, "Spiritual Warfare," 114–18.

60. Powlison, *Power Encounters*, 148–52; Powlison, "The Classical," 92–98; Lowe, *Territorial*, 129–41. MacNutt differentiates between protection, simple deliverance and heavy deliverance. MacNutt, *Deliverance from*, 142–80.

61. Gross, *Miracles, Demons*, 166–67.

62. See "The Nature and Character" (pp.13–18) and "Chapter 5 Introduction" (pp.108–110) sections above.

claim, his unique contribution to trinitarian theology.⁶³ In chapter five, with the help of other panentheists such as Gregersen and von Balthasar, an adjusted and refined version of Fiddes' panentheistic doctrine has been offered that makes room for all expressions of evil, especially evil caused by rebellious demonic forces who are ontologically real, subpersonal, and operate with will and volition.

Above I argued that Fiddes' panentheism is a Christian and soteriological panentheism, one into which divine hiddenness finds a natural home in this current milieu and where forgiveness and reconciliation are common occurrences given the "now-and-not-yet" dynamic of life and relationships between the first and second coming of Christ.⁶⁴ Von Balthasar's "no" in the "yes" between the Father and the Son creates infinite distance and space for the freewill rebellion of creation (both physical and spiritual) to continually happen within the omnipresence of God without making God the primary cause of all evil and sin in the world. Applying the above-developed accounts of the omniscience and omnipotence of God offers reasons to believe that the panentheistic reality of God will be all-in-all and will permeate the new heavens and new earth once fully consummated by God in the eschaton.⁶⁵

It has been shown that the panentheism of Fiddes demonstrates the covenantal validity and biblical underpinnings of his omnipresence doctrine. Not only is the biblical-theological foundation for God's universal omnipresence a hallmark of Fiddes' doctrine but he has also shown the impact of panentheism upon the narrative world of literature and theology and our understanding of the church.⁶⁶ Therefore, this begs the question of what are the implications of God's universal and interweaving presence for the individual person's struggle with the evil triptych and what difference does it make framing SW as happening *within* the one in whom "we live, move and have our being"?

The extent to which every human capacity is fallen is borne out by what Caird entitles "the bondage of corruption." Whether it is nature, humanity's relationship with nature, the presence and prevalence of different powers and principalities, or the many different thorns in the flesh, humanity is, and lives in a world, marred by a permanent corruption, decline and decay (Romans 8). This is internally and externally the human

63. See "Panentheism Defined" (pp.112–120) section above.
64. See "Panentheism Defined" (pp.112–120) section above.
65. See "Ontological Evil and" (pp.123–130) section above.
66. See "Covenant Theology of Panentheism" (pp.110–112) section above.

experience and condition, and no human being, except the second Adam, is exempt from it.[67] In this sense, SW against the flesh is living in and under the potential reconciliation to God wrought by Christ through his crucifixion and resurrection. Caird articulates this reality stating "upon this divine plan to sum up all things in Christ there had intruded the contradiction of sin; man had come under God's judgement, the heavenly powers had become world-rulers of this darkness, the subhuman creation had been subjected to futility; and all must now be reconciled to God by the blood of the Cross."[68]

Powlison concurs and avers that, in the main, SW is spiritual conflict in order to override and transform the bondage of corruption while recognizing that it will not be fully possible until the eschaton. Emphasizing preaching, teaching, and living the truth as expressions of spiritual disciplines, Powlison focuses on the believer in Christ being alert and fully aware of their new status in Christ in order to adopt a humble and teachable posture as life-long learners of the way of Jesus so that they can successfully fight against the enticements of their fallen, sinful fleshly nature. While it is not necessary to reject that true Christian believers can be demonized, Powlison uses this preclusion to assert that while the Bible presents a balance of the three members of the evil triumvirate, the focus in most of the NT is, contrary to what some teach,[69] primarily on the human heart, i.e. the flesh.[70]

The relevance of Powlison when it relates to the individual lies very much in his strong pastoral approach. It is intertwined with a conviction of God's decretive will and absolute sovereignty which plays out in his advocacy of sitting under biblical preaching, prayer, and discipleship as SW engagement. This comes out clearly in the globally-derived anecdotes he offers in order to prove his point such as the story of Bob and his "demons of lust, anger, uncleanness and pride" who following attempts of deliverance starts to make progress once he embarks on some Christian counselling and discipleship; a post-deliverance stage of Christian discipleship and journey from spiritual milk to meat (Hebrews 5:12–14).[71]

---

67. Caird, *Principalities*, 54–79.

68. Caird, *Principalities*, 79.

69. Powlison accuses Wagner and Greenwood of holding to a theology in which the Devil completely drowns out the world and the flesh. Powlison, "Response to C. Peter," 204.

70. Powlison, *Power Encounters*, 93–120.

71. Powlison, "The Classical," 106–8; Powlison, *Power Encounters*, 142–52.

With a different focus, Boyd's "warfare worldview" offers a substantive theology and praxis for the individual Christian's engagement in spiritual warfare that specifically focusses upon evil systems and values at work in the world, and the demonic influences and structures that seek to create chaos and undermine the worship of God. Boyd's developed warfare worldview biblical theology, the kernel of which is what he calls the "normativity of evil,"[72] based primarily on Daniel 10:12–20, is that because evil and suffering are a normal part of human existence we need to be spiritually engaged and overcoming it instead of intellectually questioning *why* evil is present.[73] This worldview, he argues, is truly global and adopted by countless individual Christians across the world.[74]

Globally as a church and individual believers we need to, states Boyd, be in allegiance with the kingdom of God, not the kingdoms of the world. As Jesus pointedly infers in his kingdom teaching, allegiance to the kingdom of God immediately sets a person on a collision course with the kingdom of the world, for the kingdom of God is on the offensive (Matthew 16:18–19) and this will cause a worldly kingdom response of violence against those in the kingdom of God (Matthew 11:12) who are committed to non-violence.[75] Moreover, to avoid an overly-forced dichotomy between the world and the devil, Boyd reminds us that the Johannine literature, despite having no accounts of deliverance, uses strong dualistic language and states that the ruler of the world, together with its values and idols, is Satan himself (1 John 5:19 cf. 2 Corinthians 4:4).[76] Hence militant adherence to the kingdom of God is not just an act of SW against the world but simultaneously against Satan.

Ultimately, declaring warfare on the world, its value systems and idols will be ongoing and costly for each Christian believer. Boyd is under no illusion that when it comes to discerning kingdom values from

---

72. Not normative in the sense that it reflects God's original design but rather it is normal to the current fallen world state of play.

73. Kelsey reiterates the "normativity of naked evil" and states that there is a very real "naked evil," that seeks to destroy, which we need to accept, and one cannot reduce the horrors of Nazi death camps to basically an "absence of the good." Kelsey, *Discernment*, 74–75, 97–103; Kelsey, *Healing & Christianity*, 249–52, 282–84.

74. Boyd, *God at War*, 9–11.

75. Boyd, *God at War*, 216–18; 222–26. Ambiguity remains as to whether Boyd's firm conviction that the kingdom of God is characterized by a commitment to pacifistic non-violence naturally aligns him with Wink on this issue. Wink, *Engaging the Powers*, 209–29.

76. Boyd, *God at War*, 227–30.

worldly norms it can often be problematic but Christians in the west need to "wake up" to the warfare context in which they live and stop what he calls "holiday-living."[77] Part of this waking up is realizing that the kingdom of God does not look or sound like Christendom that is slowly disappearing, and any attempt to re-establish Christendom through the use of SW is erroneous and should be opposed.[78]

When it concerns Satan and the demonic, Boyd argues that warfare is a recurrent theme in the Scriptures which can form a hermeneutical lens through which to read scripture. Reading the Hebrew Bible reveals that it is replete with images and symbolism which points to the fact that God has to engage in battle with demonic powers in order to establish his will and purposes.[79] Whether that be locking up the raging creational cosmic forces of the sea,[80] slaying diabolical mythical beasts such as Leviathan or Behemoth,[81] conflict with and judgement of others "gods,"[82] or even rebuking the arch-enemy Satan himself,[83] Boyd argues that all these Old Testament examples and echoes force us to formulate a nuanced definition of God's enemies: fallen spiritual beings with freedom, a will and sentience which are hell bent against individual Christian believers.

This warfare hermeneutic, argues Boyd, continues into the New Testament writings and era. Due to the oppression of the Jews during the second temple period, the idea of spiritual battles intensifies and so Jesus appears when the biblical writers had no problem viewing Satan as the *functional* lord of the earth while still maintaining the non-dualistic metaphysical superiority of the uncreated God over the created and fallen archenemy Satan.[84] Jesus heals and delivers people in a functionally dualistic way while maintaining metaphysical superiority over Satan.[85]

---

77. Boyd, "The Ground-Level," 151–52.

78. Boyd criticizes the triumphant-sounding theology of Wagner and Greenwood. Boyd, "Response to C. Peter," 213–15.

79. Boyd and Eddy, "Evil," 288.

80. Boyd, *God at War*, 73–92; Boyd, "The Ground-Level," 130–32; cf. Longman III and Reid, *God is a Warrior*, 72–82. For a theological exploration of malevolent spiritual forces at work in the sea see Hart, *The Doors*.

81. Boyd, *God at War*, 93–113; Boyd, "The Ground-Level," 132–33; cf. Day, *God's Conflict*, 87.

82. Boyd, *God at War*, 114–42; cf. Boyd, "The Ground-Level," 133–35.

83. Boyd, *God at War*, 143–67; cf. Boyd, "The Ground-Level," 135.

84. Boyd, "Powers and Principalities," 611–12; Boyd, "The Ground-Level," 136; Boyd, *God at War*, 283–90.

85. Twelftree has arguably written the most scholarship on all matters relating

These actions, together with his kingdom of God declarations, form the warfare context; one in which kingdom advancement must take place through spiritual force so that the gates of hell will not prevail.[86]

Like others,[87] Boyd draws heavily on the gospels in order to flesh out the warfare worldview and demonstrate that the demonic is ontologically real and the conflict between the kingdoms is real and stark. The Lord's Prayer only makes sense if God's will is not being done, and the duality language of John's gospel paints the reality of the darkness.[88] This is why Boyd, in the spirit of Aulen and others, sees Christ's death and resurrection primarily in warfare and cosmic terms as the ultimate act of God's victory over Satan's functional domination of the earth.[89] Not only is this a demonstrable plain reading of the gospels,[90] but is also supported by countless global accounts of the reality of spirits and demon possession,[91] which have actually caused numerous anthropologists and ethnographers to re-evaluate their framework of naturalism.[92]

In concluding this final section of part A, let us return to the question of what, if any, impact there is in reframing the individual's battle with the evil triumvirate within God's interweaving omnipresence? It seems, given the ubiquity of humanity's fallen fleshly nature, the global-worldly values and systems, and the diabolical but sentient enemy of God who is currently the prince/ruler of this world (John 12:31; 14:40; 16:11; Ephesians 2:2; 2 Corinthians 4:4), that the counter-ubiquity of God himself should, at the very least, be accented in any theological account.

This means that all experiences and encounters of spiritual warfare take place, *de facto,* within the very relations of the triune God and so all divine attributes of God can be called upon and used in the spiritual fight. There is no dualistic sacred-secular divide, no gnostic material-spiritual bifurcation, and most importantly no fear in the face of evil as every

---

to exorcism in the history of the church. For more see Twelftree, *Christ Triumphant*; Twelftree, *Jesus the Exorcist*; Twelftree, *In the Name of Jesus*.

86. Boyd, *God at War*, 184–214; cf. Boyd, "The Ground-Level," 136–38.

87. Others who base their doctrine of Satan and evil in the gospels include Kallas, *Jesus and the Power*, 118–201; Park, "Hermeneutics and Spiritual," 85–103; Story, "Jesus' 'Enemy' in," 43–63; Swartley, "Biblical Faith," 100–113.

88. Boyd, *God at War*, 215–37.

89. Aulen, *Christus*; Wright, *Evil and*, 114.

90. An approach perfectly justified by Frei. Frei, *The Eclipse*, 1.

91. Boyd, *God at War*, 11–17.

92. Boyd, "The Ground-Level," 143–47.

individual believer is surrounded by the perfect love of God, a love that will conquer all things and not allow anyone in Christ to be separated from his love by any angels or demons, principalities or powers (Romans 8:37–39).

Of course, no individual believer is *only* that. Each Christian person is also part of a corporate body of God's people known as the church of Jesus Christ. Therefore, it is imperative to analyze and discuss whether or not situating the church's engagement in SW within a doctrine of God will aid understanding and elicit greater explanatory power of the scriptural witness and experiential phenomena related to all matters related to evil and the demonic. To this task we now turn.

PART B: TERRITORIES, POWERS AND PRINCIPALITIES—SPIRITUAL WARFARE THEOLOGY ON THE CORPORATE LEVEL

With the appearance in 1970 of the term "spiritual warfare"[93] as a new nomenclature to describe the spiritual battle in every Christian's life, it did not take long—approximately two decades—for the term to become a broad rubric under which was housed not just every aspect of the individual believer's fight against the flesh, world and devil but also apparent corporate demonic forces and systems of evil, known as principalities and powers, that needed to be opposed by collective groups of people, especially church gatherings of Christian believers. By 1987 Christians in their thousands gathered in the UK and other parts of the world for a global "March for Jesus," predicated on the claim that there are demonic spiritual beings at the top of demonic hierarchies who have geographical and strategic jurisdiction over large swathes of society and cities and need to be opposed in the spiritual realm.[94]

This new claim concerning evil territorial spirits received more publicity when the Lausanne conference on evangelism in 1993 released a cautious statement of recognition.[95] The involvement of Wagner in

---

93. Widely attributed to Michael Harper in his 1970 text *Spiritual Warfare*.

94. Ediger, "Strategic-Level Spiritual Warfare," 126–29; Wright, "Charismatic," 159–62.

95. The conference admitted their involvement in the promotion process through facilitating a track on spiritual warfare at Lausanne II 1989 conference in Manila under the aegis of then Fuller Seminary professor of church growth C. Peter Wagner and then continuing the life of that track under the sponsorship of the AD2000 and Beyond

Lausanne led to a tacit acknowledgement that there could be a number of different levels in the theology and practice of SW, as taught by Wagner: "ground-level" warfare which seeks to free individual persons from demonic bondage, "occult-level" warfare which attempts to deal with demonic oppression within Satanism, the occult, etc., and "strategic (or cosmic)-level" warfare (SLSW hereafter), based upon Ephesians 6:12, which involves a direct confrontation in the spirit world through prayer and praise against principalities and powers, otherwise known as corporate, territorial spirits.[96] As stated above, for the purpose of this chapter these claims will be accepted at face value without any critique or defense.[97]

Deeper penetration into the world and practice of SLSW reveals three other unique assertions of orthopraxis that are new to Christian theology or practice. To begin, there is "spiritual mapping" which is "the practice of identifying the spiritual conditions at work in a given community, city or nation."[98] This, so claimed, is achieved by looking at secular and Christian history, identifying prophets, intercessors, and spiritual elders, studying various demographics,[99] and, controversially, using new ageism's ley lines of a city to identify ancient landmarks and places of idol worship.[100] Second, when good spiritual mapping reveals the geographical areas that need to be surrounded by a wall of prayer, then "intentional prayer walking" and prayer marches like March for Jesus need to be organized and actioned.[101] Imitating Israel's marching

---

movement. Wagner, *Spiritual*, 16–21. In 1993 they stated, "We are cautious about the way in which the concept of territorial spirits is being used and look to our biblical scholars to shed more light on this recent development." "Lausanne Statement."

96. Wagner, *Spiritual Warfare Strategy*, 20–22; Greenwood, *Authority to Tread*, 22–30; Wagner and Greenwood, "The Strategic," 178–81. Cf. Eddy and Beilby, "Introduction," 40–43.

97. See "Introduction: Systematic Theology" (pp.xxii–xxvi) section above.

98. Wagner and Greenwood, "The Strategic," 182.

99. Dawson, "Seventh Time Around," 140–41.

100. It is claimed, somewhat hyperbolic, that all this research can reveal hidden spiritual truths such as prevailing bondages in the city and the systemic root bondage which often concern land defilement such as bloodshed, war, broken land covenants, sexual immorality or idolatry. Greenwood, *Authority*, 92–98; Wagner and Greenwood, "The Strategic," 183–87. The reason for the controversy is that others identify ley lines as a central part of witchcraft. Perry *Deliverance*, 66–71.

101. Greenwood, *Authority*, 81–99; Wagner and Greenwood, "The Strategic," 181–91. Obviously using Old Testament historical narrative, i.e. Joshua 5:13—6:27, as biblical justification opens a Pandora's box of hermeneutical challenges.

around Jericho, focused intercessory prayer with eyes open is a key tactic in seeing the spiritual atmosphere of a town or city positively change.[102]

Finally, if more SLSW is needed then there is another tool in the armory known as "identificational repentance," which seeks to deal with original sin(s) of peoples, cities or nation committed a long time ago by providing prayer intercessors (ideally *bloodline* descendants of those who committed the original sins) who will stand in the gap and repent on behalf of the historic offenders, can be used.[103] Overall, practitioners of SLSW purport that it is a gift of spiritual technology from God whereas critics rebut by claiming that SLSW needs a more rigorous method and should not mainly rely on the open-ended potential of experience to determine one's theology.[104]

SLSW is, of course, a new development in the scholarship of spiritual warfare on the corporate level. As previously mentioned,[105] there is a sizeable history of biblical scholarship on the powers and principalities which concludes that Pauline language on the powers refers more to societal and structural powers, not spiritual ones as previously thought.[106] More recently there has been an attempt, following the path first started by Cullmann, to seek a malleable and dialectical understanding of the powers, one that views them as both political and spiritual in an attempt to move beyond the binary positions of the past. No one has done more to develop this case than Walter Wink whose trilogy *The Powers* sought to relate the New Testament's witness of "principalities and powers" to the pervasive social systems and structures of the modern era.[107]

Having claimed that his work is the first ever comprehensive study of the language of principalities and powers,[108] Wink suggests that the language of power pervades the entire New Testament and while somewhat malleable, the use of the language shows some clear patterns of synonymous

---

102. Wagner and Greenwood, "The Strategic," 190–91.

103. Greenwood, *Authority*, 76, 122–23. The primary text that argues identificational repentance is biblically sound and rooted in Nehemiah's prayer of corporate repentance (Nehemiah 1:5–9) is Dawson, *Healing America's*.

104. Lowe, *Territorial Spirits*, 113–27; Powlison, "Response to C.," 207–9. Wink and Hardin, "Response to C. Peter," 199–203; cf. Girard, "To Double Business; Girard, *The Scapegoat*.

105. See "Methodology - Challenges and Solutions" (pp.136–138) section above.

106. Key texts include Berkhof, *Christ and*; Caird, *Principalities*; Van Den Heuvel, *These Rebellious Powers*; E. Rupp, *Principalities and Powers*.

107. Wink, *Naming*; Wink, *Unmasking*; Wink, *Engaging*.

108. Wink, *Naming*, 6.

usage. Most importantly, based upon Colossians 1:16, the powers stated in the New Testament text are heavenly *and* earthly, divine *and* human, spiritual *and* political, invisible *and* structural, good *and* evil, with the majority of usage referring to human bearers and social structures.[109]

With these introductory comments in mind, let us now proceed to consider the theological implications and assessment for the doctrine of God when we encase Wagner and Wink's corporate spiritual warfare models, together with other varying positions, within God's ontological and metaphysical reality. Following Wright's comments about the theology of an angelic fall,[110] what are the *theological* benefits of taking Wink's panentheistic world-systems paradigm and Wagner's strategic-level warfare model, together with all else in between, to form a lens through which to better understand the nature and character of the God who is in conflict with fallen forces of evil in the corporate spirit realm?

Corporate Warfare Foreknowledge: The Exhaustive Presentiment of God

Of the three omni-characteristics of God, his omniscience is the least considered metaphysical divine property when it concerns corporate level SW, especially against principalities and powers. Despite how critical and central they are to a fuller understanding of SW on the corporate level, questions such as "what does God know about principalities and powers?," "when does he know it?," and "what foreknowing knowledge and understanding about the future destination of all principalities and powers does he possess?," are rarely considered in scholarly discussions about the powers.[111]

As is known, within the nexus of Fiddes' doctrine of God is the question of divine passibility and its specific connection with evil and theodicy: in a world with so much suffering and misery it is only a suffering God who could have created it. To use Baukham's phraseology, "only a suffering God can help." There is, for Fiddes, an inextricable link between the passibility of God and the challenge of evil and theodicy and so this presents the opportunity for an analysis of this link and the related

---

109. Wink, *Naming*, 7–12.

110. Wright, *A Theology*, 70–73.

111. Even in the three volumes of his magnum opus on *The Powers*, Wink never mentions the omniscience or foreknowledge of God.

implications there are for corporate SW, especially with concern to the battle with principalities and powers, whether defined as political and societal forces *or* spiritual beings *or* both.

The uncommon use of the term divine "presentiment" presents an opportunity to explore the connections made by Fiddes between divine passibility and evil without arriving at similar conclusions to Fiddes which contain some already identified problematic elements.[112] While fully acknowledging the anthropomorphic and anthropopathic qualities of the term "presentiment," it seems justifiable to predicate it of God since it specifically elicits the idea of some kind of feeling of foreboding about future events that are likely to be of an evil kind. The emphases on feeling and potential future knowledge concerning malevolent events or happenings strongly suggest it is a term to be procured theologically and applied to this question regarding the nature of God's knowledge when in confrontation with principalities and powers.

As we have already discovered, the strengthened version of Fiddes' divine passibility, without the Achilles heels of presentism and mutability, offers a pliable and dynamic doctrine of divine suffering without the need for ontological change or lack of infinite divine prescience, hence the use of the term "exhaustive presentiment."[113] Tanner's non-competitive, ultimate gift-giver articulation of God allows us to maintain libertarian freewill and full divine foreknowledge without denying that God can and does indeed suffer, but not in the way envisaged by Fiddes. It is possible, as we know, to articulate the passibility of God without divine change or lack of foreknowledge, which in turn removes the imperative to define time *only* in a tensed manner.[114]

Of the previous interlocutions Young and von Balthasar present versions of divine passibility without change that hold most potential for synthesis with Tanner's non-competitive model. Young, in essence, states that what can be predicated of God is the experience humans have of evil and tragedy, an experience which sometimes demands fellow suffering with

112. See "Two Realms Warfare Theology" (pp.141–144) section above.

113. It could be averred that "Exhaustive Presentiment" is an oxymoronic idea. My rationale for why it is not, is that it perfectly captures God's passible response to future malevolent and nefarious events without inferring that these events take God by surprise. Similarly, a person can fully know that a loved one is going to die a painful death in the near future and yet still respond very emotionally when the loved one passes.

114. See "The Passibility and Mutability of God" section above. Of the three interlocutors only Young and von Balthasar actually maintain passibility whereas Weinandy denies it in favor of divine impassibility.

the victim and at other times needs a helper of static resolve who demonstrates imperviousness to the situation and goes beyond suffering and self-involvement. Slightly differently, von Balthasar locates all suffering of God *within* God himself, a theology of the cross which involves divine recklessness of the Father and Son in the power of the Spirit. Both constructs of divine passibility can be located within the necessary, non-contingent plane of existence occupied by God without any needed trade-off between divine sovereignty and creaturely libertarian freedom. In his uncreated realm of existence and being, God can freely choose to operate as the fellow sufferer or not without diminishing the reality of his divine passibility since suffering is known within the triune relations of the Trinity and is therefore not contingent on God's interaction with creation.[115]

However, in the other-worldly realm of spiritual conflict, God does interact with the created reality, albeit the created spiritual realm of the excluded middle. If, following Surin, divine passibility with both creaturely libertarian freedom and unlimited divine foreknowledge, presents the best answers for any Auschwitz theodicy while maintaining that God is a God of love,[116] what ramifications does this "eschatological and inverted theodicy" have for greater understanding of the content of God's epistemological base when confronting and warring against fallen societal, political or spiritual powers that seek to tyrannize and bring chaos to corporate gatherings of people?[117]

As we consider God's exhaustive presentiment when in conflict with the powers, it is vital that terms are defined regarding powers and principalities. Building on the brief mention above and following the lead of

---

115. This suggested construction of divine passibility enables a new possible route instead of the usual well-worn paths between Calvinism and Arminianism. To illustrate, when critiquing open theist Boyd, Carson exemplifies the usual concession between divine sovereignty and human freewill as he argues in favor of a compatibilist definition of freedom in order to embolden his definition of divine sovereignty. He does this because he claims that any form of presentism denies the complexity of time and a God who does not know the future is no help regarding the problem of evil. Yet, for a theology of SW, the articulation of freedom in compatibilist terms is restrictive and lacks explanatory power. Carson, "God, the Bible," 262–66.

116. See "The Contemporary Need" (pp.4–9) and "Divine Passibility of Suffering" (pp.18–21) sections above.

117. Rooting his divine passibility doctrine in God's unconditional love, Surin looks to the incarnation to show that God can suffer which leads to an inverted theodicy since God gave to human beings the freedom that he knew with full knowledge they would use one day to kill him. Surin, "The Impassibility of God," 97–115.

Cullmann,[118] recast more recently in work by Wink and others, it can be asserted that all principalities and powers are both political/structural *and* spiritual. Indeed, it is largely accepted that Cullmann was the first to offer a non-binary both/and interpretation of the principalities and powers,[119] which has produced the possibility of finding common interpretive ground between thinkers of different theological frameworks. For example, both Wagner and Wink give credit to Cullmann for his dialectical interpretation of Paul's concept of "authorities" (ἐξουσίαι) in Romans 13:1 and 1 Corinthians 2:8, referring to *both* human governments and state authority *and* supernatural, angelic principalities, powers and rulers that stand *behind* the human government.[120] In fact, Cullmann goes on to say, as suggested in Ephesians 6:12, that the state is the executive agent (i.e. the physical face) of the invisible spiritual powers.[121] Dialectically, once structural power (internal or external) moves from being a created good for the service of humanity to an idolatrous system of domination then it can be proffered that this idol is fueled and enhanced by demonic spiritual beings.[122] Put differently, ontological, sentient, and parasitical demons feed off diabolical structures and powers and in turn exacerbate the demonic system of domination by applying their own conscious, nefarious desire to kill, steal and destroy (John 10:10).

Having established a unified, non-binary definition of the powers, that God is passible without any change or reduction of God's infinite foreknowledge, and that divine exhaustive presentiment does not reduce or eradicate the divine dynamism and emotion involved in conflict

---

118. See "Part B - Territories, Powers and Principalities" (pp.154–170) section above.

119. Cullmann, *The State*, 95–114; Cullmann, *Christ*, 191–205. O'Brien refers to Cullmann's "double reference theory," arguing that principalities and powers refer to civil authorities and angelic powers, being brought into the scholarly debate for the first time and this catalyzed similar work by others such as Schmidt and Dehn. O'Brien, "Principalities and Powers," 117–19.

120. Wink, *Naming*, 11–17. cf. Cullmann, "The Subjection," 218–19.

121. Cullmann, *Christ*, 195. In order not to mislead with erroneous assimilation, it does need acknowledged that Wagner imports *a posteriori* the idea of territorial, "super-spirits" into Cullmann's understanding of principalities and powers. This was never proposed by Cullmann.

122. Wink's understanding that the powers, both in New Testament times and today, consist of an outer manifestation together with an inner spirituality or interiority is what leads him to postulate that the term "principalities and powers" is generic, and refers to the physical, psychic and social forces encountered in everyday life. Wink, *Unmasking*, 4.

against all principalities and powers,[123] does this mean that what God knows we can know and how should this affect our engagement and participation in spiritual warfare? Regarding the final destiny of the powers and principalities, when it comes to structural and societal powers, there is a scholarly consensus that God has foreordained that one day their original design as gifts and goods to be enjoyed will be restored and the powers fully redeemed. Missiologist Sider for example, when arguing that activist non-violence is superior to non-resistive pacifism, stakes his claim on the biblical witness that the principalities and powers are part of a good creation (Colossians 1:16), became fallen, have been disarmed (Colossians 2:15) and will one day be reconciled with their creator.[124]

If this is the case for political and structural principalities, will it be the same outcome of reconciliation for the spiritual powers behind the societal powers?[125] On this matter, there is no agreement. Sider argues that the powers in 1 Corinthians 15:24 will be rendered powerless, not destroyed.[126] Newbigin disagrees and states that they will ultimately be destroyed.[127] In an attempt to solve the scholarly *impasse* concerning the future outcome for all principalities and powers, Kellermann offers a dialectical solution based on the apparent paradoxical antinomy between Romans 13 and Revelation 13. Whether it is the history of Satan and demons or of a structure such as the law for example, we can see as illustrated in Romans 13 the creation of something or someone which is good and there to serve the people (the law or Lucifer) which becomes in Revelation 13 a fallen creation in a state of frenzy and chaos having received the focus of idolatry after giving into blasphemous pretensions.[128]

Therefore, in terms of the exhaustive divine presentiment which directs his divine actions against the demonic, whether structural or

123. Just like Jesus weeping while knowing full well his intention to bring Lazarus back from the dead (John 11:1–44), God can indeed weep because of the evil in the world despite exhaustively knowing the future defeat of the powers. Mott, *Biblical Ethics*, 19–21; Stewart, "On a Neglected," 292–301.

124. Sider, "Christ and Power," 12–20. Other redemptionists of the powers include Berkhof, *Christ and*, 36–46; Caird, *Principalities*, 26–30; Linthicum, *City of God*, 68–73; Wink, *The Powers*, 13–36.

125. Powell reveals that there are various treatments of these principalities and powers in the New Testament. They are brought to a new knowledge and understanding (Ephesians 3:10), reconciled (Colossians 1:20), triumphed over (Colossians 2:16), and destroyed (1 Corinthians 15). Powell, *The Biblical Concept*, 161–72.

126. Sider, "Christ and Power," 14–15.

127. Newbigin, *The Gospel*, 204.

128. Kellermann, *Seasons of Faith*, 81–85.

spiritual, God operates in a separate non-contingent realm from that which is created. He alone, with proleptic insight concerning future divine interaction into an eschatological kingdom, knows which powers, while operating under the broad sovereignty of God, are too far gone in their bombastic self-idolatry and thereby beyond redemption (Revelation 20). However, from the perspective of creation the foreknown final outcome of all principalities and powers is a mystery and so corporate gatherings of Christians need to participate with God in the specific divine conflict they face and seek divine empowerment to fight each battle without exact knowledge about the details of the end of the war. Let us now consider what that empowerment is.

Corporate Kenoticism: Spiritual Warfare Power for God's People

> All authority and rule is now under Christ. This is the under-lying fact of this era, even though not fully recognised by many of its participants! The Christian, living in the times of tension between the Resurrection and the End, is denizen of a world whose rulers, both terrestrial and celestial, *do not yet all recognize Christ's authority*. Because of this, perplexing questions are continually raised about the Christian's allegiance. (emphasis mine).[129]

Having framed God's omnipotent power within the context of spiritual conflict on the individual level as dual power which manifests itself simultaneously and dialectically as divine full and varying kenotic power,[130] what are the implications of this model if mapped onto SW on the corporate level, especially claimed global-systemic and territorial expressions of the demonic? Obviously, there are various nuanced articulations of demonic powers on the corporate level but if we want to form a voluminous theology of omnipotence in SW that helps explicate a doctrine of God, then we need to tether our understanding of who God is to a dialectical and unified theology, what has been called an "exousiology,"[131] of SW on the corporate level.

The greatest dialectic is formed using polar opposite models as thesis and antithesis and harmonizing them into a unified model. In the literature on corporate principalities, as hinted at in this section's

---

129. Powell, *The Biblical Concept*, 171–72.
130. See "Dual Power Warfare Theology" (pp.145–148) section above.
131. Yoder, *The Politics*, 141–44.

introduction above,¹³² the paradigms of Wagner and of Wink are arguably the two most polar opposite voices in the debate.¹³³ In the recent past they have clashed over matters pertaining to the ontology of the demonic, too broad a definition of intercessory prayer, flat use of the Bible, scapegoating and the use of the myth of redemptive violence, and a focus on American exceptionalism and Christendom.¹³⁴ In the wider debate, both positions have their critics from scholars who would define themselves as more centrist on matters pertaining to structural and territorial spirits.¹³⁵

That said, notwithstanding the clear differences, there is a unified and dialectical theology that can be formed. Three points of overlap come to the fore: First, as already established, both models deal primarily with SW against corporate and strategic principalities and powers, despite differing understandings of the powers. Wink defines them as the inner and outer spiritual aspects of any given manifestation of power, especially within organizations, structures and systems that quickly become demonic if they become idols.¹³⁶ This definition naturally catalyzes the didactic task of re-defining Satan in a non-personal and non-ontological

---

132. See "Part B - Territories, Powers and Principalities" (pp.154–170) section above.

133. Breuninger states that Wink and Wagner represent the two extremes of "powers theology." Breuninger, "Where Angels Fear," 41–42.

134. To be more specific, in the most recent and final direct debate between the two proponents Wink and co-author Hardin accuse Wagner and his co-author Greenwood of using scripture in a hermeneutically flat way that is full of anachronisms. They also make gross generalizations of other religions under the rubric "witchcraft" without noting the differences. Most concernedly is re-telling the story of their SLSW against an abortion clinic which, despite their denial and protestations, seemed somehow linked to the killing of the lead abortion doctor of the clinic as though this was part of "binding and victory" over the abortion demon called "Lilith." Wink and Hardin, "Response to C.," 200–203.

135. To exemplify critiquing Wagner, Arnold broadly welcomes SLSW and its emphasis upon territorial spirits, but he cautions the reader about discerning and praying down territorial spirits instead of letting God do the tearing down. Arnold, *3 Crucial*, 143–99. Also, Gilbert is highly critical of SLSW (also known as "third-wave") theology's cosmological dualism and its tendency to give demons too much power. Gilbert, "The Third Wave," 155–64. Focused upon Wink, critics are very dubious about the varied sources Wink draws upon for his "integral-panentheist worldview" including Jung, process philosophy and new physics which has led to the accusation that he is a liberal and postmodern revisionist who eisegetically imports human psychology into the biblical text. Gaston, Review of *Unmasking*, 153; Malina, Review of *Naming*, 75–76; Noll, "Thinking About," 23–26; Powlison, "Response to Walter," 77.

136. Wink, *Naming*, 5.

way, which Wink does; Satan is no longer a noun but rather an adjective.[137] Conversely, Wagner believes the powers to be demons with full ontology, spirit-principalities that govern territories and are in rebellion against God.[138]

Both paradigms refer to the same scriptures (Deuteronomy 32:8 and Daniel 10) to buttress their articulation of geographically wide angels and demons over urban areas or corporate gatherings of human beings. Wagner builds his biblical theology of territorial spirits around these passages together with Psalm 82.[139] Wink, in line with his integrated approach, takes these verses and adds to them non-canonical passages that talk of angels over nations, such as First Enoch 89–90.[140] Once he establishes these angels of nations and their connection to the "sons of God" in Genesis 6:4 he applies this understanding to the angels of the seven churches in Revelation 2–3 arguing that the seven ἀγγέλοι are not human messengers but spiritual angels and that each angel is held accountable for the behavior of the church. If the church turns its back on God, then the angel could become demonic.[141]

Finally, both insist on the central importance of intercessory prayer. There is considerable consensus that persevering intercessory prayer directly influences what God does and God responds *because* of the intercessions.[142] As Wink succinctly puts it, "history belongs to the intercessors" so long as biblical prayer is modelled on examples such as

---

137. Wink's main reason for doing this is that the traditional understanding of Satan does not commend itself to the modern mind and so, despite all the surrounding evidence of evil's existence, nobody takes Satan intellectually seriously even though we also lack the intellectual capacity to understand and explain evil. Wink and Higgins, "The World Systems," 47–48; Wink, *Unmasking*, 9–11.

138. Wagner, "Territorial Spirits," 72–73; Wagner, *Spiritual*, 211–13; cf. Eddy and Beilby, "Introduction," 41.

139. Wagner, *Spiritual*, 167–69. Heiser makes a very strong and convincing case that these passages used by Wagner make most sense when Yahweh is compared to other gods who actually do exist and that because Yahweh is uncreated and necessary whereas other gods are subsequent and contingent, monotheism means for Israel not a denial of other gods but that Yahweh is "species-unique." Heiser, "Monotheism, Polytheism," 1–30. He also strongly argues that these passages, Deuteronomy 32:8 and Daniel 10, are source material for the apostle Paul when he writes about principalities and powers in his letters. Heiser, *The Unseen Realm*, 113–22

140. Wink, *Naming*, 26–35; Wink, *Engaging*, 87–107.

141. Wink, *Engaging*, 69–82.

142. Wagner agrees with the emphasis upon intercessory prayer but disagrees with Wink's definition of an intercessor believing it to be too broad and outside of the Christian faith. See Wagner and Greenwood, "Response to Walter," 86–87.

Abraham and Moses whose prayers are more like haggling God of the cosmic, oriental bazaar than the unctuous prayers of most churches.[143]

Viewing, therefore, all powers as visible structural or societal principalities that have become idolatrous and in their mode as idols are invisibly empowered and exacerbated by demonic volitional-spiritual beings, how does God's omnipotence demonstrate itself in the midst of divine conflict in which corporate gatherings of believers participate? The answer, it seems, is a two-pronged spiritual and physical approach, namely intelligent intercessory prayer and benevolent, non-violent resistive force.

To best explicate this approach, let me reconstruct and develop an illustration used by Wagner and Greenwood. Greenwood describes a SLSW "prayer assignment" against gentlemen's clubs in the Houston area. When praying outside these clubs, not only did they see a number of men reach the door of the club, turn and leave promptly while they were praying for men not to go in, but over the following two months these clubs were exposed for fraudulent and corrupt practices which resulted in some of them closing, and this was then followed by the most fruitful evangelistic effort among the club girls that had ever been seen in this part of the city.[144]

The demonstration of God's divine power operating concurrently on full and changeable kenotic power is summed up in Greenwood's later statement: "some of the Gentlemen's Clubs are still in operation in this area of the city."[145] The desired outcome was only partially realized. For a SLSW-only approach, especially the type that seeks to tell a territorial spirit to leave a city or area, is a one-prong approach which does not address the physical, structural power that is present. If some of the clubs remain and the people of the city are still thinking and living according to sinful patterns, then this will reinforce the demonic right for evil spirits to remain. Instead, "the people of God need to do hand-to-hand combat on the streets by proclaiming the message of deliverance and *ministering* to those victimized by sin and the demonic."[146]

A two-pronged effective approach, which could see varying levels of God's kenotic power at work, could be intercession teams praying strategically over the area and clubs, evangelism teams spreading the gospel on the streets near the vicinity, engagement with the diabolical structures

143. Wink, *Engaging*, 297–317; Wink and Higgins, "The World Systems," 61–71.
144. Greenwood, *Authority*, 28–30.
145. Greenwood, *Authority*, 30.
146. Arnold, *3 Crucial*, 166.

and systems of the sex-club industry by non-violent political lobbying, and pastoral intervention in the lives of the involved girls that seeks to help them work through the personal root bondages that force them to choose this vocation. Collectively, this response would seek to address both the worldly diabolical principality structures and its symbiotically tied demonic ontological powers behind the systems of domination.[147]

Viewing varying kenotic power as the *sine qua non* of God's omnipotence serves as a powerful antidote to any spiritual hubris which may reside in the practitioners of SW on the corporate level.[148] It also holds much explanatory power for the varying degrees of "success" that is experienced in the world of deliverance ministry.[149] Most vitally, it presents a theological foundation for using God's power to serve one another,[150] and mobilizing God's people to be a church that comes alongside those who are marginalized and have no voice.[151] The more effective the global church is in this, the greater the presence of God through his church, which will have greater implications for the panentheistic reality of God; a matter to which we now turn.

Divine Panentheistic Omnipresence and Ubiquitous Powers and Principalities

Fiddes' Christian and soteriological panentheism governed by his trinitarian "persons as relations" concept and full creaturely participation within the relations of the Trinity implies that evil, the demonic and fallen principalities and powers are, in some way, situated *within* God himself. Simultaneously, evil defined as the negative expression of irrevocable libertarian freedom means that God is not the primary origin or

---

147. A really creative and fully-orbed approach could include developing a prophetic voice in culture via Christian art, media, music, and film that confronts the cheap-sex message by presenting a biblical theology of sexuality in which covenant commitment is extolled and the demand for illicit sexual services jettisoned. This would certainly go far in rebutting Wink's criticism that by "attempting to fight the demons 'in the air,' evangelicals and charismatics will continue largely to ignore the institutional sources of the demonic." Wink, *Engaging*, 314.

148. Something Fiddes is very sensitive to and critical of. See "Omnipotence's Kenotic Warfare" (pp.98–106) section above.

149. Seen of course in the life of Jesus when Mark recorded that Jesus "could not do" any works of signs and wonders because of the unbelief in Nazareth. (Mark 6:4–6).

150. Murphy, "Toward a Theology," 51–53.

151. Pannell, "Evangelism and Power," 49–55.

cause of evil and subsequent suffering. With the help of von Balthasar, the above-developed doctrine of God's omnipresence enables one to explain where evil resides and exercises its malevolent will within the relations of the triune God while ensuring that culpability for much evil remains with Satan, his demonic forces and the visible frontage of the powers and principalities.[152]

The worldwide ubiquity of internal and external structural powers and the sub-personal, volitional demonic forces behind them is attested to in many different contexts. Whether it is in the desert-nomadic animistic cultures of Africa,[153] the capitalist-consumerist urban centers around the globe,[154] tyrannical despotic states who are main players in the global arms-dealing trade,[155] or all parts of the world where human beings gather and form societies and culture based on hierarchy and privilege,[156] the existence and manifestation of evil in different forms is an accepted presupposition. Through his social-scientific prism on the powers, Hiebert reminds us that the scriptural witness is that the earth is the Lord's and that God's key objective when participating in spiritual conflict is to establish God's reign on earth and throughout the universe, just as it is in the heavenly realm.[157] Moreover, O'Brien contends that understanding principalities and powers as personal, supernatural agents who can penetrate social, political, judicial structures significantly helps us to see the global ubiquity of the powers and also why not all structures become tyrannical.[158]

Von Balthasar's "yes" and "no" between the Father and Son's relations creates relational divine kenotic acts that result in a fathomless separation of God from himself in which exist all forms of dark and wicked separation, including hell. This means it is a non-static and open distance that can morph in order to contain all mutational types of evil, whether that be personalist-ontological, structural and societal or even

---

152. See "Ontological Evil and" (pp.123–130) section above.

153. Ferdinando, *The Triumph of Christ*; Igenoza, "Christian Theology," 39–48.

154. Padilla, "Spiritual Conflict," 208–13.

155. Murphy, "Toward a Theology," 48–54.

156. Lohfink, *Jesus and Community*, 115–21; Lohfink, *Option for the Poor*, 5–15.

157. Hiebert, "Spiritual Warfare," 118–23.

158. O'Brien, "Principalities and Powers and," 9–10. O'Brien and others make the point that it is vital to note that the powers of evil work in and through people and that if we equate the powers only with human structures then false conclusions will be arrived at. Cf. Lynch, "How Convincing," 262–65.

territorial. This has to be the case given the malleable nature of the demonic and principalities and powers. For example, as Wink has amply demonstrated, in scripture and church history Satan is a fluid category, one that changes with every historical epoch. In the Old Testament he is presented as God's dark side, his *agent provocateur*.[159] This representation is continued into the New Testament,[160] which delineates a picture of Satan as a subtle tempter from God, a legalist, a being who knows his place, and a means of deliverance.[161]

It is as we enter early church history, with an increasing ubiquity of evil, that church fathers like Justin Martyr and Abbot Richalm of Schontal portray Satan as the origin of evil and fully responsible for every evil act.[162] So this very unsystematic picture of Satan from scripture and church history should preclude any attempt to define Satan mono-archetypally or mono-theologically. Rather Satan should be seen as a changeable category between the poles of God's purposes intertwined with humanity's choices and thereby located in all his different descriptive characteristics in the significant and rebellious "no" within the "yes" between the Father and the Son.

To frame all accounts and evidence of evil as existing within the relations of the triune God in this way not only reinforces the mainline view that principalities and powers are still, despite their malevolent and nefarious spirit and action, under the broad sovereignty of God, but also all forms of territorial spirits are not independent of God and do not operate in a separate, dualistic fashion outside of the presence of God.[163] One of the repeated criticisms of Wagner's SLSW teaching is that because

---

159. 2 Samuel 24:1; Zechariah 3:1–5; Job 1–2.

160. Luke 22:31–34; 1 Corinthians 5:1–5; 1 Timothy 1:20; Matthew 4:1–13 cf. Luke 4:1–13.

161. Wink and Higgins, "The World Systems," 51–56; Wink, *Unmasking*, 14–22. This claim by Wink from these passages is contested. Brown, for example, commenting on 1 Cor 5:1–5 states that "it cannot be claimed that Satan functions as an (unwitting) agent of God in 1 Cor 5:5. The verse does not refer to Satan himself, but primarily to the realm of existence outside the Christian community over which Satan rules." Brown, *The God of This Age*, 151.

162. Wink, *Unmasking*, 22–23, 36–37.

163. Gilbert persuasively argues the problem with the third-wave movement that proffers territorial spirits theology is their cosmological worldview which, contrary to a Christian worldview, has violence, mythologized accounts, and a pantheon of demons all at the center of their creation account and so this goes a long way to creating a "paranoid universe," outside of God's providence and governed primarily by fear and a defensive mentality. Gilbert, "The Third Wave," 153–61.

of its emphasis upon large geo-political areas under the complete influence and oppression of superior territorial spirits, it often demonizes "secular" culture and develops "us versus them" language. Critics assert that this quickly moves the model of SW in the direction of nationalism, mimetic practice of scapegoating, or a Constantinian, postmillennial vision that seeks to get power in order to legislate Christianity back into the host culture.[164]

Viewing all powers and principalities together with the bolstering spiritual forces behind them as situated within the triune relations of God and therefore within the very broad providence of God, does not mean, however, that SW is neat and tidy.[165] There exists too many accounts of explicit demonic and evil events often adversely affecting Christians to accept a pedestrian account of SW.[166] Rather, within the omnipresence of God subsists the *collective* omnipresence of principalities and powers and so this needs to be acknowledged and engaged with by the church globally. At this juncture, therefore, there is an imperative that apparent opposite paradigms of SW, as represented by Wagner and Wink, are viewed as the two sides of the same "powers" coin which determine a two-pronged attack, one that deals with both spiritual and worldly systemic root issues together in an effective way.

Being sensitive to the global presence of evil Wagner, together with Greenwood, purports that SLSW is a gift of spiritual technology for the world from God. First, it is an effective means to the end goal of global evangelism, bringing people into belief in Christ.[167] Also, it never underestimates the activity of the demonic since Satan's origin as fallen Lucifer means that his complete *modus operandi* is to rebel against God and his

---

164. Wink and Hardin, "Response to C.," 199–203; Boyd, "Response to C.," 210–15.

165. Similarly, Foster reminds the reader that even though the Holy Spirit is omnipresent he still regularly acts territorially and manifests himself with particular weightiness in different regions or places, often in ways that are messy and chaotic, just like Pentecost. Foster, "Preface," xi.

166. Wagner retells an account of a Ghanaian Presbyterian pastor who, after instructing a tree used as a satanic shine to be cut down, collapsed and died the moment the tree was felled. Wagner, "Spiritual Warfare," 49. Bennett cites a typical testimony of a convert to Christianity in Madagascar, "Before I was converted to Christianity, the devils had power over me. . . When the demons saw that I wanted to be a Christian they appeared to me with knives and spears and wanted to kill me. One day they wanted to throw me into the fire." Bennett, *I Am Not Afraid*, 76–77. Even Wink's journey into studying the Powers started after he nearly lost his life under the spiritual weight and oppression of the powers in South America. Wink, *Naming*, ix–x.

167. Wagner, *Spiritual*, 151–54.

creation by inducing as much suffering and misery as possible.[168] Third, SLSW is one specific part of a global rise in intercessory prayer that seeks to constantly and permanently cover the world in prayer.

This mention of global intercessory prayer presents the most significant tool in the spiritual arsenal to be used by the global church as she participates in spiritual conflict with the ubiquitous powers, both structural and spiritual. Without repeating on the *power* of prayer,[169] both Wagner and Wink maintain that intercessory prayer really does matter and is really effective. While history does not belong to the intercessor alone, history belongs to the God of the intercessor who partners (albeit as the stronger partner) with the intercessor and brings things about in response to prayer.[170] The omnipresent element concerning prayer, agree Wagner and Wink, is that prayer is dynamic, has some sort of causal effect regarding God's interaction with creation,[171] and this is primarily because God in us (i.e. the Holy Spirit) fuels our prayers and so in a sense it is God interceding to God on creation's behalf.[172] This theology of prayer therefore opens the door for less traditional, prophetic-type action in the belief that God's unction of the Spirit will call and raise an intercessor to stand in the gap and mediate a corporate act of identificational repentance for past sins, speak blessings over geographical areas via prayer walks, or confront a town or city about its idolatrous behavior.[173]

---

168. Wagner and Greenwood criticize Boyd for not including the fall of Lucifer in his account of Satan's functional lordship. See Wagner and Greenwood, "Response to Gregory," 169–70.

169. See "Corporate Kenoticism" (pp.162–166) section above.

170. The qualifications of an intercessor is where Wagner and Wink disagree the most. Wink's theology of prayer contends that Revelation 5–8 clearly teaches that all humans intervene in heavenly liturgy. Wink and Higgins, "The World Systems," 61–67; cf. Wink, *Engaging*, 298–304. Wagner and Greenwood absolutely disagree by retorting that there is a spiritual anointing, qualification and calling on the lives of the intercessors and so is not open to anyone. Greenwood, *Authority*, 59–64, 103–7; Wagner, *Spiritual*, 36–37.

171. Wagner, *Spiritual*, 23–24.

172. Wink, *Engaging*, 304–8.

173. Wink and Hardin, "Response to C.," 199–200; Wagner and Greenwood, "The Strategic," 187–91; Wagner, *Spiritual*, 256; Greenwood, *Authority*, 74–76.

CONCLUSION

> The existence of both God and the evil from which God is entreated to deliver us are integral and central ingredients in their religious worldview; the notion that there might be some logical incompatibility between the two simply does not come to mind.[174]

Hasker may be overstating his case in order to prepare his answer on whether or not God and evil are compatible. However, while questions of theodicy may prevent people from becoming Christian believers,[175] it seems the majority of Christians do practice their faith within the tension of an all-powerful, all-knowing, benevolent God and all-pervasive and prevalent evil, be that moral, natural, or spiritual. This chapter has sought to examine this tension by constructing a unified and dialectical theology of evil and SW. To do this Fiddes' doctrine of God has been utilized in order to undergird the constructed theology of SW in a way commensurate and congruent to the presented theology.

The adaption and development of Fiddes' theology has formed a doctrine of God well-suited to explain the various aspects of a spiritual warfare theology that explains spiritual conflict involving individual Christian believers. In this doctrine, God's nature is dynamic, with a freely chosen ability to absorb the pain and suffering of the world without ontological mutability or limitation of foreknowledge. He is relationally malleable and able to genuinely respond to the irrevocable, libertarian freewill decisions of his creation, both spiritual and physical. All this he does while concurrently and non-competitively holding all knowledge of the past, present, future, and operating with varying degrees of full and kenotic power. This elicits a globally pervasive atonement of *Christus Victor*, which collectively enables Christian believers to battle and overcome their fallen nature, live in allegiance to the kingdom of God, and remind Satan of his yet-to-be-fully consummated defeat by Christ through his crucifixion and resurrection.

In the same way as the rubric "spiritual warfare" has evolved to include not just individual demons or forces of evil but also the claims of territorial principalities and powers, so has the articulated doctrine of God in this chapter grounded and sustained the depicted theology of SW on the

---

174. Hasker, *The Triumph*, 55.

175. "In the mind of the latter [the non-believer] it [evil] stands as a major obstacle to religious commitment." Hick, *Evil and*, 3.

geo-political corporate level. Situating all of God's knowledge within his exhaustive presentiment has enabled a theological connection to be made between God's infinite knowledge of all future events of evil and suffering and his genuine divine pathos. His ability to suffer and be passible without ontological change maintains the realness of his conflict with all forms of principalities and powers while knowing the full outcome of their final destination. God's omnipotence as defined above in kenotic concepts reflects in real terms the various outcomes of the SW two-pronged approach of non-violent activism and continuous prayer. Finally, the omnipresence of God matches the ubiquity of evil by manifesting itself through the global, continual prayers of all believing intercessors who are not praying apart from God but are interceding within the very relations of the triune God, counteracting the "no" within the "yes" of Father and Son by participating in the "yes" within the triune relations.

Having reached the end of the chapter, all that now remains to be done in conclusion form is an articulated theological definition of spiritual warfare. This will include a summary of the entire thesis, a verdict on whether or not the research thesis statement has been demonstrated, and some comments on the outcome of using Fiddes' theology as a congenial framework to build a doctrine of God robust enough to construct a unified theology of SW. From these final judgements it will be possible to identify areas of potential further study and research.

Conclusion

INTRODUCTION

As well demonstrated, the key themes of Fiddes' theological project have not altered during a career now spanning over 40 years. In his most recent published writings, Fiddes' vision of who God is and how he acts deviates little from the picture set out earlier in CSG and other texts. For instance, having thoroughly analyzed and critiqued Iris Murdoch's engagement and synthesis with theology in her philosophy and prose, Fiddes concludes that in order to develop a theology of a suffering God which goes beyond sentimentality—a charge brought by Murdoch—one needs to hold "a theology that takes divine passibility seriously. . . is willing to work out the implications of passibility and empathy in terms of a radical self-limiting of divine knowledge and power and a mutability of God in the sense of divine openness to new experience arising from creation."[1] Moreover, having made the surprising claim that he sourced the theological concept "divine perichoresis" from Lewis, not Moltmann,[2] Fiddes delineates the historical, theological, and relational contours of Lewis' development of perichoresis through his "co-inherent" friendship with Charles Williams, both of whom came to their perichoretic understanding through the work of G.L. Prestige.[3]

The stability and consistency of Fiddes' theology has been crucial to the justification of him as dialogue partner for this construction of

---

1. Fiddes, *Iris Murdoch*, 200, cf. CSG, 68–71.

2. See "Covenant Theology of Panentheism" (pp.110–112) section above.

3. Fiddes, *Charles Williams*. For an overview of Fiddes' perichoretic and co-inherent thesis about Lewis and Williams, see Cuthbert, Review of *Charles Williams*, 44–47.

a doctrine of God which coheres well with a theology of SW. As noted in the introduction, modern thinking about SW has taken place since the beginnings of the charismatic renewal in the late 1960s.[4] Therefore, using Fiddes—a theologian whose corpus of work approximately mirrors the epoch of renewal—in conversation has created a genuine case of contemporary, constructive theology using sources which are both systematic and subject-based.[5] Also in drawing from Fiddes, a theologian who grounds both literary and ecclesial theology in a doctrine of God, has enabled emergent analysis to come forth from tragic literature and pastoral and practical theology, both of which are important considerations in a theology of SW. So, Fiddes' doctrine of God is useful for theologizing SW.

SUMMARY OF THESIS

The research question asked in the introduction was "does the contemporary theology of Paul S. Fiddes offer a better framework than traditional theologies to explain the nature and character of God that best fits with a theology of SW?" More specifically, is it indeed the case that a critical evaluation and reconstruction of Fiddes' theology offers the best paradigm to construct a doctrine of God suitable for a spiritual conflict theology. Chapters one through six answer this research question. Before articulating a succinct answer to the question by giving a theological account of SW, let us first summarize where we have been in the book, part by part.

Chapters one and two laid crucial groundwork by delineating a broad picture of Fiddes' doctrines of God and of evil, accounts that highlight the *sine qua non* themes in his key works. Fiddes aligns well with other theologians who argue that divine passibility of suffering love is the only appropriate response to evil and spiritual conflict in the current post-Auschwitz milieu.[6] There is a cross in the heart of God, an experience of pain and suffering from the crucifixion of Christ and cry of

---

4. See "Introduction: Setting the Scene" (pp.xix–xxi) section above.

5. Some of Fiddes' earliest work was critiquing the charismatic renewal. See "The Place of *Experience*" (pp.9–13) section above. For an account how Fiddes' trinitarian theology differed from charismatic theology in the UK, see Cuthbert, "Participatory and Perichoretic," 45–59.

6. Davis informs that before the holocaust, *the* evil event which emboldened all theodicies was the Lisbon earthquake in 1755. It is interesting that the quintessential paradigm of evil has changed from an event of natural evil to a moral one and so is now perhaps easier to explain. Davis, *Encountering Evil*, 6.

dereliction. Human affliction and pain at the hands of evil and malevolent forces is analogous to divine nature and experience. Evil *befalls* God and so a practical theodicy should be rooted in divine passibility and pathos, without collapsing Calvary into a general account of divine suffering. Fiddes' theological definition of evil is that it is primarily *privatio boni*, which emerges from nothingness. Satan may have sub-personhood and so there is no sentience or willful volition in evil but rather a parasitic quiddity which maintains ambiguity and resists definition. For reasons I explicate in part two, Fiddes' non-ontological definition of evil is a weakness and more at odds with his doctrine of God than a personal-ontological account of evil.

Chapters three, four and five offered three developed and nuanced accounts of God's necessary omni-attributes, i.e. his omniscience, omnipotence and omnipresence, which collectively establish a doctrine of God commodious enough to situate a spiritual warfare theology. Because God is both passible and mutable, Fiddes denies EDF; God knows *only* what can be known. A theology of SW, however, is better suited to a tenseless, not tensed, view of time, and as shown can avoid a zero-sum game between divine sovereignty and creaturely freedom thereby guaranteeing full divine knowledge of the future, including the eschatological full abolishment of evil, while maintaining full creaturely and angelic freedom and will.

In chapter four the use of Martensen's kenotic theology enabled the formulation of a journey of kenosis power that was able to be mapped onto the kenotic Christ hymn of Philippians chapter two. Fiddes strongly proffers a non-coercive power definition, one freely realized in God by self-limitation which has a range of power outage depending upon the stages of kenosis, plerosis or theosis. Taking this definition of kenotic power helps elucidate in chapter five the plausibility of evil's location falling within the omnipresent, panentheistic domain of God. Situated in the "yes" of relations between the Father and Son, this development of von Balthasar's trinitarian theology allows for the twisted knot of rebellion to be present in the relations of the triune God, whether those rebellious acts originate with human or spiritual beings.

In chapter six a constructive dialectical theology of SW was presented, one in which Fiddes' nuanced doctrine of God could be located. Bifurcated into the individual and corporate, a theology of SW was depicted through the lenses of God's prescience, kenotic power, and panentheistic presence. Whether it is the spiritually evil triptych of the flesh, world and devil or the corporate territories, principalities or powers, forces of malevolence do contribute to the tension faced by all humans, Christian or otherwise, created by the co-existence of an all-powerful, good God and ubiquitous forces of evil, whether natural, moral, spiritual or existential. This tension was examined and explained by a dialectical theology of SW, a theology of which a succinct account will now be presented.

A THEOLOGICAL ACCOUNT OF SPIRITUAL WARFARE

> Evil is not merely a lack of something, but an effective agent, a living spiritual being, perverted and perverting, a terrible reality, mysterious and frightening . . . It is not a question of one devil but of many . . . This question of the devil and the influence he can exert on individual persons as well as on communities, whole societies and events is a very important chapter of Catholic doctrine.[7]

Theologically, what is SW? Who is involved in the conflict? Pope Paul VI's declaration to an audience of Catholic believers in 1972 perfectly encapsulates a doctrine of evil which needs embedded in any theology of SW. As the four acts of the biblical narrative strongly suggest, together with the fifth act currently being written,[8] God and his church are at war with a common enemy. The people of God participate in the divine conflict taking place in the heavenly realms; that excluded middle, which does not war against flesh and blood but rather spiritual beings, principalities and powers (Ephesians 6:12).

As the previous section concludes, the use of the contemporary theology of Paul S. Fiddes, adapted, integrated and nuanced because of my interlocution with Fiddes,[9] does offer a better schematic framework than more traditional theologies to construct a doctrine of God that best grounds a theology of SW. The proposed qualifications indeed strengthen the Fiddesian doctrine of God as an optimum model to make sense of the surrounding SW reality. Fundamentally, God is ultimately responsible for the presence and problem of evil. As the uncreated, non-contingent, necessary being, all other beings in created, necessary and contingent form owe their existence, ontology and irrevocable libertarian freedom

---

7. Faricy S.J., "Deliverance from Evil," 73.
8. Bartholomew and Goheen, *The Drama of Scripture.*
9. Drawn from various sources, both direct and indirect critics of Fiddes.

to God, whether that freedom is used for ill or good. Therefore, God cannot be completely exonerated of all culpability for the existence of evil and warfare reality currently prevalent in the heavenly, spiritual realms.

However, via revelation of scripture, God guarantees that the days of evil's presence and activity are finite and the future, full consummation of the eschaton will realize the final and exhaustive destruction of Satan and all demonic principalities and powers. Because God is a non-contingent, necessary being, he exists and operates on a completely different and distinct plane of reality from the created universe. Therefore, there is no need to reduce creaturely libertarian freedom, God's EDF of the future, or his unlimited sovereignty and providence, in order to assert absolute co-existence of full creaturely freedom alongside infinite divine knowledge of the past, present and future.

Moreover, due to residual culpability remaining with God for the existence of malevolent, nefarious spirit beings who cause much evil, divine possibility of suffering love is *inter alia* a necessary attribute of God. "Only the suffering God can help,"[10] one whose interaction with the spiritual and physical creation determines divine relational mutability whilst maintaining ontological immutability. His non-contingent, uncreated nature cannot change while his approach, dealings and interactions with all created reality can. Through the mystery of the incarnation, the two distinct planes of ontological reality coalesce, and the suffering of God takes on a singular form because of divine possibility directly caused by creation via human agency. There is no collapsing of Golgotha into a general account of divine suffering; rather the crucifixion of Christ univocally actualizes the cross permanently located within the heart of God.

Situating the cross in the heart of the triune God enables a kenotic Christology that maps out kenosis, plerosis and theosis power onto the incarnation, life, death, resurrection and ascension of Christ which consequently establishes a kenotic Trinitarianism and cosmology. Atonement power through Christ's death and resurrection is both humanward and Satanward and releases combative and transformative power over Satan and the demonic, as well as the hold and tyranny of evil over the creation. Moreover, taking the singularity of the cross and the consequent defeat of the demonic, together with the universality of God's triune presence, establishes a panentheistic reality to God's ontology, one into which all sentient rebellion and opposition is situated within the infinite distance

---

10. Bauckham, "Only the Suffering," 6–7.

of the "yes" between the Father and Son, which distance was caused by the rupturing of divine relations at the moment of dereliction at Calvary.

Finally, as worked out above,[11] an adapted Fiddesian doctrine of God offers an effective model of God that explicates evil and spiritual warfare taking place on the level of the individual, whether that be on the frontline of the sinful flesh, worldly values or devilish assignments. Concurrently, it also explains what impact corporate evil—be that fallen creation, principalities and powers, or even so called "territorial spirits,"—has on God and, therefore, what we can expect in terms of his response and divine action in the face of the evil befalling him.

POTENTIAL FURTHER RESEARCH

The scope of this book has been determined by which subjects under the general rubrics of "spiritual warfare" and "evil and the demonic" have been addressed by Fiddes in his sizeable corpus of scholarship. The connectional nature of his theological enterprise made him a very suitable dialogue partner for constructing a theology of SW.[12] However, Fiddes does not address every relevant question or issue. There is an *ad infinitum* quality to the entire debate concerning evil and divine conflict which can be tackled from various perspectives, many of which are unaddressed by Fiddes and thereby outside of the scope of this book.

So, what follows are some areas of research not addressed in this book but very germane to the theological subject matter of evil and SW. To begin, given the practical nature of much SW teaching and scholarship, it would be prudent and relevant to examine the three constructions of God's knowledge, power and presence through the lens of practical theology and see what impact, if any, the above theology of SW has on prayer ministry for deliverance or even a full exorcism.

Also, Fiddes' denial of an ontology of the demonic in favor of *privatio boni* means that much more could have been explored and argued in terms of Satan's origins and ontology, from both biblical scholarship and theology. For instance, what to make of Wright's claim that it is theologically vital to acknowledge the libertarian freewill fall of Lucifer and the angels despite the lack of favorable biblical evidence.[13]

11. See Chapter 6 (pp.135–172) above.
12. See "Introduction: Systematic Theology" (pp.xxii–xxvi) section above.
13. Wright, *A Theology*, 70–73.

Finally, the use of Fiddes' oeuvre as a primary source for this academic thesis could lead to a broad horizon of further research focused on analysis and critique of Fiddes' doctrine of God. Building upon the development of Fiddes' doctrines of omniscience, omnipotence, and omnipresence, further inquiry is invited concerning other attributes of God, both communicable and incommunicable, in terms of their explication when situated within a triune God model of "persons as relations." Moreover, since little examination of Fiddes' use of sources has taken place above, this leaves an expansive amount of groundwork to be covered concerning his understanding and use of his central six twentieth-century theologians,[14] as well as other thinkers from various disciplines such as Kristeva, Hopkins, Girard, Murdoch, Levinas, etcetera. Given the copious amount and prolific rate of writings in Fiddes' corpus, together with the wide range of inter-disciplinary connections in his work, it seems indubitably the case that the scholarship of Fiddes will continue to be analyzed and critiqued for many future generations, both within Baptist theological circles and further afield.

---

14. See "The Place of *Experience*" (pp.9–13) section above.

Bibliography

Aguilar, Mario. *Theology, Liberation and Genocide: A Theology of the Periphery*. London: SCM, 2009.
Alighieri, Dante. *The Divine Comedy 1: Hell*. Translated by Dorothy L. Sayers. London: Penguin, 1949.
———. *The Divine Comedy: Inferno, Purgatorio, Paradiso*. Translated by Robin Kirkpatrick. London: Penguin, 2012.
Allen, Robert Francis. "St. Augustine's Free Will Theodicy and Natural Evil." *Ars Disputandi* 3:1 (2003) 84–90.
Allen, Thomas B. *Possessed: The True Story of an Exorcism*. Lincoln: iUniverse, 2000.
Amorth, Gabriele. *An Exorcist Tells His Story*. Translated by Nicoletta V. MacKenzie. San Francisco: Ignatius, 1999.
Anderson, Gordon L. Review of *God at War* and *Satan and the Problem of Evil*, by Gregory A. Boyd. *PNEUMA: The Journal of the Society for Pentecostal Studies* 25.1 (Spring 2003) 125–29.
Anderson, Neil T. *The Bondage Breaker*. Tunbridge Wells: Monarch, 1990.
———. *Victory Over the Darkness*. Oxford: Lion, 1992.
Anderson, Pamela Sue and Paul S. Fiddes. "Creating a New Imaginary for Love in Religion." *Angelaki* 25:1–2 (2020) 46–53.
Anselm. *Proslogion: With a Reply on Behalf of the Fool by Gaunilo and the Author's Reply to Gaunilo*. Translated by M. J. Charlesworth. Notre Dame: University of Notre Dame Press, 1979.
Aquinas, Thomas. *Summa Contra Gentiles*. II. Translated by James F. Anderson. Notre Dame: University of Notre Dame Press, 1975.
Arnold, Clinton E. *3 Crucial Questions about Spiritual Warfare*. Grand Rapids: Baker Academic, 1997.
———. *Ephesians: Power and* Magic. Cambridge: Cambridge University Press, 1989.
Astley, Jeff., David Brown and Ann Loades (eds.). *Evil: A Reader*. London: T&T Clark, 2003.
Aulen, Gustaf. *Christus Victor: An Historical Study of the Three Main Types of the Idea of the Atonement*. London: SPCK, 1931.
Balthasar, Hans Urs von. *Dare We Hope That All Men Be Saved? With a Short Discourse on Hell*, 2nd ed. Translated by David Kipp and Lothar Krauth. San Francisco: Ignatius, 2014.

―――. *Epilogue*. Translated by Edward T. Oakes, S.J. San Francisco: Ignatius, 2004.

―――. *Mysterium Paschale*. Translated by Aidan Nichols, O.P. Edinburgh: T&T Clark, 1990.

―――. *Theo-Drama: Theological Dramatic Theory. Vol. IV—The Action*. Translated by Graham Harrison. San Francisco: Ignatius, 1994.

Barbour, Ian G. "God's Power: A Process View." In *The Work of Love: Creation as Kenosis*, edited by J. Polkinghorne, 1–20. London: SPCK, 2001.

Barrett, Lee C. "Martensen as Systematic Theologian: The Architectonics of Incarnation." In *Hans Lassen Martensen: Theologian, Philosopher and Social Critic*, edited by Jon Stewart, 73–98. Copenhagen: Museum Tusculanum, 2012.

Barth, Karl. *The Doctrine of Creation*. Vol. 3.3 of *Church Dogmatics*. Edited by G. W. Bromiley and T. F. Torrance. Translated by G. W. Bromiley and R. J. Ehrlich. Peabody: Hendrickson, 2010.

―――. *The Doctrine of God*. Vol. 2.1 of *Church Dogmatics*. Edited by G. W. Bromiley and T. F. Torrance. Translated by T.H.L. Parker, W. B. Johnston, Harold Knight and J.L.M Haire. Peabody: Hendrickson, 2010.

―――. *The Doctrine of God*. Vol. 2.2 of *Church Dogmatics*. Edited by G. W. Bromiley and T. F. Torrance. Translated by G.W. Bromiley, J.C. Campbell, Iain Wilson, J. Strathearn McNab, Harold Knight and R. A. Stewart. Peabody: Hendrickson, 2010.

―――. *The Doctrine of Reconciliation*. Vol. 4.1 of *Church Dogmatics*. Edited by G. W. Bromiley and T. F. Torrance. Translated by G. W. Bromiley. Peabody: Hendrickson, 2010.

―――. *The Doctrine of Reconciliation*. Vol. 4.3.1 of *Church Dogmatics*. Edited by G. W. Bromiley and T. F. Torrance. Translated by G. W. Bromiley. Peabody: Hendrickson, 2010.

Bartholomew, Craig and Michael W. Goheen, *The Drama of Scripture: Finding Our Place in the Biblical Story* 2nd rev ed. London: SPCK, 2014.

Basinger, David. *The Case for Freewill Theism: A Philosophical Assessment*. Downers Grove: IVP, 1996.

―――. "Divine Persuasion: Could the Process God Do More?" *Journal of Religion* 64.3 (1984) 332–47.

―――. "Divine Power: Do Process Theists Have a Better Idea?" In *Process Theology*, edited by Ronald H. Nash, 197–213. Grand Rapids: Baker Book House, 1987.

―――. "Human Freedom and Divine Providence: Some New Thoughts on an Old Problem." *Religious Studies* 15 (1979) 491–510.

Bauckham, Richard. "'Only the Suffering God Can Help:' Divine Passibility in Modern Theology." *Themelios* 9/3 (1984) 6–12.

―――. *The Theology of the Book of Revelation*. Cambridge: Cambridge University Press, 1993.

Beck, Richard. *Reviving Old Scratch: Demons and the Devil for Doubters and the Disenchanted*. Minneapolis: Fortress, 2016.

Beilby, James K. and Paul R. Eddy (eds.). *The Nature of the Atonement: Four Views*. Downers Grove: IVP Academic, 2006.

―――. *Understanding Spiritual Warfare: Four Views*. Grand Rapids: Baker Academic, 2012.

Bennett, Robert H. *I Am Not Afraid: Demon Possession and Spiritual Warfare*. Saint Louis: Concordia House, 2013.

Berkhof, Hendrikus. *Christ and the Powers*. Harrisonburg: Herald, 1977.
Blocher, Henri. *Evil and the Cross: Christian Thought and the Problem of Evil*. Leicester: Apollos, 1994.
Boethius. The Consolation of Philosophy. Translated by P. G. Walsh. Oxford: Oxford University Press, 1999.
———. 'A Treatise Against Eutyches and Nestorius,' The Theological Tractates. Translated by H. F. Stewart. London: Heinemann, 1918.
Boyd, Gregory A. *Crucifixion of the Warrior God: Interpreting the Old Testament's Violent Portraits of God in Light of the Cross*, Vol. 1. Minneapolis: Fortress, 2017.
———. *Crucifixion of the Warrior God: Interpreting the Old Testament's Violent Portraits of God in Light of the Cross*, Vol. 2. Minneapolis: Fortress, 2017.
———. *God at War: The Bible & Spiritual Conflict*. Downers Grove: InterVarsity, 1997.
———. *God of the Possible: A Biblical Introduction to the Open View of God*. Grand Rapids: Baker Book House, 2000.
———. "The Ground-Level Deliverance Model." In *Understanding Spiritual Warfare: Four Views*, edited by James K. Beilby and Paul Rhodes Eddy, 129–57. Grand Rapids: Baker Academic, 2012.
———. *Is God to Blame? Beyond Pat Answers to the Problem of Suffering*. Downers Grove: InterVarsity, 2003.
———. *The Myth of a Christian Nation*. Grand Rapids: Zondervan, 2005.
———. "Powers and Principalities." In *Dictionary of Scripture and Ethics*, edited by Joel Green, 611–13. Grand Rapids: Baker Academic, 2011.
———. "Response to C. Peter Wagner and Rebecca Greenwood." In *Understanding Spiritual Warfare: Four Views*, edited by James K. Beilby and Paul Rhodes Eddy, 210–15. Grand Rapids: Baker Academic, 2012.
———. "Response to David Powlison." In *Understanding Spiritual Warfare: Four Views*, edited by James K. Beilby and Paul Rhodes Eddy, 117–22. Grand Rapids: Baker Academic, 2012.
———. "Response to Walter Wink." In *Understanding Spiritual Warfare: Four Views*, edited by James K. Beilby and Paul Rhodes Eddy, 78–83. Grand Rapids: Baker Academic, 2012.
———. *Satan and the Problem of Evil: Constructing a Trinitarian Warfare Theodicy*. Downers Grove: InterVarsity, 2001.
———. "The Self-Sufficient Sociality of God: A Trinitarian Revision of Hartshorne's Metaphysics." In *Trinity in Process: A Relational Theology of God*, edited by Joseph A. Bracken and Marjorie Hewitt Suchocki, 73–94. New York: Continuum, 1997.
Boyd, Greg and Paul R. Eddy. "Evil." In *Dictionary of Scripture and Ethics*, edited by Joel Green, 288–89. Grand Rapids: Baker Academic, 2011.
Braaten, Carl E. "Powers in Conflict: Christ and the Devil." In *Sin, Death and the Devil*, edited by Carl E. Braaten and Robert W. Jenson, 94–107. Grand Rapids: Eerdmans, 2000.
Braaten, Carl E. and Robert W. Jenson (eds.). *Sin, Death and the Devil*. Grand Rapids: Eerdmans, 2000.
Bracken, Joseph. "The End of Evil." In *World without End: Christian Eschatology from a Process Perspective*, edited by Joseph A. Bracken, 1–11. Grand Rapids: Eerdmans, 2005.
———. "Panentheism from a Process Perspective." In *Trinity in Process: A Relational Theology of God*, edited by Joseph A. Bracken and Marjorie Hewitt Suchocki, 95–113. New York: Continuum, 1997.

———. *The Triune Symbol: Persons, Process and Community*. Lanham: University Press of America, 1985.

———. (ed.). *World without End: Christian Eschatology from a Process Perspective*. Grand Rapids: Eerdmans, 2005.

Bracken, Joseph A. and Marjorie Hewitt Suchocki (eds.). *Trinity in Process: A Relational Theology of God*. New York: Continuum, 1997.

Bradnick, David. *Evil, Spirits, and Possession: An Emergent Theology of the Demonic*. Leiden: Brill, 2017.

———. Review of *Understanding Spiritual Warfare: Four Views*, edited by James K. Beilby and Paul Rhodes Eddy. *Religious Studies Review* 39.4 (2013) 240.

Bradshaw, Timothy. Review of *The Openness of God: a biblical challenge to the traditional understanding of God*, by Clark H. Pinnock, Richard Rice, John Sanders, William Hasker, and David Basinger. *Themelios* 21.3 (Apr 1996) 29.

Breuninger, Christian. "Where Angels Fear to Tread: Appraising the Current Fascination with Spiritual Warfare." *Covenant Quarterly* 53 (1995) 37–43.

Breytenbach, C. and P. L. Day. "Satan." In *Dictionary of Deities and Demons in the Bible*, edited by Karel van der Toorn, Bob Becking and Pieter W. van der Horst, 1369–80. Leiden: E. J. Brill, 1995.

Brierley, Michael W. "Naming a Quiet Revolution: The Panentheistic Turn in Modern Theology." In *In Whom We Live and Move and Have Our Being: Panentheistic Reflections on God's Presence in a Scientific World*, edited by Philip Clayton and Arthur Peacocke, 1–15. Grand Rapids: Eerdmans, 2004.

Bromiley, Geoffrey W. *Introduction to the Theology of Karl Barth*. Edinburgh: T&T Clark, 1979.

Brown, David. *Divine Humanity: Kenosis and the Construction of a Christian Theology*. Waco: Baylor University Press, 2011.

Brown, Derek R. *The God of This Age: Satan in the Churches and Letters of the Apostle Paul*. Tubingen: Mohr Siebeck, 2015.

Brueggemann, Walter. *Isaiah 40–66*. Louisville: Westminster John Knox, 1998.

Brunner, Emil. *Dogmatics. Vol.2, The Christian doctrine of creation and redemption*. Translated by Olive Wyon. London: Lutterworth, 1952.

Burkholder, Lawrence. "The Theological Foundations of Deliverance Healing." *The Conrad Grebel Review* 19.1 (2001) 38–68.

Cady, Linell E. "Extending the boundaries of theology: The writings of John B Cobb, Jr." *Religious Studies Review* 19.1 (1993) 15–17.

Caird, George B. *Principalities and Powers: A Study in Pauline Theology*. Oxford: Clarendon, 1956.

Cameron, Nigel M. de S. (ed.). *The Power and Weakness of God: Impassibility and Orthodoxy*. Edinburgh: Rutherford House, 1990.

Carr, Wesley. *Angels and principalities: the background, meaning and development of the Pauline phrase hai archai kai hai exousiai*. Cambridge: Cambridge University Press, 1981.

Carson, D.A. 'God, the Bible and Spiritual Warfare: A Review Article.' *Journal of Evangelical Theology Society* 42.2 (1999): 251–69.

Clanchy, M. T. *Abelard: A Medieval Life*. Oxford: Blackwell, 1997.

Clark, Kelly J. "Hold Not Thy Peace At My Tears: Methodological Reflections on Divine Impassibility." In *Our Knowledge of God: Essays on Natural and Philosophical Theology*, edited by Kelly J. Clark, 167–93. Dordrecht: Kluwer Academic, 1992.

Clarke, Anthony. "Introduction." In *Within the Love of God: Essays on the Doctrine of God in Honour of Paul S. Fiddes*, edited by Anthony Clarke and Andrew Moore, 1–15. Oxford: Oxford University Press, 2014.

Clarke, Anthony J. and Paul S. Fiddes. *Dissenting Spirit: A History of Regent's Park College, 1752–2017*. Centre for Baptist History and Heritage Studies. Oxford: Regent's Park College, 2017.

Clarke, Anthony and Andrew Moore (eds.). *Within the Love of God: Essays on the Doctrine of God in Honour of Paul S. Fiddes*. Oxford: Oxford University Press, 2014.

Clayton, Philip. "Panentheism in Metaphysical and Scientific Perspective." In *In Whom We Live and Move and Have Our Being: Panentheistic Reflections on God's Presence in a Scientific World*, edited by Philip Clayton and Arthur Peacocke, 73–91. Grand Rapids: Eerdmans, 2004.

———. 'The Panentheistic Turn in Christian Theology.' *Dialog* 38.4 (1999) 289–93.

Clayton, Philip and Arthur Peacocke (eds.). *In Whom We Live and Move and Have Our Being: Panentheistic Reflections on God's Presence in a Scientific World*. Grand Rapids: Eerdmans, 2004.

Coakley, Sarah. "Kenosis: Theological Meanings and Gender Connotations." In *The Work of Love: Creation as Kenosis*, edited by J. Polkinghorne, 192–210. London: SPCK, 2001.

Cobb, John B. and David R. Griffin. *Process Theology: An Introductory Exposition* Philadelphia: Westminster, 1976.

Cobb Jr, John B. and Clark H. Pinnock (eds.). *Searching for an Adequate God: A Dialogue between Process and Free Will Theism*. Grand Rapids: Eerdmans, 2000.

Collins, James M. *Exorcism and Deliverance Ministry in the Twentieth Century*. Milton Keynes, Paternoster, 2009.

Colwell, Jason. "Chaos and Providence." *International Journal for Philosophy and Religion* 48 (2000) 131–38.

Colwell, John. "The Contemporaneity of the Divine Decision: Reflections on Barth's Denial of Universalism." In *Universalism and the Doctrine of Hell*, edited by Nigel M. de S. Cameron, 139–60. Carlisle: Paternoster, 1992.

Cook, David. "Weak Church, Weak God." In *The Power & Weakness of God: Impassibility and Orthodoxy*, edited by Nigel M De S. Cameron, 69–92. Edinburgh: Rutherford House, 1990.

Cook, Robert. "Devils and Manticores: Plundering Jung for a Plausible Demonology." In *The Unseen World: Christian Reflections on Angels, Demons and the Heavenly Realm*, edited by Anthony N. S. Lane, 165–84. Grand Rapids: Baker, 1996.

Cooper, John W. *Panentheism: The Other God of the Philosophers*. Nottingham: Apollos, 2007.

Cox, Harvey G. *On Not Leaving it to the Snake*. London: SCM, 1968.

Craig, William Lane. *God, Atonement and the Death of Christ: An Exegetical, Historical and Philosophical Exploration*. Waco: Baylor University Press, 2020.

———. *God, Time and Eternity*. Dordrecht: Kluwer Academic, 2001.

———. *The Tensed Theory of Time: A Critical Examination*. Dordrecht: Kluwer Academic, 2000.

———. *The Tenseless Theory of Time: A Critical Examination*. Dordrecht: Kluwer Academic, 2000.

———. "Timelessness and Omnitemporality." In *God and Time: Four Views*, edited by Gregory E. Ganssle, 129–60. Downers Grove: Inter Varsity, 2001.

Creel, Richard E. *Divine Impassibility: An Essay in Philosophical Theology.* Eugene: Wipf and Stock, 1986.

Crisp, Oliver D. *Divinity and Humanity: The Incarnation Reconsidered.* Cambridge: Cambridge University Press, 2007.

———. *Jonathan Edwards on God and Creation.* Oxford: Oxford University Press, 2013.

Cross, F. L. and E. A. Livingstone (eds.). *Oxford Dictionary of the Christian Church.* third ed. Oxford: Oxford University Press, 1997.

Cullmann, Oscar. *Christ and Time.* rev ed. London: SCM, 1962.

———. *The State in the New Testament.* New York: Scribner, 1956.

———. "The Subjection of the Invisible Powers." In *Territorial Spirits: Practical Strategies for how to Crush the Enemy through Spiritual Warfare*, edited by C. Peter Wagner, 215-24. Shippensburg: Destiny Image, 2012.

Cuthbert, Alistair J. "Participatory and Perichoretic Doctrine of the Trinity: A Theological Account for Grounding the True Ministry of the Holy Spirit in the Life of the Local Church." *Scottish Bulletin of Evangelical Theology* 42.1 (2024) 45-59.

———. Review of *Charles Williams and C.S. Lewis: Friends In Co-Inherence*, by Paul S. Fiddes. *Pacific Journal of Theological Research* 17.1 (2022) 44-47.

———. Review of *Church Militant: Spiritual Warfare in the Anglican Charismatic Renewal*, by Graham R. Smith. *PNEUMA: The Journal of the Society for Pentecostal Studies* 40.4 (2018) 580-82.

Daunton-Fear, Andrew. *Healing in the Early Church: The Church's Ministry of Healing and Exorcism from the First to the Fifth Century.* Milton Keynes, Paternoster, 2009.

Davis, Stephen T (ed.). *Encountering Evil: Live Options in Theodicy.* Edinburgh: T&T Clark, 1981.

———. "Free Will and Evil." In *Encountering Evil: Live Options in Theodicy*, edited by Stephen T. Davis, 69-99. Edinburgh: T&T Clark, 1981.

———. *Logic and the Nature of God.* London: Macmillan, 1983.

Dawe, D. G. *The Form of a Servant: A Historical Analysis of the Kenotic Motif.* Philadelphia: Westminster, 1963.

———. "A Fresh Look at the Kenotic Christologies." *Scottish Journal of Theology* 15 (1962): 337-49.

Dawson, John. *Healing America's Wounds.* Ventura: Regal, 1994.

———. "Seventh Time Around: Breaking Through a City's Invisible Barriers to the Gospel." In *Territorial Spirits: Insights on Strategic-Level Spiritual Warfare from Nineteen Christian Leaders*, edited by C. Peter Wagner, 135-42. Chichester: Sovereign World, 1991.

Day, John. *God's Conflict with the Dragon and the Sea.* Cambridge: Cambridge University Press, 1985.

Dearman, J. Andrew. *The Book of Hosea.* Grand Rapids: Eerdmans, 2010.

Delbanco, Andrew. *The Death of Satan: How Americans Have Lost the Sense of Evil.* New York: Farrar, Straus and Giroux, 1995.

Duffey, John M. *Lessons Learned: The Anneliese Michel Exorcism: The Implementation of a Safe and Thorough Examination, Determination, and Exorcism of Demonic Possession.* Eugene: Wipf and Stock, 2011.

Eddy, Paul R. and James Beilby. "The Atonement: *An Introduction.*" In *The Nature of the Atonement: Four Views*, edited by James Beilby and Paul R. Eddy, 9–21. Downers Grove: IVP Academic, 2006.

———. "Introduction." In *Understanding Spiritual Warfare: Four Views*, edited by James K. Beilby and Paul Rhodes Eddy, 1–45. Grand Rapids: Baker Academic, 2012.

Ediger, Gerald. "Strategic-Level Spiritual Warfare in Historical Retrospect." *Direction: A Mennonite Brethren Forum* 29.2 (2000) 125–41.

Edwards, Denis. "A Relational and Evolving Universe Unfolding Within the Dynamism of the Divine Communion." In *In Whom We Live and Move and Have Our Being: Panentheistic Reflections on God's Presence in a Scientific World*, edited by Philip Clayton and Arthur Peacocke, 199–210. Grand Rapids: Eerdmans, 2004.

Edwards, Jonathan. *The Works of Jonathan Edwards, Vol. 8: Ethical Writings*, edited by Paul Ramsey. New Haven: Yale University Press, 1989.

Evans, G. R. *Anselm and a New Generation*. Oxford: Clarendon, 1980.

Evans, C. Stephen (ed.). *Exploring Kenotic Christology: The Self-Emptying of God*. Oxford: Oxford University Press, 2006.

———. "Kenotic Christology and the Nature of God." In *Exploring Kenotic Christology: The Self-Emptying of God,* edited by C. Stephen Evans, 190–217. Oxford: Oxford University Press, 2006.

Faber, Ronald. "Introduction to Process Theology." In *Models of God and Alternative Ultimate Realities*, edited by Jeanine Diller and Asa Kasher, 311–21. Netherlands: Springer, 2013.

Faricy S.J., Robert. "Deliverance from Evil: Private Exorcism." In *Deliverance Prayer*, edited by Matthew & Dennis Linn, 72–85. New York: Paulist, 1981.

Fee, Gordon D. "The New Testament and Kenosis Christology." In *Exploring Kenotic Christology: The Self-Emptying of God,* edited by C. Stephen Evans, 25–44. Oxford: Oxford University Press, 2006.

Feenstra, Ronald J. "A Kenotic Christological Method for Understanding the Divine Attributes." In *Exploring Kenotic Christology: The Self-Emptying of God*, edited by C. Stephen Evans, 139–64. Oxford: Oxford University Press, 2006.

Ferdinando, Keith. *The Battle is God's*. Nigeria: Africa Christian, 2012.

———. *The Message of Spiritual Warfare*. London: Inter-Varsity, 2016.

———. "Screwtape Revisited: Demonology Western, African and Biblical." In *The Unseen World: Christian Reflections on Angels, Demons and the Heavenly Realm*, edited by Anthony N. S. Lane, 103–32. Grand Rapids: Baker, 1996.

———. *The Triumph of Christ in African Perspective: A Study of Demonology and Redemption in the African Context*. Carlisle: Paternoster, 1999.

Ferguson, Everett. *Demonology of the Early Christian World*. New York: Edwin Mellen, 1984.

Fiddes, Paul S. "Acceptance and Resistance in a Theology of Death." *Modern Believing* 56.2 (2015) 223–36.

———. "Ambiguities of the Future: Theological Hints in the Novels of Patrick White." *Pacifica* 23.3 (2010) 281–98.

———. "Ancient and Modern Wisdom: The Intersection of Clinical and Theological Understanding of Health." In *Wisdom, Science and the Scriptures: Essays in Honour of Ernest Lucas*, edited by Stephen Finamore and John Weaver, 75–98. Centre for Baptist History and Heritage and Bristol Baptist College, 2012.

———. "The Atonement and the Trinity." In *The Forgotten Trinity 3: A Selection of Papers Presented to the BCC Study Commission on Trinitarian Doctrine Today*, edited by Alasdair I. C. Heron, 103–22. London: British Council of Churches, 1991.

———. "Atonement, Forgiveness and the Nature of God." In *Atonement. Proceedings of the Second Symposium of the Russian Society of Christian Philosophers*, edited by Mel Stewart, 198–211. St. Petersburg: International Scholars, 1999.

———. "Atonement in the Life of the Church." In *Care Împarte Drept Cuvântul Adevărului: Volum Omagial Ioan Bunaciu*, edited by Otniel Bunaciu, Radu Gheorghița, and Emil Bartoș, 195–208. Oradea: Editura Reformatio, 2005.

———. "Attending to the Sublime and the Beautiful: Theological Reflection on Iris Murdoch and Emmanuel Levinas." In *Theology of Beauty*, edited by Alexei Bodrov and Michael Tolstoluzhenko, 70–89. Moscow: St Andrew's, 2013.

———. "Authority in Pastor-People Relationships." In *Baptist Faith and Witness, The Papers of the Study and Research Division of the Baptist World Alliance 1990–95*, edited by William H. Brackney and T.A. Cupit, 59–63. Samford: Samford University Press, 1995.

———. "Baptism and Creation." In *Reflections on the Water: Understanding God and the World Through the Baptism of Believers*. Regent's Study Guides 4, edited by Paul S. Fiddes, 47–67. Oxford: Regents Park College with Marcon: Smyth & Helwys, 1996.

———. "Baptism and Membership of the Body of Christ: A Theological and Ecumenical Conundrum." In *Gemeinschaft der Kirchen und gesellschaftliche Verantwortung: die Würde des Anderen und das Recht anders zu denken; Festschrift für Professor Dr. Erich Geldbach*, edited by Lena Lybæk et al, 83–93. Oekumenische Studien 30: LIT Verlag Berlin-Hamburg-Münster, 2004.

———. "Baptism and the Process of Christian Initiation." *Ecumenical Review* 54.1 (2002) 48–65.

———. "Baptism and the Process of Initiation." In *Dimensions of Baptism: Biblical and Theological Studies*, edited by Stanley E. Porter and Anthony R. Cross, 280–303. London: Sheffield Academic, 2002.

———. "Baptism of Believers." In *Baptism Today: Understanding, Practice, Ecumenical Implications, edited by* Thomas F. Best, 73–80. Collegeville: Liturgical, 2008.

———. "Baptist Concepts of the Church and their Antecedents." In *The Oxford Handbook of Ecclesiology*, edited by Paul Avis, 293–315. Oxford: Oxford University Press, 2018.

———. "Baptist Ecclesiology." In *T & T Clark Handbook of Ecclesiology*, edited by Kimlyn J. Bender and D. Stephen Long, 225–40. London: T & T Clark, 2020.

———. "Baptist Ecclesiology: A Response to David Carter's Article Review of *Tracks and Traces*." *Ecclesiology* 1.3 (2005) 87–100.

———. "Baptist Theology." in *The Cambridge Dictionary of Christian Theology*, edited by David Fergusson, Karen Kilby, Ian A. McFarland, and Iain Torrance, 54–56. Cambridge: Cambridge University Press, 2010.

———. "Baptist Union of Great Britain." In *The Oxford Dictionary of the Christian Church*, edited by Andrew Louth. Oxford: Oxford University Press, 2022. Accessed February 23, 2025. https://www-oxfordreference-com.ezproxy.st-andrews.ac.uk/view/10.1093/acref/9780199642465.001.0001/acref-9780199642465/

———. "Baptist World Alliance." In *The Oxford Dictionary of the Christian Church*, edited by Andrew Louth. Oxford: Oxford University Press, 2022. Accessed February 23, 2025. https://www-oxfordreference-com.ezproxy.st-.andrews.ac.uk/view/10.1093/acref/9780199642465.001.0001/acref-9780199642465/

BIBLIOGRAPHY 189

———. "Baptists." In *The Oxford Dictionary of the Christian Church*, edited by Andrew Louth. Oxford: Oxford University Press, 2022. Accessed February 23, 2025. https://www-oxfordreference-com.ezproxy.st-andrews.ac.uk/view/10.1093/acref/9780199642465.001.0001/acref-9780199642465/

———. "Baptists and the Leuenberg Documents on Baptism." In *Dialog zwischen der Europäischen Baptistischen Föderation und der Gemeinschaft Evangelischer Kirchen in Europa zur Lehre und Praxis der Taufe*, edited by Wilhelm Hüffmeier and Tony Peck, 189–99. Frankfurt am Main: Verlag Otto Lembech, 2005.

———. "Baptists and Theological Education: A Vision for the Twenty-First Century." In *Baptist Identity into the 21stCentury: Essays in Honour of Ken Manley*, edited by Frank Rees, 183–98. Melbourne: Whitley College, 2016.

———. "Baptists and 1662: The Effect of the Act of Uniformity on Baptists and its Ecumenical Significance for Baptists Today." *Ecclesiology* 9.2 (2013) 183–204.

———. "Baptists in the Age of Brahms' *German Requiem*." *Baptist Quarterly* (2022) 1–17. Accessed February 23, 2025. doi: 10.1080/0005576X.2021.1904725.

———. "'Believer's Baptism. An act of inclusion or exclusion?' Signposts for a New Century." In *Exploring Baptist Distinctives*, 1–20. Hertfordshire Baptist Association, 1999.

———. (ed.). *Believing and Being Baptized: Baptism, so-called re-baptism, and children in the church*. The Faith and Unity Executive Committee. Doctrine and Worship Committee. London: Baptist Union, 1996.

———. "The Body as Site of Continuity and Change." In *New Topics in Feminist Philosophy of Religion: Contestations and Transcendence Incarnate*, edited by Pamela Sue Anderson, 261–78. Dordrecht: Springer, 2010.

———. "Can God Face Up to Evil?" Accessed February 23, 2025, (https://closertotruth.com/video/fidpa-001/?referrer=8043)

———. "The Canon as Space and Place." In *Die Einheit der Schrift und die Vielfalt des Kanons/The Unity of Scripture and the Diversity of the Canon. Beihefte zur Zeitschrift für die neutestamentliche Wissenschaft und die Kunde der älteren Kirche*, edited by John Barton and Michael Wolter, 127–49. Bd. 118, Berlin: W. de Gruyter, 2003.

———. *Charismatic Renewal: A Baptist View*. London: Baptist, 1980.

———. *Charles Williams and C.S. Lewis: Friends in Co-Inherence*. Oxford: Oxford University Press, 2021.

———. "Charles Williams and the Problem of Evil." In *Essays and Memoirs from the Oxford C. S. Lewis Society*, edited by Judith Wolfe and Brendan Wolfe, 65–88. New York: Oxford University Press, 2015.[1]

———. "Christian Doctrine and Free Church Ecclesiology: Recent Developments among Baptists in the Southern United States." *Ecclesiology* 7.2 (2011) 195–219.

———. "Christianity, Atonement and Evil." In *The Cambridge Companion to the Problem of Evil*, edited by Paul Mosser and Chad Meister, 210–29. Cambridge: Cambridge University Press, 2017.

———. "Christianity, Culture and Education: A Baptist Perspective." In *The Scholarly Vocation and the Baptist Academy: Essays on the Future of Baptist Higher* Education, edited by R. Ward and D. Gushee, 1–25. Macon: Mercer University Press, 2008.

---

1. Contains full and developed content of previous essay: Paul S. Fiddes, "Charles Williams and the Problem of Evil," in *Learning from Beauty. Baptist Reflections on Christianity and the Arts*, eds. D. Rayburn, D. Kari and D. Gwaltney. (Lampeter: Edwin Mellen, 1997), 89–116.

———. "The Church and Salvation: A Comparison of Orthodox and Baptist Thinking." In *Ecumenism and History: Studies in Honour of John H. Y. Briggs*, edited by Anthony R. Cross, 120–48. Carlisle: Paternoster, 2002.

———. "Church and Sect: Cross-currents in Early Baptist Life." In *Exploring Baptist Origins*, edited by Anthony R. Cross and Nicholas J. Wood, 33–60. Centre for Baptist History and Heritage Studies Volume 1. Oxford: Regent's Park College, 2010.

———. "The Church Local and Universal: Catholic and Baptist Perspectives on Koinonia Ecclesiology." In *Revisioning, Renewing, Rediscovering the Triune Center: Essays in Honor of Stanley J. Grenz*, edited by Derek J. Tidball, Brian S. Harris and Jason S. Sexton, 97–120. Eugene: Cascade, 2014.

———. "Church, Trinity and Covenant: An Ecclesiology of Participation." In *Gemeinschaft am Evangelium: Festschrift für Wiard Popkes zum 60. Geburtstag*, edited by Paul S. Fiddes, Edwin Brandt and Joachim Molthagen, 37–54. Leipzig: Evangelische Verlagsanstalt, 1996.

———. "The Church's Ecumenical Calling. A Challenge to Baptists and Pentecostals." In *The Many Faces of Global Pentecostalism*, edited by Harold D. Hunter and Neil Ormerod, 36–61. Cleveland: CPT, 2013.

———. "Concept, Image and Story in Systematic Theology." *International Journal of Systematic Theology* 11.1 (2009) 3–23.

———. "A Conversation in Context: An Introduction to the Report, The Word of God in the Life of the Church." *American Baptist Quarterly*, 31.1 (2012) 7–27.

———. (Co-Chair). *Conversations Around the World: 2000–2005: Report of the International Conversations Between the Anglican Communion* and the *Baptist World Alliance*. London: Anglican Communion Office, 2005.

———. "Covenant." In *The Oxford Dictionary of the Christian Church*, edited by Andrew Louth. Oxford: Oxford University Press, 2022. Accessed February 23, 2025. https://www-oxfordreference-com.ezproxy.st-andrews.ac.uk/view/10.1093/acref/9780199642465.001.0001/acref-9780199642465/

———. "Covenant and Participation: A Personal Review of the Essays." *Perspectives in Religious Studies* 44.1 (2017) 119–37.

———. "Covenant and the Inheritance of Separatism." In *The Fourth Strand of the Reformation: The Covenant Ecclesiology of Anabaptists, English Separatists, and Early General Baptists*, edited by Paul S. Fiddes, William H. Brackney and Malcolm B. Yarnell III, 63–91. Centre for Baptist History and Heritage Studies, Volume 17. Oxford: Regent's Park College, 2018.

———. "Covenant—Old and New." In *Bound to Love: The Covenant Basis of Baptist Life and Mission*, 9–23. Baptist Union, 1985.

———. "Creation in Freedom and Love." In *Theology of Freedom. Religious and Anthropological Foundations of Freedom in a Global Context. Essays in Honour of Alexei Bodro*, edited by Irina Yazykova, 26–42. Moscow: St Andrews, 2020.

———. "Creation Out of Love." In *The Work of Love: Creation as Kenosis*, edited by John Polkinghorne, 167–91. London: SPCK, 2001.

———. *The Creative Suffering of God*. Oxford: Clarendon, 1988.

———. "The Cross of Hosea Revisited: The Meaning of Suffering in the Book of Hosea." *Review & Expositor* 90 (Spring 1993) 175–90.

———. "C. S. Lewis the Myth-Maker." In *A Christian for All Christians: Essays in Honour of C. S. Lewis*, edited by Andrew Walker and James Patrick, 132–55. London: Hodder & Stoughton, 1991.

———. "Daniel Turner and a Theology of the Church Universal." In *Pulpit and People: Studies in Eighteenth Century Baptist Life and Thought*, edited by John H. Y. Briggs, 112–27. Milton Keynes: Paternoster, 2009.

———. "The Demand Beyond the Commands." In *Proclaiming Baptist Vision: The Bible*, edited by Walter B. Shurden, 51–61. Macon: Smyth and Helwys, 1994.

———. "Do Heaven and Hell Really Exist?" Accessed February 23, 2025, (https://closertotruth.com/video/fidpa-002/?referrer=8359)

———. (ed.). *Doing Theology in Baptist Way*. Oxford: Whitley, 2000.

———. "Dual Citizenship in Athens and Jerusalem: The Place of the Christian Scholar in the Life of the Church." In *Questions of Identity: Studies in Honour of Brian Haymes*, edited by A. R. Cross and R. Gouldbourne, 119–40. Centre for Baptist History and Heritage Studies Volume 6. Oxford: Regent's Park College, 2011.

———. "Dystopia, Utopia and the Millennium: Competing Images of Presence in an Anxious World." *Perspectives in Religious Studies* 43.1 (2016) 7–21.

———. "Ecclesiology and Ethnography: one world revisited," *Journal Teologic*, 15.1 (2016) 5–35.

———. "Ecclesiology and Ethnography: Two Disciplines, Two Worlds?" In *Perspectives on Ecclesiology and Ethnography*, edited by Pete Ward, 13–35. Grand Rapids: Eerdmans, 2012.

———. "An Ecclesiology of an Undivided Christ." In *Worship, Tradition, and Engagement: Essays in Honor of Timothy George*, edited by David S. Dockery, James Earl Massey and Robert Smith Jnr, 200–216. Eugene: Pickwick, 2018.

———. "Ecumenical Relations and the Creation of Liturgy." In *Reconciling Rites: Essays in Honour of Myra N. Blyth*, edited by Andy Goodliff, Anthony Clarke and Beth Allison-Glenny, 146–69. Oxford: Regents Park College, Centre for Baptist Studies, 2020.

———. *The Escape and the City. Old Testament Study. Baptist Union Christian Training Programme*. London: Baptist Union, 1974.

———. "*Ex Opere Operato*: Rethinking a Historic Baptist Rejection." In *Baptist Sacramentalism 2*. Studies in Baptist History and Thought Volume 25, edited by Anthony R. Cross and Philip E. Thompson, 219–38. Milton Keynes: Paternoster, 2008.

———. "Facing the End: The Apocalyptic Experience in Some Modern Novels." In *Called To One Hope: Perspectives on the Life to Come*, edited by John Colwell, 191–209. Carlisle: Paternoster, 2000.

———. "Faith and Baptism in the New Testament and Christian Doctrine." In *Dialog zwischen der Europäischen Baptistischen Föderation und der Gemeinschaft Evangelischer Kirchen in Europa zur Lehre und Praxis der Taufe*, edited by Wilhelm Hüffmeier and Tony Peck, 134–45. Frankfurt am Main: Verlag Otto Lembech, 2005.

———. (ed.). *Faith in the Centre: Christianity and Culture*. Macon: Smyth & Helwys, 2001.

———. "Father, Son, and Holy Spirit": The Triune Creator in Hymn and Theology." In *Gathering Disciples. Essays in Honour of Christopher J. Ellis*, edited by Myra Blyth and Andy Goodliff, 204–20. Eugene: Wipf & Stock, 2017.

———. "'For the Dance all Things Were Made:' The Great Dance in C.S. Lewis' Perelandra." In *C. S. Lewis's Perelandra: Reshaping the Image of the Cosmos*, edited by Judith Wolfe and Brendan Wolfe, 33–49. Kent: Kent State University Press, 2013.

———. "Foreword" to William H. Brackney, *The Early English General Baptists and Their Theological Formation*. Oxford: Regent's Park College, 2017.

———. "Forgiveness, Empathy and Vulnerability: An Unfinished Conversation with Pamela Sue Anderson." *Angelaki* 25.1–2 (2020) 109–25.

———. (ed.). *Forms of Ministry among Baptists: Towards and Understanding of Spiritual Leadership*. The Faith and Unity Executive Committee. Doctrine and Worship Committee. London: Baptist Union, 1994.

———. "A Fourth Strand of the Reformation. Editorial." *Ecclesiology* 13 (2017) 153–59.

———. *Freedom and Limit: A Dialogue between Literature and Christian Doctrine*. Basingstoke Macon: Macmillan, 1991.

———. "Glaube und Taufe im Neuen Testament und in christlicher Lebe." In *Wer Glaubt Und Getauft Wird*, edited by Uwe Swarat, 139–48. Kassel: Oncken, 2010.

———. "G. M. Hopkins." In *The Blackwell Companion to the Bible in English Literature*, edited by R. Lemon and C. Rowland, 563–76. Oxford: Wiley-Blackwell, 2009.

———. "God and History." *Baptist Quarterly* 30 (1983) 74–90.

———. "God and Story in the Church and in Doctrine. Reflections on the Ecclesial Basis of Method in Theology." *Ecclesial Practices* 2 (2015) 5–22.

———. "God is love: but is love God? Towards a Theology of Love as Knowledge." In *Love as Common Ground. Essays in Love in Religion*, edited by Paul S. Fiddes, 1–30. Lanham: Lexington, 2021.

———. "The Holocaust and Divine Suffering." In *Holocaust Theology: A Reader*, edited by Dan Cohn-Sherbok, 127–29. New York: New York University Press, 2002.

———. "How does God Relate to the World?" Accessed February 23, 2025, (https://closertotruth.com/video/fidpa-003/?referrer=8317)

———. "'I would as lief be a Brownist. . .' Puritanism and Spirituality in Shakespeare's *Twelfth Night*." In *Christian Shakespeare: Question Mark. A Collection of Essays on Shakespeare in his Christian Context*, edited by Michael Scott and Michael J. Collins, 15–34. Washington: Georgetown University Press, 2022.

———. "Imagination, Theology, and Literature." *Theology in Scotland*, 29.1 (2022) 7–22.

———. "Immortality and Personal Consciousness?" Accessed February 23, 2025, (https://closertotruth.com/video/fidpa-004/?referrer=8427)

———. "Internal and External Powers. A Response to 'Journeying in Hope; Paul's Letter to the Romans and John Bunyan's *The Pilgrim's Progress* and *The Holy War* in Conversation,' by Scott C. Ryan." *American Baptist Quarterly* 33.3–4 (2014) 319–25.

———. "Introduction: A Fourth Strand?" In *The Fourth Strand of the Reformation: The Covenant Ecclesiology of Anabaptists, English Sepratists, and Early General Baptists*, Centre for Baptist History and Heritage Studies, Vol. 17, edited by Paul S. Fiddes, William H. Brackney and Malcolm B. Yarnell III, 1–14. Oxford: Regent's Park College, 2018.

———. "Introduction: A Theology of Public Prayer." In *Prayers of the People*, edited by Karen E. Smith and Simon P. Woodman, 1–16. Oxford: Regents's Park College, 2011.

———. "Introduction: David Jones: Christian Traveller on the Paths of Modernity." In *David Jones: A Christian Modernist? Approaches to His Art, Poetry and Cultural Theory*. Studies in Religion and the Arts, edited by Paul S. Fiddes, Jamie Callison, Anna Johnson and Erik Tonning, 1–13. Leiden: Brill, 2018.

———. "Introduction: Love as Common Ground." In *Love as Common Ground. Essays in Love in Religion*, edited by Paul S. Fiddes, vii–xvii. Lanham: Lexington, 2021.

———. "Introduction: The Novel and the Spiritual Journey Today." In *The Novel, Spirituality and Modern Culture. Eight Novelists Write about their Craft and their Context*, edited by Paul S. Fiddes, 1–21. Cardiff: University of Wales Press, 2000.

———. *Iris Murdoch and the Others: A Writer in Dialogue with Theology*. London: T&T Clark, 2022.

———. "Is God All-Knowing?" Accessed February 23, 2025, (https://closertotruth.com/video/fidpa-005/?referrer=8283)

———. "Is God All-Powerful?" Accessed February 23, 2025, (https://closertotruth.com/video/fidpa-006/?referrer=8285)

———. "Is the Future Open?" Accessed February 23, 2025, (https://closertotruth.com/video/fidpa-005/?referrer=8319)

———. "Is this the Promised End? Shakespearean Tragedy and a Christian Tragic Theology for Today." Paper presented at the Institute for Theology, Imagination & the Arts Seminar, St Mary's School of Divinity, University of St Andrews, St Andrews, Fife, 15 April 2016.

———. "'Is this the Promised End?' Shakespearean Tragedy and Christian Tragic Theology for Today." In *The Transformation of Tragedy. Christian Influence from Early to Modern*, edited by Fionnuala O'Neill Tonning, Erik Tonning and Jolyon Mitchell, 219–42. Studies in Theology and the Arts 16. Leiden: Brill, 2019.

———. "A Journey of Discovery: Christian Initiation, Archbishop Rowan Williams and Ecumenism." *Ecclesiology* 8.2 (2012) 153–61.

———. "Koinonia Ecclesiology among Roman Catholics and Baptists: Hermeneutics, Perichoresis and Personhood." *Pages* (The Journal of St. Andrew's Biblical Theological Institute) 18/2 (2014) 250–69.

———. "'*Koinonia*: The Church in and for the World.' Comment on the Final Part of *The Church—Towards a Common Vision* (Faith and Order Paper 214)." In *Baptist Faith and Witness, Book 5*, edited by Eron Henry, 37–49. Papers of the Commission on Mission, Evangelism and Theological Reflection of the Baptist World Alliance 2010–2015. Mclean: BWA, 2016.

———. "The Late-Modern Reversal of Spirit and Letter: Derrida, Augustine and Film." In *The Spirit and the Letter: A Tradition and a Reversal*, edited by Günter Badder and Paul S. Fiddes, 105–30. London: Bloomsbury, 2013.

———. "Law and Divine Mercy in Shakespeare's Religious Imagination: *Measure for Measure* and *The Merchant of Venice*." In *Poetry and the Religious Imagination*, edited by Francesca B. Knox and David Lonsdale, 109–28. Aldershot: Ashgate: 2015.

———. *A Leading Question: The Structure and Authority of Leadership in the Local Church*. London: Baptist, 1986.

———. "Learning from Others: Baptists and Receptive Ecumenism." *Louvain Studies* 33 (2008) 54–75.

———. "Liturgy, Shakespeare, and Defamiliarisation: A Contribution to the Ethnography of Worship." In *Being Attentive: Explorations in Practical Theology in Honour of Robert Ellis*, edited by Anthony Clarke, 209–32. Oxford: Regent's Park College, 2021.

———. (ed.). *Love as Common Ground. Essays on Love in Religion*. Lanham: Lexington, 2021.

———. "The Making of a Christian Mind." In *Faith in the Centre: Christianity and Culture*, edited by Paul S. Fiddes, 1–24. Macon: Smyth & Helwys, 2001.

———. "Mary in the Theology of Karl Barth." In *Mary in Doctrine and Devotion*, edited by Alberic Stacpoole, 111–26. Blackrock: Columba, 1990.

———. "Memory, Forgetting and the Problem of Forgiveness: Reflecting on Volf, Derrida and Ricoeur." In *Forgiving and Forgetting. At the Margins of Soteriology.* Series: *Religion in Philosophy and Theology*, edited by Johannes Zacchuber and Hartmut Von Sass, 117–33. Tübingen: Mohr Siebeck, 2015.

———. "Millennium and Utopia: Images of a Fuller Presence." In *Apocalyptic in History and Tradition*, edited by C. Rowland and J. Barton, 7–25. Sheffield: Sheffield Academic, 2002.

———. "Ministry and Ordination." *The Fraternal: Journal of the Baptist Ministers' Fellowship*, 211 (1985) 11–19.

———. "Ministry and Poetry." In *Ministry in Conversation: Essays in Honour of Paul Goodliff*, edited by Andy Goodliff and John Colwell, 33–55. Eugene: Wipf & Stock, 2022.

———. *More Things in Heaven and Earth: Shakespeare, Theology, and the Interplay of Texts.* Charlottesville: University of Virginia Press, 2022.

———. "Murdoch, Derrida and *The Black Prince*." In *Iris Murdoch: Texts and Contexts*, edited by Anne Rowe and Avril Horner, 91–109. Basingstoke: Palgrave Macmillan, 2012.

———. (ed.). *The Nature of the Assembly and the Council of the Baptist Union of Great Britain.* The Faith and Unity Executive Committee. Doctrine and Worship Committee. London: Baptist Union, 1994.

———. "Not Anarchy but Covenant: A Nonconformist Response to Matthew Arnold's view of Religion and Culture." In *Theology and Human Flourishing: Essays in Honor of Timothy J. Gorringe*, edited by Mike Higton, Jeremy Law and Christopher Rowland, 141–56. Eugene: Cascade, 2011.

———. (ed.). *The Novel, Spirituality and Modern Culture. Eight Novelists Write about their Craft and their Context.* Cardiff: University of Wales Press, 2000.

———. "On God the Incomparable: Thinking about God with John Macquarrie." In *In Search of Humanity and Deity: A Celebration of John Macquarrie's Theology*, edited by Robert Morgan, 179–99. London: SCM, 2006.

———. "On Theology." In *The Cambridge Companion to C. S. Lewis*, edited by R. MacSwain and M. Ward, 89–104. Cambridge: Cambridge University Press, 2010.

———. "One Baptism: A Baptist Contribution." In *Pushing at the Boundaries of Unity: Anglicans and Baptists in Conversation*, Council of Christian Unity/Baptist Union of Great Britain, 31–57. London: Church House, 2005.

———. "Old Testament Principles of Wholeness." In *Iosif Ton—orizonturi noi in spiritualitate si slujire*, edited by Sorin Sabou and Dorothy Ghitea, 35–48. Oradea: Editura Cartea Crestina, 2004.

———. *Participating in God: A Pastoral Doctrine of the Trinity.* London: Darton, Longman, & Todd, 2000.

———. "Participating in the Trinity." *Perspectives in Religious Studies* 33.3 (2006) 375–91.

———. "The Passion Story in Literature." In *The Oxford Handbook of English Literature and Theology*, edited by Andrew W. Hass, David Jasper and Elisabeth Jay, 742–59. Oxford: Oxford University Press, 2007.

———. *Past Event and Present Salvation: The Christian Idea of Atonement*. London: Darton, Longman, & Todd, 1989.

———. "Patterns of hope and images of eternity: listening to Shakespeare, Blake and T.S. Eliot." In *Art, Imagination and Christian Hope*, edited by Trevor Hart, Jeremy Begbie and Gavin Hopps, 31–50. Farnham: Ashgate, 2012.

———. "Pentecost. The Rhythm of God on Monday." In *Rhythms of Faithfulness. Essays in Honour of John E. Colwell*, edited by Andy Goodliff and Paul W. Goodliff, 194–210. Eugene: Pickwick, 2018.

———. "The Place of Christian Theology in the Modern University." *Baptist Quarterly* 42 (Apr 2007) 71–88.

———. "Preaching Forgiveness." *Preaching Today* 36.1 (1993) 11–15.

———. "Preface." In *Covenant and Church for Rough Sleepers. A Baptist Ecclesiology in Conversation with the Trinitarian Pastoral Theology of Paul S. Fiddes*, by Daniel Sutcliffe-Pratt, 1–4. Centre for Baptist History and Heritage Studies, Occasional Papers 14. Oxford: Regent's Park College, 2017.

———. "Preface." In *Tradition and the Baptist Academy*, edited by Roger A. Ward and Philip E. Thompson, xi–xviii. Studies in Baptist History and Thought 31. Milton Keynes: Paternoster, 2011.

———. "Preface: Poetry and War." In *Step Into Your Place. The First World War and Baptist Life and Thought*. Centre for Baptist History and Heritage Studies Volume 9, edited by Larry Kreitzer, 1–22. Oxford: Regent's Park College, 2014.

———. "Process Theology." In *The Blackwell Encyclopaedia of Modern Christian Thought*, edited by Alister E. McGrath, 472–76. Oxford: Blackwell, 1993.

———. "Process Theology." In *Microsoft Encarta Electronic Encyclopaedia*. Microsoft/Websters, 1996.

———. *The Promised End: Eschatology in Theology and Literature*. Oxford: Blackwell, 2000.

———. "*The Promised End*: Response to a Review by Jennifer L. Geddes." *Conversations in Religion and Theology* 2.2 (2004) 191–95.

———. "Prophecy, Corporate Personality, and Suffering: Some Themes and Methods in Baptist Old Testament Scholarship." In *The "Plainly Revealed" Word of God? Baptist Hermeneutics in Theory and Practice*, edited by Helen Dare and Simon Woodman, 72–94. Macon: Mercer University Press, 2011.

———. "The quest for a place which is not-a-place: the hiddenness of God and the presence of God." In *Silence and the Word: Negative Theology and Incarnation*, edited by O. Davies and D. Turner, 35–60. Cambridge: Cambridge University Press, 2002.

———. "Question and Answer Session." Institute for Theology, Imagination & the Arts Seminar, St Mary's School of Divinity, University of St Andrews, St Andrews, Fife, 15 April 2016.

———. "Receiving One Another: The History and Theology of the Church Covenant, 1780." In *A Protestant Catholic Church of Christ: Essays on the History and Life of New Road Baptist Church, Oxford*, edited by Rosie Chadwick, 65–105. Oxford: New Road Baptist Church, 2003.

———. (ed.). *Reflections on the Water: Understanding God and the World Through the Baptism of Believers*. Regent's Study Guides 4. Oxford: Regents Park College with Marcon: Smyth & Helwys, 1996.

———. "Regent's Park College, Oxford: A Typology of Baptist Theological Education." *American Baptist Quarterly* 18.2 (1999): 106–17

———. "Rejoinder Comments and Clarification." In *Two Views on the Doctrine of the Trinity*, edited by Jason Sexton, 204–6. Grand Rapids: Zondervan, 2014.

———. "Relational Trinity: Radical Perspective." In *Two Views on the Doctrine of the Trinity*, edited by Jason Sexton, 159–85. Grand Rapids: Zondervan, 2014.

———. "Religious Rights and Freedoms within the Baptist Tradition: Theological Foundations." In *Crossing Baptist Boundaries. A Festschrift in Honor of William Henry Brackney*, edited by Erich Geldbach, 36–55. Macon: Mercer University Press, 2019.

———. (ed.). "Response from the Baptist World Alliance to A Common Word Between Us and You. 26 December, 2008." In *A Common Word Between Us and You*. 5th Anniversary Edition. MABDA Monograph Series 20, 213–34. Amman: MABDA, 2012.

———. "A Response to Andrew Moore." Paper presented at the one-day colloquium on the Doctrine of God in conversation with Paul Fiddes, St Mary's School of Divinity, University of St Andrews, St Andrews, Fife, 16 April 2016.

———. "A Response to John Webster." Paper presented at the one-day colloquium on the Doctrine of God in conversation with Paul Fiddes, St Mary's School of Divinity, University of St Andrews, St Andrews, Fife, 16 April 2016.

———. "Response to Paul D. Molnar." In *Two Views on the Doctrine of the Trinity*, edited by Jason Sexton, 104–8. Grand Rapids: Zondervan, 2014.

———. "A Response to Stephen R. Holmes." Paper presented at the one-day colloquium on the Doctrine of God in conversation with Paul Fiddes, St Mary's School of Divinity, University of St Andrews, St Andrews, Fife, 16 April 2016.

———. "Restorative Justice and the Theological Dynamic of Forgiveness." *Oxford Journal of Law and Religion* (2015) 1–12.[2]

———. Review of *Christology in Conflict. The Identity of a Saviour in Rahner and Barth*, by Bruce Marshall. *Journal of Theological Studies* 40.2 (1989) 700–703.

———. Review of *Coleridge as Poet and Religious Thinker*, by David Jasper. *The Modern Churchman* 28.3 (1986) 56

———. Review of *Eberhard Jüngel. An Introduction to his Thought*, by John Webster. *Journal of Theological Studies* 38.1 (1987) 265–69.

———. Review of *Faith, Theology and Imagination* by John McIntyre. *Modern Churchman* 30.2 (1988) 58–59.

———. Review of *God in Creation. An Ecological Doctrine of Creation*, by Jürgen Moltmann. *Journal of Theological Studies* 38.1 (1987) 262–65.

———. Review of *God, Sexuality and the Self: An Essay 'On the Trinity'*, by Sarah Coakley. *Ecclesial Practices* 3.1 (2016) 142–46.

———. Review of *How to Read Karl Barth: The Shape of His Theology* by George Hunsinger. *The Expository Times* 103.8 (1992) 248–49.

———. Review of *Karl Barth: A Theological Legacy* by Eberhard Jüngel. *Journal of Theological Studies* 40.2 (1989) 696–99.

———. Review of *Karl Barth: Centenary Essays* by S. W. Sykes (ed.). *Journal of Theological Studies* 42.2 (1991) 790–93.

---

2. Also listed as Paul S. Fiddes, "Restorative Justice and the Theological Dynamic of Forgiveness," *Oxford Journal of Law and Religion*, 5/1 (2016) 54–65.

———. Review of *Material Eucharist*, by David Grumett. *Ecclesiology* 13.3 (2017) 387–92.

———. Review of *Persuade us to Rejoice. The Liberating Power of Fiction*, by Robert McAfee Brown. *Literature and Theology* 9.1 (1995) 110–11.

———. Review of *T&T Clark Companion to Nonconformity*, edited by Robert Pope. *Ecclesiology* 13 (2017) 113–17.

———. Review of *The Critical Spirit and the Will to Believe* by David Jasper and T.R. Wright (eds.). *The Modern Churchman* 33.4 (1992) 52–54.

———. Review of *The Glory of the Lord VII. Theology: The New Covenant*, by Hans Urs Von Balthasar. *The Expository Times* 102.11 (1991) 349–50.

———. Review of *The New Oxford Book of Christian Verse*, edited by Donald Davie. *The Modern Churchman* 25.2 (1982) 61–62.

———. Review of *The New Testament and the Literary Imagination*, by David Jasper. *Literature and Theology* 3.2 (1989) 254–56.

———. "The Root of Religious Freedom: Interpreting Some Muslim and Christian Sacred Texts." *Oxford Journal of Law and Religion* (2012) 169–84.

———. "Sacraments in a Virtual World: A Baptist Approach." In *Baptist Sacramentalism 3*, edited by Anthony R. Cross and Philip E. Thompson, 81–100. Eugene: Pickwick, 2020.

———. "Sacraments in a Virtual World?" *The Kate Boardman Blog*. Accessed May 25, 2017. http:// kateboardman.me.uk/blog/wp-content/uploads/2011/04/virtual-communion.doc.

———. "The Sacramental Modernism of David Jones and the World as Text." In *David Jones. The Furrowed Line*, edited by Rebecca White, 51–73. Oxford: Fellowship of St Alban and St Sergius, 2014.[3]

———. "A Sacramental World: Refiguring the Sacred and the Secular in David Jasper's 'Sacred' Trilogy." In *Sacred Modes of Being in a Postsecular World*, edited by Andrew Hass, 31–58. Cambridge: Cambridge University Press, 2021.

———. "Sacrifice, Atonement and Renewal: Intersections between Girard, Kristeva and Von Balthasar." In *Sacrifice and the Modern World*, edited by Johannes Zachhuber and Julia Meszaros, 48–65. Oxford: Oxford University Press, 2013.

———. "Salvation." In *The Oxford Handbook of Systematic Theology*, edited by J. Webster, K. Tanner and I. Torrance, 176–96. Oxford: Oxford University Press, 2007.

———. *Seeing the World and Knowing God: Hebrew Wisdom and Christian Doctrine in a Late-Modern Context*. Oxford: Oxford University Press. 2013.

———. *Shakespeare and Religion*. Studies in Modernism 7. Tbilisi: Ilia University Press, 2015.

———. "Shakespeare and Spirituality." In *Re-Membering the Body: The Witness of History, Theology, and the Arts in Honour of Ruth M. B. Gouldbourne*, edited by Anthony Cross and Brian Haymes, 257–77. Eugene: Pickwick, 2021.

———. "Shakespeare in Church: Reflection on an Intertextual Liturgy Based on *A Midsummer Night's Dream*." *Ecclesial Practices* 4.2 (2017) 199–217.

3. Same essay and title later reprinted in Paul S. Fiddes, "The Sacramental Modernism of David Jones and the World as Text." In *David Jones: A Christian Modernist? Approaches to His Art, Poetry and Cultural Theory. Studies in Religion and the Arts*, eds. Paul S. Fiddes, Jamie Callison, Anna Johnson and Erik Tonning, (Leiden: Brill, 2018), 227–48.

———. *Sharing the Faith at the Boundaries of Unity*. A Report Commissioned by The Council for Christian Unity of the Church of England & the Faith and Society Team of the Baptist Union of Great Britain (2015).

———. (ed.). *Sharing the Faith at the Boundaries of Unity: Further Conversations between Anglicans and Baptists*. Centre for Baptist History and Heritage Studies, Vol. 12. Oxford: Regent's Park College, 2015.

———. "A Short History of the Angus Library and Archives, Regent's Park College, Oxford." *Baptist Quarterly* 52.3 (2021) 125–40.

———. "The Signs of Hope." In *A Call To Mind: Baptist Essays Towards a Theology of Commitment*, 33–45. London: Baptist Union, 1981.

———. "Social Implications of Hebrew Wisdom Literature." In *The Economic and Social Teaching of the Hebrew Scriptures*, edited by Richard Turnbull, 45–56. Oxford: Centre for Enterprise, Markets and Ethics, 2021.

———. "Soelle, Dorothee." In *The Oxford Dictionary of the Christian Church*, edited by Andrew Louth. Oxford: Oxford University Press, 2022. Accessed February 23, 2025. https://www-oxfordreference-com.ezproxy.st-.andrews.ac.uk/view/10.1093/acref/9780199642465.001.0001/acref-9780199642465/

———. "Something will come of nothing: on *A Theology of the Dark Side*." In *Challenging to Change: dialogues with a radical Baptist theologian. Essays presented to Dr Nigel G. Wright on his sixtieth birthday*, edited by Pieter J. Lalleman, 87–104. London: Spurgeon's College, 2009.

———. "Spirituality as Attentiveness: Stillness and Journey." In *Under the Rule of Christ: Dimensions of Baptist Spirituality*. Regent's Study Guides 14, edited by Paul S. Fiddes, 25–57. Oxford: Regent's Park College with Macon: Smith & Helwys, 2008.

———. "The Status of Women in the Thought of Karl Barth." In *After Eve: Women, Theology & the Christian Tradition*, edited by J. Soskice, 138–55. London: Collins, 1990.

———. "Story and Possibility: Reflections on the Last Scenes of the Fourth Gospel and Shakespeare's The Tempest." In *Revelation and Story: Narrative Theology and the Centrality of Story*, edited by H. Sauter and J. Barton, 29–52. Aldershot: Ashgate, 2000.

———. "The Story and the Stories: Revelation and the Challenge of Postmodern Culture." In *Faith in the Centre: Christianity and Culture*, edited by Paul S. Fiddes, 75–96. Macon: Smyth and Helwys, 2001.

———. "The Sublime and the Beautiful: Intersections Between Theology and Literature." In *Literature and Theology: New Interdisciplinary Spaces*, edited by Heather Walton, 127–52. Farnham: Ashgate, 2011.

———. "The Sublime, the Conflicted Self and Attention to the Other: Towards a Theopoetics with Iris Murdoch and Julia Kristeva." In *Theopoetic Folds: Philosophizing Multifariousness*, edited by Roland Faber, 159–78. New York: Fordham University Press, 2013.

———. "Suffering, Divine." In *The Blackwell Encyclopaedia of Modern Christian Thought*, edited by Alister E. McGrath, 633–36. Oxford: Blackwell, 1993.

———. "Suffering in Theology and Modern European Thought." In *The Oxford Handbook of Theology and Modern European Thought*, edited by Nicholas Adams, Graham Ward and George Pattison, 169–92. Oxford: Oxford University Press, 2013.

———. "Suffering, Slavery and Participating in the Triune God." In *Slavery-Free Communities: Emerging Theologies and Faith Responses to Modern Slavery*, edited by Dan Pratt, 154–76. London: SCM, 2021.

———. "Thanksgiving Address: Revd Dr Barrington Raymond White. New Road Baptist Church, Oxford, 28 November 2016." *Baptist Quarterly*, 48.2 (April 2017) 66–68.

———. "Theology and a Baptist Way of Community." In *Doing Theology in a Baptist Way*, edited by Paul S. Fiddes, 19–38. Oxford: Whitley, 2000.

———. "Theology of Covenant." In *A Dictionary of European Baptist Life and Thought*, edited by John. H. Y. Briggs, 124–26. Studies in Baptist History and Thought Volume 33. Milton Keynes: Paternoster, 2009.

———. "The Theology of the Charismatic Movement." In *Strange Gifts? A Guide to Charismatic Renewal*, edited by D. Martin and P. Mullen, 19–40. Oxford: Blackwell, 1984.

———. "A Theological Reconsideration of 'the Wild': A Response to Elizabeth O'Donnell Gandolpho." *Louvain Studies* 41.3 (2018) 317–27.

———. "Time for Vision and Revision." Foreword in *On Being the Church. Revisioning Baptist Identity*, Studies in Baptist History and Thought Volume 21, edited by Brian Haymes, Ruth Gouldbourne and Anthony R. Cross, xiii-xv. Milton Keynes: Paternoster, 2008.

———. "Towards a New Millennium: Doctrinal Themes of Strategic Significance for Baptists." In *Baptist Faith and Witness Book 2: The Papers of the Study and Research Division of the Baptist World Alliance, 1995–2000*, edited by L. A. Cupit, 13–22. Baptist World Alliance, 1999.

———. *Tracks and Traces: Baptist Identity in Church and Theology*. Carlisle: Paternoster. 2003.

———. "Tragedy as Rhetoric of Evil." In *Rhetorik des Bösen / The Rhetoric of Evil. Studien des Bonner Zentrums* für Religion und Gesellschaft, edited by Paul S. Fiddes and Jochen Schmidt, 165–92. Würzburg: Ergon Verlag, 2013.

———. "The Trinity in Process Thought." Unpublished Paper, 1987.

———. *The Trinity in Worship and Preaching*. London: London Baptist Preachers' Association. 1991.

———. "The Trinity, Modern Art, and Participation in God." In *Christian Theology and the Transformation of Natural Religion: From Incarnation to Sacramentality. Essays in Honour of David Brown*, edited by Christopher R. Brewer, 81–100. Leuven: Peeters, 2018.

———. "The Understanding of Salvation in the Baptist Tradition." In *For Us and for Our Salvation: Seven Perspectives on Christian* Soteriology, edited by Rienk Lanooy, 15–37. Utrecht: Interuniversitair Instituut voor Missiologie en Oecumenica, 1994.

———. (ed.). *Under the Rule of Christ: Dimensions of Baptist Spirituality*. Regent's Study Guides 14. Oxford: Regent's Park College with Macon: Smith & Helwys, 2008.

———. *A Unicorn Dies. A Novel of Mystery and Ideas*. Oxford: Firedint, 2017.

———. "Unity and Universality, Locality and Diversity according to Baptist Thinking about the Church." In *Receptive Ecumenism as Transformative Ecclesial Learning: Walking the Way to a Church Re-formed*, edited by Paul D. Murray, Gregory A. Ryan and Paul Lakeland, 12–24. Oxford: Oxford University Press, 2022.

———. "Versions of Ecclesiology: Stanley Hauerwas and Nicholas Healy," *Ecclesiology* 12.3 (2016) 331–53.

———. "Versions of the Wasteland. The Sense of an Ending in Theology and Literature in the Modern Period." In *Modernism, Christianity and Apocalypse*, edited by Erik Tonning, Matthew Feldman & David Addyman, 29–52. Brill: Leiden, 2014.

———. "'Walking Together:' The Place of Covenant Theology in Baptist Life Yesterday and Today." In *Pilgrim Pathways: Essays in Baptist History in Honour of B. R. White*, edited by Paul S. Fiddes, William H. Brackney, and John H. Y. Briggs, 47–74. Macon: Mercer University Press, 1999.

———. "The Web of Peacemakers." In *'A World-Order of Love': Baptists and the Peace Movements of 1914*. Centre for Baptist History and Heritage Studies, Vol. 15, edited by Paul S. Fiddes, 1–8. Oxford: Regent's Park College, 2017.

———. (ed.). "What Are Baptists? On the Way to Expressing Baptist Identity in a Changing Europe." The Division for Theology and Education of the European Baptist Federation (1993).

———. "What is God?" Accessed February 23, 2025, (https://closertotruth.com/video/fidpa-008/?referrer=8522)

———. "What we get Wrong about the Trinity." *Mission Catalyst* 4 (2016) 10–11.

———. "Whatever Happened to a Pauline Text? 2 Corinthians 3.6 and its Afterlife." In *The Spirit and the Letter: A Tradition and a Reversal*, edited by Paul S. Fiddes and Günter Badder, 3–27. London: T & T Clark, 2013.

———. "When Text Becomes Voice: *You've Got Mail*." In *Flickering Images: Theology and Film in Dialogue*, edited by Paul S. Fiddes and A. Clarke, 97–111. Macon: Smyth and Helwys, 2005.

———. "'Where Shall Wisdom Be Found?': Job 28 as a Riddle for Ancient and Modern Readers." In *After the Exile: Essays in Honour of Rex Mason*, edited by John Barton and David J. Reimer, 171–90. Macon: Mercer University Press, 1996.

———. "Wisdom and the Spirit: The Loss and Re-making of a Relationship." *Perspectives in Religious Studies* 41.2 (2014) 151–67.

———. "'Woman's Head is Man': A Doctrinal Reflection upon a Pauline Theme." *Baptist Quarterly* 31 (1986) 370–83.

———. (ed.). *The Word of God in the Life of the Church*. A Report of International Conversations between the Catholic Church and the Baptist World Alliance. *American Baptist Quarterly*, 26.1 (2012) 28–122.

———. (ed.). *'A World-Order of Love': Baptists and the Peace Movements of 1914*. Centre for Baptist History and Heritage Studies, Vol. 15. Oxford: Regent's Park College, 2017.

Fiddes, Paul S. and Peter Ward. "Affirming Faith at a Service of Baptism in St Aldates Church, Oxford." In *Explorations in Ecclesiology and Ethnography: Studies in Ecclesiology and Ethnography*, edited by Christian Scharen, 51–70. Grand Rapids: Eerdmans, 2012.

Fiddes, Paul S. and Stephen Finamore. "Baptists and Spirituality: A Rule of Life." In *Under the Rule of Christ. Dimensions of Baptist Spirituality*, edited by in Paul S. Fiddes, 1–24. Oxford: Regent's Park College with Macon: Smith & Helwys, 2008.

Fiddes, Paul S., Brian Haymes and Richard Kidd. *Baptists and the Communion of Saints: A Theology of Covenanted Disciples*. Waco: Baylor University Press, 2014.

Fiddes, Paul S., Brian Haymes and Richard Kidd. *Communion, Covenant, and Creativity: An Approach to the Communion of Saints Through the Arts*. Eugene: Cascade, 2020.

Fiddes, Paul S., Jamie Callison, Anna Johnson and Erik Tonning. (eds.). *David Jones: A Christian Modernist? Approaches to His Art, Poetry and Cultural Theory*. Studies in Religion and the Arts. Leiden: Brill, 2018.

Fiddes, Paul S. and Malkaz Songulashvili. "A Dialogue between the Orthodox Church of Georgia and the 'Evangelical Christians-Baptists' of Georgia (1979–1980) with its wider Baptist Context." *International Journal for the Study of the Christian Church*, 13.3 (2013) 222–54.

Fiddes, Paul S. and Judith Pollinger (eds.). *A Festivity of Love: Poems, Verse, and Prose from St Endellion*. Oxford: Firedint Pub, 2018.

Fiddes, Paul S. and A. Clarke. (eds). *Flickering Images: Theology and Film in Dialogue* Macon: Smyth and Helwys, 2005.

Fiddes, Paul S., William H. Brackney and Malcolm B. Yarnell III (eds.). *The Fourth Strand of the Reformation: The Covenant Ecclesiology of Anabaptists, English Separatists, and Early General Baptists*. Centre for Baptist History and Heritage Studies, Vol. 17. Oxford: Regent's Park College, 2018.

Fiddes, Paul S., E. Brandt and J. Molthagen. (eds.). *Gemeinschaft am Evangelium. Festschrift für Wiard Popkes zum 60. Geburtstag*. Leipzig: Evangelische Verlagsanstalt, 1996.

Fiddes, Paul S. and Bill Lees. "How are People Healed Today? The relation between the 'Medical' and the 'Spiritual' in Healing." In *Christian Healing. What can we Believe?* edited by Ernest Lucas, 5–30. London: Lynx Communications, SPCK, 1997.

Fiddes, Paul S. and John H. Y. Briggs. "Introduction." In *Peoples of God. Baptists and Jews Over Four Centuries*. Centre for Baptist History and Heritage Studies, edited by Paul S. Fiddes and John H. Y. Briggs, 1–9. Oxford: Centre for Baptist History, 2019.

Fiddes, Paul S., Brian Haymes, Richard Kidd and Michael Quicke, *On the Way of Trust*. Oxford: Whitley, 1997.

Fiddes, Paul S., W. H. Brackney and John H.Y. Briggs. (eds.). *Pilgrim Pathways. Essays in Baptist History in Honour of B.R. White*. Macon: Mercer University Press, 1999.

Fiddes, Paul S. and Jochen Schmidt. (eds). *Rhetorik des Bösen / The Rhetoric of Evil. Studien des Bonner Zentrums* für Religion und Gesellschaft. Würzburg: Ergon Verlag, 2013.

Fiddes, Paul S. and Andrew Taylor. "Seeing More Clearly with the Eyes of Love: A Liturgy for Voices Based on *A Midsummer Night's Dream*." In *New Places: Shakespeare and Civic Creativity*, edited by Paul Edmonson and Ewan Fernie, 83–108. London: Bloomsbury, Arden Shakespeare, 2018.

Fiddes, Paul S., Brian Haymes, Richard Kidd and Michael Quicke, *Something to Declare. A Study of the Declaration of Principle of the Baptist Union of Great Britain*. Oxford: Whitley, 1996.

Fiddes, Paul S. and Günter Badder. (eds). *The Spirit and the Letter: A Tradition and a Reversal*. London: T & T Clark, 2013.

Finger, Thomas N. *A Contemporary Anabaptist Theology: Biblical, Historical, Constructive*. Downers Grove: InterVarsity, 2004.

Forsyth, Neil. *The Old Enemy: Satan and the Combat Myth*. Princeton: Princeton University Press, 1987.

Forsyth, P. T. *The Person & Place of Jesus Christ*. Grand Rapids: Eerdmans, 1965.

Foster, Roger. "Foreword." In *Territorial Spirits: Insights on Strategic-Level Spiritual Warfare from Nineteen Christian Leaders*, edited by C. Peter Wagner, vii–xv. Chichester: Sovereign World, 1991.

Fox, Rory. "Can there be a Reason to Believe in Angels and Demons?" *The Downside Review* 115 (April 1997) 112–38.
France, R. T. *The Gospel of Matthew*. Grand Rapids: Eerdmans, 2007.
Frei, Hans W. *The Eclipse of the Biblical Narrative: A Study in Eighteenth and Nineteenth Century Hermeneutics*. New Haven: Yale University Press, 1974.
Fretheim, Terence E. "The Repentance of God: A Key to Evaluating Old Testament God-Talk." *Horizons in Biblical Theology* 10 (1988) 47–70.
———. *The Suffering of God: An Old Testament Perspective*. Philadelphia: Fortress, 1984.
Friesen, Randy. "Equipping Principles for Spiritual Warfare." *Direction* 29.2 (2000) 142–52.
Frohlich, Ida. "Evil in Second Temple Texts." In *Evil and the Devil*, edited by Ida Frohlich and Erkki Koskenniemi, 23–50. London: Bloomsbury T&T Clark, 2013.
Fudge, Edward William. *The Fire That Consumes: A Biblical and Historical Study of the Doctrine of Final Punishment*. third ed. Eugene: Cascade, 2011.
Ganssle, Gregory E. (ed.). *God and Time: Four Views*. Downers Grove: Inter Varsity, 2001.
Garrett, Susan R. *The Demise of the Devil: Magic and the Demonic in Luke's Writings*. Minneapolis: Fortress, 1989.
Gaston, Lloyd. Review of *Unmasking the Powers: The Invisible Forces that Determine Human Existence*, by Walter Wink. *Theology Today* 44.1 (1987) 153.
Gavrilyuk, Paul L. *The Suffering of the Impassible God*. Oxford: Oxford University Press, 2004.
Gilbert, Pierre. "The Third Wave Worldview: A Biblical Critique." *Direction* 29.2 (2000) 153–68.
Girard, Rene. *I See Satan Fall Like Lightning*. Translated by James G. Williams. New York: Orbis, 2001.
———. *The Scapegoat*. Translated by Yvonne Freccero. Baltimore: John Hopkins University Press, 1986.
———. *"To Double Business Bound": Essays in Literature, Mimesis, and Anthropology*. London, Athlone, 1978.
Godlove, Terry (ed.). *Between Hegel and Kierkegaard: Hans L. Martensen's Philosophy of Religion*. Translated by Curtis L. Thompson and David J. Kangas. Atlanta: Scholars, 1997.
Goodman, Felicitas D. *The Exorcism of Anneliese Michel*. Eugene: Resource, 2005.
———. *How About Demons? Possession and Exorcism in the Modern World*. Bloomington: Indiana University Press, 1988.
Gray, Tony. and Christopher Sinkinson (eds.). *Reconstructing Theology: A Critical Assessment of the Theology of Clark Pinnock*. Carlisle: Paternoster, 2000.
Green, Michael. *I Believe in Satan's Downfall*. London: Hodder & Stoughton, 1981.
Greenwood, Rebecca. *Authority to Tread: An Intercessor's Guide to Strategic-Level Spiritual Warfare*. Tonbridge: Sovereign World, 2005.
Gregersen, Niels Henrick. "Three Varieties of Panentheism." In *In Whom We Live and Move and Have Our Being: Panentheistic Reflections on God's Presence in a Scientific World*, edited by Philip Clayton and Arthur Peacocke, 19–35. Grand Rapids: Eerdmans, 2004.
Gregg, Steve. *Revelation: Four Views—A Parallel Commentary*. Nashville: Thomas Nelson, 1997.

Grenz, Stanley J. and Roger E. Olson. *20th-Century Theology: God & the World in a Transitional Age.* Cumbria: Paternoster, 1992.

Griffin, David R. *God, Power and Evil: A Process Theodicy.* Philadelphia: Westminster, 1976.

Gross, Edward N. *Miracles, Demons & Spiritual Warfare: An Urgent Call for Discernment.* Grand Rapids: Baker Book House, 1990.

Gruenler, Royce Gordon. *The Inexhaustible God: Biblical Faith and the Challenge of Process Theism.* Grand Rapids: Baker Book House, 1983.

Gunton, Colin E. (ed.). *Becoming and Being: The Doctrine of God in Charles Hartshorne and Karl Barth.* new ed. London: SCM, 2001.

———. *Trinity, Time and the Church: A Response to the Theology of Robert W. Jenson.* Grand Rapids: Eerdmans, 2000.

Hagner, Donald A. *Word Biblical Commentary Volume 33A: Matthew 1–13.* Dallas: Word, 1993.

Hall, Christopher A. Review of *Satan and the Problem of Evil: Constructing a Trinitarian Warfare Theodicy*, by Gregory A. Boyd. *Christianity Today* 47.2 (Feb 2003) 89–92.

Hallowell, Billy. *Playing With Fire: A Modern Investigation into Demons, Exorcism and Ghosts.* Nashville: Emanate, 2020.

Hammond, Frank and Ida Mae. *Pigs in the Parlour.* Kirkwood: Impact, 1973.

Harper, Michael. *Spiritual Warfare.* London: Hodder & Stoughton, 1970.

Hart, David B. *The Beauty of the Infinite: The Aesthetics of Christian Truth.* Grand Rapids: Eerdmans, 2003.

———. *The Doors of the Sea: Where was God in the Tsunami?* Grand Rapids: Eerdmans, 2005.

———. "No Shadow of Turning: On Divine Impassibility." *Pro Ecclesia* (2002) 184–206.

———. *That All Shall Be Saved: Heaven, Hell & Universal Salvation.* New Haven: Yale University Press, 2019.

Hart, Trevor A. and Daniel P. Thimell (eds.). *Christ in Our Place: The Humanity of God in Christ for the Reconciliation of the World.* Exeter: Paternoster, 1989.

Hartshorne, Charles. *The Divine Relativity: A Social Conception of God.* New Haven: Yale University Press, 1962.

———. *The Logic of Perfection.* La Salle: Open Court, 1962.

Hartshorne, Charles and William L Reese (eds.). *Philosophers Speak of God.* Chicago: University of Chicago Press, 1976.

Hasker, William. *God, Time and Knowledge.* Ithaca: Cornell University Press, 1989.

———. *The Triumph of God Over Evil: Theodicy for a Suffering World.* Downers Grove: IVP Academic, 2008.

Hebblethwaite, Brian. "MacKinnon and the Problem of Evil." In *Christ, Ethics and Tragedy: Essays in Honour of Donald MacKinnon*, edited by Kenneth Surin, 131–45. Cambridge: Cambridge University Press, 1989.

Hegel, Georg Wilhelm Friedrich. *Lectures on the Philosophy of Religion*, vol. 1. Edited by Peter C. Hodgson. Translated by R. F. Brown, P. C. Hodgson, and J. M. Stewart. Los Angeles: University of California Press, 1984.

Heiser, Michael S. "Co-Regency in Ancient Israel's Divine Council as the Conceptual Backdrop to Ancient Jewish Binitarian Monotheism." *Bulletin for Biblical Research* 26.2 (2015) 195–225.

———. "Monotheism, Polytheism, Monolatry, or Henotheism? Toward an Assessment of Divine Plurality in the Hebrew Bible." *Bulletin for Biblical Research* 18.1 (2008) 1–30.

———. *The Unseen Realm: Recovering the Supernatural Worldview of the Bible.* Bellingham: Lexam, 2015.

Herbert, T. D. *Kenosis and Priesthood.* Milton Keynes: Paternoster, 2008.

Herrick, Vanessa. *Limits of Vulnerability.* Cambridge: Grove, 1997.

Herrick, Vanessa and Ivan Mann. *Jesus Wept: Reflections on Vulnerability in Leadership.* London: DLT, 1998.

Heschel, Abraham J. *The Prophets.* New York: Harper and Row, 1962.

Hick, John. *Evil and the God of Love.* second ed. London: MacMillan, 1977.

———. "An Irenaean Theodicy." In *Encountering Evil: Live Options in Theodicy*, edited by Stephen T. Davis, 39–68. Edinburgh: T&T Clark, 1981.

Hiebert, Paul G. "The Flaw of the Excluded Middle." *Missiology* 10.1 (Jan 1982) 35–47.

———. "Spiritual Warfare and Worldviews." *Direction* 29.2 (2000) 114–24.

Highfield, Ron. "The Function of Divine Self-Limitation in Open Theism: Great Wall or Picket Fence?" *Journal of the Evangelical Theological Society* 45.2 (2002): 279–99.

Hinton, James. *The Mystery of Pain: A Book for the Sorrowful.* London: Smith, Elder & Co, 1866.

Holmes, Steve. "Edwards on the Will." *International Journal of Systematic Theology* 1.3 (1999) 266–85.

———. *The Holy Trinity: Understanding God's Life.* Milton Keynes: Paternoster, 2012.

———. "Response to Paul S. Fiddes." In *Two Views on the Doctrine of the Trinity*, edited by Jason Sexton, 186–90. Grand Rapids: Zondervan, 2014.

———. "Who Can Count How Many Crosses?: Paul Fiddes on Salvation." In *Within the Love of God: Essays on the Doctrine of God in Honour of Paul S. Fiddes*, edited by Anthony Clarke and Andrew Moore, 120–33. Oxford: Oxford University Press, 2014.

Holt, Kathy. Review of *God at War: The Bible & Spiritual Conflict*, by Gregory A. Boyd. *Stone-Campbell Journal* 2.1 (Spring 1999) 129–30.

Holvast, René. *Spiritual Mapping in the United States and Argentina, 1989–2005: A Geography of Fear.* Leiden: Brill, 2008.

Horn, Robert Leslie. *Positivity and Dialectic: A Study of the Theological Method of Hans Lassen Martensen.* Copenhagen: CA Reitzel, 2007.

Horrobin, Peter. *Healing Through Deliverance.* Lancaster: Sovereign World, 1995.

Hubbard, David Allan. *Joel and Amos: An Introduction and Commentary.* Nottingham: InterVarsity, 1989.

Hume, David. *Dialogues Concerning Natural Religion.* New York: Social Sciences, 1948.

Hunt, David P. "Divine Providence and Simple Foreknowledge." *Faith and Philosophy* 10 (July 1993) 394–414.

———. "If God knows the future, what is free will? (Part 1)" Accessed February 23, 2025, (https://closertotruth.com/video/hunda-001/?referrer=7839)

———. "If God knows the future, what is free will? (Part 2)" Accessed February 23, 2025, (https://closertotruth.com/video/hunda-009/?referrer=7839)

———. "Two Problems with Knowing the Future." *American Philosophical Quarterly* 34 (April 1997) 273–85.

Hunt, David P. and Seth Shabo. "Frankfurt cases and the (in)significance of timing: a defense of the buffering strategy." *Philosophical Studies: An International Journal for Philosophy in the Analytic Tradition* 164.3 (July 2013): 599–622.

Instone-Brewer, David. "Jesus and the Psychiatrists." In *The Unseen World: Christian Reflections on Angels, Demons and the Heavenly Realm*, edited by Anthony N. S. Lane, 133–44. Grand Rapids: Baker, 1996.

Inwagen, Peter van. (ed.). *Christian Faith and the Problem of Evil*. Grand Rapids: Eerdmans, 2004.
James, Graham. "The Enduring Appeal of a Kenotic Christology." *Theology* 86 (1983) 7–14.
Jenkins, Philip. *The Next Christendom: The Coming of Global Christianity*. Oxford: Oxford University Press, 2002.
Jenson, R. W. *Systematic Theology Vol. 1: The Triune God*. Oxford: Oxford University Press, 1997.
Jones, Paul Dafydd. "A Hopeful Universalism." *The Christian Century* 129 (2012) 22–27.
Jüngel, Eberhard. *God as the Mystery of the World*. Translated by D. Guder. Edinburgh: T&T Clark, 1983.
Kallas, James. *Jesus and the Power of Satan*. Philadelphia: Westminster, 1968.
Kay, William K. and Robin Parry (eds.). *Exorcism & Deliverance: Multi-Disciplinary Studies*. Milton Keynes: Paternoster, 2011.
Keener, Craig S. *A Commentary on the Gospel of Matthew*. Grand Rapids: Eerdmans, 1999.
Keller, Catherine. "The Mystery of the Insoluble Evil: Violence and Evil in Marjorie Suchocki." In *World Without End: Christian Eschatology from a Process Perspective*, edited by Joseph A. Bracken, 46–71. Grand Rapids: Eerdmans, 2005.
Keller, Tim. *Preaching: Communicating Faith in an Age of Scepticism*. London: Hodder & Stoughton, 2015.
Kellermann, Bill Wylie. *Seasons of Faith and Conscience: Explorations in Liturgical Direct Action*. Eugene: Wipf & Stock, 2008.
Kelly, Henry Ansgar. *Towards the Death of Satan: The Growth and Decline of Christian Demonology*. London: G. Chapman, 1968.
Kelsey, Morton. *Discernment: A Study in Ecstasy and Evil*. New York: Paulist, 1987.
———. *Healing & Christianity*. Minneapolis: Augsburg Fortress, 1995.
Koch, Kurt E. *Between Christ and Satan*. Grand Rapids: Kregel, 1971.
Laato, Antti. "The Devil in the Old Testament." In *Evil and the Devil*, edited by Ida Frohlich and Erkki Koskenniemi, 1–22. London: Bloomsbury T&T Clark, 2013.
Ladd, G.E. *The Presence of the Future*. Grand Rapids: Eerdmans, 1974.
Lane, Anthony. (ed.). *The Unseen World: Christian Reflections on Angels, Demons and the Heavenly Realm*. Grand Rapids: Baker, 1996.
Lausanne Movement. "Lausanne Statement on Spiritual Warfare (1993)." Accessed February 23, 2025, (https://lausanne.org/content/statement/statement-on-spiritual-warfare-1993)
Law, David R. *Kierkegaard's Kenotic Christology*. Oxford: Oxford University Press, 2013.
Lee, Jung Y. *God Suffers for Us: A Systematic Enquiry into the Concept of Divine Passibility*. The Hague: Martinus Nijhoff, 1974.
Leftow, Brian. *Time and Eternity*. Ithaca: Cornell University Press, 1991.
Levenson, Jon D. *Creation and the Persistence of Evil: The Jewish Drama of Divine Omnipotence*. San Francisco: Harper, 1988.
Lincoln, Andrew T. *Word Biblical Commentary Volume 42: Ephesians*. Dallas: Thomas Nelson, 1990.
Linn, Matthew and Dennis Linn. *Deliverance Prayer: Experiential, Psychological and Theological Approaches*. New York: Paulist, 1981.
Linthicum, Robert C. *City of God, City of Satan: A Biblical Theology of the Urban Church*. Grand Rapids: Zondervan, 1991.

Löfstedt, Torsten. *The Devil, Demons, Judas, and "the Jews."* Eugene: Pickwick, 2021.

———. Review of *Church Militant: Spiritual Warfare in the Anglican Charismatic Renewal*, by Graham R. Smith. *Svensk Teologisk Kvartalskrift*, 94.1–2 (2018) 111–12.

Lohfink, Gerhard. *Jesus and Community: The Social Dimension of Christian Faith.* Philadelphia: Fortress, 1984.

Lohfink, Norbert F. *Option for the Poor: The Basic Principle of Liberation Theology in the Light of the Bible.* Berkeley: Bibal, 1987.

Long, V. Philips. Review of *God at War: The Bible & Spiritual Conflict*, by Gregory A. Boyd. *Presbyterion* 23.2 (1997) 125.

Longman III, Tremper and Daniel Reid. *God is a Warrior*. Grand Rapids: Zondervan, 1995.

Loofs, Friedrich. "Kenosis." In *Encyclopaedia of Religion and Ethics VII*, edited by James Hastings, 680–87. Edinburgh: T&T Clark, 1914.

Lowe, Chuck. *Territorial Spirits and World Evangelisation?* Ross-Shire: Mentor, 1998.

Lynch, Chloe. "How Convincing is Walter Wink's Interpretation of Paul's Language of the Powers?" *Evangelical Quarterly* 83.3 (2011) 251–66.

MacGregor, Kirk R. *A Molinist-Anabaptist Systematic Theology.* Lanham: University Press of America, 2007.

MacMullen, Ramsay. *Christianizing the Roman Empire (A.D. 100–400).* New Haven: Yale University Press, 1984.

MacNutt, Francis. *Deliverance from Evil Spirits: A Practical Manual.* Grand Rapids: Chosen, 2009.

———. *Healing* (rev ed.). Notre Dame: Ave Maria, 1999.

MacQuarrie, John. "Kenoticism Reconsidered." *Theology* 77 (Mar 1974) 115–24.

———. *The Principles of Christian Theology.* rev ed. London: SCM, 1977.

Malina, Bruce J. Review of *Naming the Powers: The Language of Power in the New Testament*, by Walter Wink. *Union Seminary Quarterly Review* 40.3 (1985) 73–76.

Mallow, Vernon R. *The Demonic: A Selected Theological Study: An Examination into the Theology of Edwin Lewis, Karl Barth, and Paul Tillich.* Lanham: University Press of America, 1983.

Marenbon, John. *Abelard in Four Dimensions: A Twelfth-Century Philosopher in his Context and Ours.* Notre Dame: University of Notre Dame Press, 2013.

Martensen, H. L. *Christian Dogmatics: Compendium of the Doctrines of Christianity.* Translated by W. Urwick. Edinburgh: T&T Clark, 1866.

Martin, Malachi. *Hostage to the Devil: The Possession and Exorcism of Five Contemporary Americans.* New York: Harper Collins, 1992.

Mason, Rex. "Response to Paul Fiddes." In *The "Plainly Revealed" Word of God? Baptist Hermeneutics in Theory and Practice*, edited by Helen Dare and Simon Woodman, 95–98. Macon: Mercer University Press, 2011.

McAlpine, Thomas H. *Facing the Powers: What are the Options?* Eugene: Wipf & Stock, 2003.

McCall, Thomas H. "Response to Paul S. Fiddes." In *Two Views on the Doctrine of the Trinity*, edited by Jason Sexton, 186–90. Grand Rapids: Zondervan, 2014.

McCloskey, H. J. "The Problem of Evil." *Journal of the American Academy of Religion* 30.3 (1962) 187–97.

McCormack, Bruce. "Karl Barth's Christology as a Resource for a Reformed Version of Kenoticism." *International Journal of Systematic Theology* 8.3 (2006) 243–51.

———. "Kenoticism in Modern Christology." In *The Oxford Handbook of Christology*, edited by Francesca Aran Murphy and Troy A. Stephano, 444–57. Oxford: Oxford University Press, 2015.
McFague, Sallie. *The Body of God: An Ecological Theology*. London: SCM, 1993.
———. *Models of God: Theology for an Ecological, Nuclear Age*. Philadelphia: Fortress, 1987.
McFarland, Ian A. "The Problem with Evil." *Theology Today* 74.4 (2018) 321–39.
McGrath, Alister E. *Christian Theology: An Introduction*. third ed. Oxford: Blackwell, 2001.
McTaggart, J. M. E. *The Nature of Existence*, Vol. 2. Cambridge: Cambridge University Press, 1927.
Molina, Javier Aguilar. "The Invention of Child Witches in the Democratic Republic of Congo: Social Cleansing, Religious Commerce and the Difficulties of Being a Parent in an Urban Culture." London: Save the Children, 2005.
Molnar, Paul D. "Response to Paul S. Fiddes." In *Two Views on the Doctrine of the Trinity*, edited by Jason Sexton, 191–96. Grand Rapids: Zondervan, 2014.
Moltmann, Jürgen. *The Coming of God*. London: SCM, 1996.
———. *The Crucified God*. London: SCM, 1974.
———. *God in Creation: An Ecological Doctrine of Creation*. London: SCM, 1985.
———. *Theology of Hope: On the Ground and the Implications of a Christian Eschatology*. London: SCM, 1967.
———. "The Trinitarian History of God." *Theology* 78 (Dec 1975) 632–46.
———. *The Trinity and the Kingdom: Doctrine of God*. London: SCM, 1981.
Moore, Andrew. "Experience and the Doctrine of God." In *Within the Love of God: Essays on the Doctrine of God in Honour of Paul S. Fiddes*, edited by Anthony Clarke and Andrew Moore, 61–76. Oxford: Oxford University Press, 2014.
Morris, Leon. *The Gospel According to Matthew*. Grand Rapids: Eerdmans, 1992.
Mott, Stephen C. *Biblical Ethics and Social Change*. Oxford: Oxford University Press, 1982.
Munger, Robert Boyd. *My Heart—Christ's Home*. rev ed. Downers Grove: InterVarsity, 1986.
Murphy, Ed. *The Handbook for Spiritual Warfare*. rev ed. Nashville: Thomas Nelson, 1996.
Murphy, George L. "Toward a Theology of Technological War." *Dialog* 27 (1988) 48–54.
Nash, Ronald. (ed.). "Introduction." In *Process Theology*, edited by Ronald Nash, 7–29. Grand Rapids: Baker Book House, 1987.
———. *Process Theology*. Grand Rapids: Baker Book House, 1987.
Newbigin, Lesslie. *The Gospel in a Pluralist Society*. London: SPCK, 1989.
Noble, Thomas A. "The Spirit World: A Theological Approach." In *The Unseen World: Christian Reflections on Angels, Demons and the Heavenly Realm*, edited by Anthony N. S. Lane, 185–223. Grand Rapids: Baker, 1996.
Noll, Stephen F. *Angels of Light, Powers of Darkness: Thinking Biblically about Angels, Satan & Principalities*. Downers Grove: InterVarsity, 1998.
———. "Thinking About Angels." In *The Unseen World: Christian Reflections on Angels, Demons and the Heavenly Realm*, edited by Anthony N. S. Lane, 1–27. Grand Rapids: Baker, 1996.
Oakes, E. "The Internal Logic of Holy Saturday in the Theology of Hans Urs von Balthasar." *International Journal of Systematic Theology* 9.2 (2007) 184–99.

O'Brien, P. T. "Principalities and Powers and Their Relationship to Structures." *The Reformed Theological Review* 40.1 (1981) 1–10.

———. "Principalities and Powers: Opponents of the Church." In *Biblical Interpretation and the Church: Text and Context*, edited by D.A. Carson, 110–50. Exeter: Paternoster, 1984.

Olu Igenoza, Andrew. "Christian Theology and the Belief in Evil Spirits: An African Perspective." *The Scottish Bulletin of Evangelical Theology* 4.1 (1986) 39–48.

Olson, Roger E. "A Postconservative Evangelical Response to Panentheism." *Evangelical Quarterly* 85/4 (2013) 328–37.

———. "Trinity and Eschatology: The Historical Being of God in Jürgen Moltmann and Wolfhart Pannenberg." *Scottish Journal of Theology* 36 (1983) 213–27.

Oord, Thomas Jay. *The Uncontrolling Love of God: An Open and Relational Account of Providence*. Downers Grove: IVP Academic, 2015.

Osborn, Lawrence. "Angels: Barth and Beyond." In *The Unseen World: Christian Reflections on Angels, Demons and the Heavenly Realm*, edited by Anthony N. S. Lane, 29–48. Grand Rapids: Baker, 1996.

Padilla, C. Rene. "Spiritual Conflict." In *The New Face of Evangelicalism: An International Symposium on the Lausanne Conference*, edited by C. Rene Padilla, 205–21. London: Hodder and Stoughton, 1976.

Page, Ruth. *God and the Web of Creation*. London: SCM, 1996.

———. "Panentheism and Pansynthism: God in Relation." In *In Whom We Live and Move and Have Our Being: Panentheistic Reflections on God's Presence in a Scientific World*, edited by Philip Clayton and Arthur Peacocke, 222–32. Grand Rapids: Eerdmans, 2004.

Pagels, Elaine. *The Origin of Satan*. New York: Vintage, 1996.

Pailin, David A. Review of *The Creative Suffering of God*, by Paul S. Fiddes. *Modern Churchman* 31.1 (1989): 59–60.

Pannell, William E. "Evangelism and Power." *International Review of Mission* 69 (1980): 49–55.

Pannenberg, Wolfhart. *Introduction to Systematic Theology*. Grand Rapids: Eerdmans, 1991.

Park, Nam Shin. "Hermeneutics and Spiritual Warfare." *Didaskalia* 22 (2011) 85–103.

Peck, M. Scott. *People of the Lie: The Hope for Healing Human Evil*. New York: Simon & Schuster, 1983.

Perry, Michael (ed.). *Deliverance: Psychic Disturbances and Occult Involvement*. second ed. London: SPCK, 1996.

Peterson, Michael L. *God and Evil: An Introduction to the Issues*. Boulder: Westview, 1998.

———. "God and Evil in Process Theology." In *Process Theology*, edited by Ronald Nash, 117–39. Grand Rapids: Baker Book House, 1987.

Picirilli, Robert E. "An Arminian Response to John Sanders's *The God Who Risks: A Theology of Providence*." *Journal of the Evangelical Theological Society* 44.3 (2001) 467–91.

Pinnock, Clark H., Richard Rice, John Sanders, William Hasker, and David Basinger. *The Openness of God: A Biblical Challenge to the Traditional Understanding of God*. Downers Grove: InterVarsity, 1994.

Plantinga, Alvin. *God, Freedom and Evil*. London: Allen and Unwin, 1975.

———. *The Nature of Necessity*. Oxford: Clarendon, 1974.

Polkinghorne, John (ed.). "Kenotic Creation and Divine Action." In *The Work of Love: Creation as Kenosis*, edited by John Polkinghorne, 90–106. London: SPCK, 2001.

———. *The Work of Love: Creation as Kenosis*. Grand Rapids: Eerdmans, 2001.

Pollard, T. E. "The Impassibility of God." *Scottish Journal of Theology* 8.4 (1955) 353–64.

Pool, Jeff B. Review of *The Creative Suffering of God*, by Paul S. Fiddes. *The Journal of Religion* 70.3 (1990) 471–72.

Powell, Cyril H. *The Biblical Concept of Power*. London: Epworth, 1963.

Powell, Samuel M. Review of *In Whom We Live and Move and Have Our Being: Panentheistic Reflections on God's Presence in a Scientific World*, by Philip Clayton and Arthur Peacocke (eds.). *Scottish Journal of Theology* 61.1 (2008): 107–9.

Powlison, David. "The Classical Model." In *Understanding Spiritual Warfare: Four Views*, edited by James K. Beilby and Paul Rhodes Eddy, 89–111. Grand Rapids: Baker Academic, 2012.

———. *Power Encounters: Reclaiming Spiritual Warfare*. Grand Rapids: Baker, 1995.

———. "Response to C. Peter Wagner and Rebecca Greenwood." In *Understanding Spiritual Warfare: Four Views*, edited by James K. Beilby and Paul Rhodes Eddy, 204–9. Grand Rapids: Baker Academic, 2012.

———. "Response to Walter Wink." In *Understanding Spiritual Warfare: Four Views*, edited by James K. Beilby and Paul Rhodes Eddy, 72–77. Grand Rapids: Baker Academic, 2012.

Pyne, Robert A. Review of *God at War: The Bible & Spiritual Conflict*, by Gregory A. Boyd. *Bibliotheca Sacra* 155 (April-June 1998) 234–36.

Quay, Paul M. "Angels and Demons: The Teaching of IV Lateran." *Theological Studies* 42 (1981) 20–45.

Rahner, Karl. *The Trinity*. Translated by Joseph Donceel. Tunbridge Wells: Burns & Oats, 1970.

Rea, Michael C. *The Hiddenness of God*. Oxford: Oxford University Press, 2018.

Richards, John. *But Deliver Us from Evil. An Introduction to the Demonic Dimension in Pastoral Care*. London: Darton, Longman & Todd, 1974.

———. *Exorcism, Deliverance and Healing: Some Pastoral and Liturgical Guidelines*. Nottingham: Grove, 1990.

Ricoeur, Paul. *The Symbolism of Evil*. Boston: Beacon, 1969.

Robinson, H. Wheeler. *The Christian Experience of the Holy Spirit*. London: Nisbet, 1928.

———. *The Cross in the Old Testament*. London: SCM, 1965.

———. *Redemption and Revelation: in the Actuality of History*. London: Nisbet & Co., 1942.

———. *Suffering Human and Divine*. New York: Macmillan, 1939.

Rodin, R. Scott. *Evil and Theodicy in the Theology of Karl Barth*. New York: Peter Lang, 1997.

Rundle, Bede. *Why there is Something rather than Nothing*. Oxford: Oxford University Press, 2009.

Rupp, E. Gordon. *Principalities and Powers*. London: Wyvern, 1965.

Sanders, John. *The God Who Risks: A Theology of Providence*. Downers Grove: Inter Varsity, 1998.

Schaff, Philip (ed.). *Nicene and Post-Nicene Fathers of the Christian Church*, vol. 3. Edinburgh: T&T Clark, 1998.

Schlier, Heinrich. *Principalities and Powers in the New Testament*. Freiberg: Verlag Herder, 1961.

Schreiner, Thomas R. "Penal Substitutionary View." In *The Nature of the Atonement: Four Views*, edited by James Beilby and Paul R. Eddy, 67–98. Downers Grove: IVP Academic, 2006.

Sexton, Jason (ed.). *Two Views on the Doctrine of the Trinity*. Grand Rapids: Zondervan, 2014.

Shanks, Andrew. *Hegel's Political Theology*. Cambridge: Cambridge University Press, 1991.

Sherman, Dean. *Spiritual Warfare for Every Christian*. Seattle: YWAM, 1995.

Shults, F. LeRon. *Reforming the Doctrine of God*. Grand Rapids: Eerdmans, 2005.

Sider, Ronald J. "Christ and Power." *International Review of Mission* 69 (1980) 8–20.

Smith, Graham R. *The Church Militant: Spiritual Warfare in the Anglican Charismatic Renewal*. Eugene: Pickwick, 2016.

Southard, Samuel. "Demonizing and Mental Illness (II): The Problem of Assessment, Los Angeles." *Journal of Pastoral Psychology* 34.4 (1986) 264–87.

Southard, Samuel and Donna Southard. "Demonizing and Mental Illness: The Problem of Identification, Hong Kong." *Journal of Pastoral Psychology* 33.3 (1985) 173–88.

Southard, Samuel and Donna Southard. "Demonizing and Mental Illness (III): Explanations and Treatment, Seoul." *Journal of Pastoral Psychology* 35.2 (1986) 132–51.

Sponheim, Paul. Review of *The Creative Suffering of God*, by Paul S. Fiddes. *Interpretation: A Journal of Bible & Theology* 43.2 (1989) 216–18.

Stafford, Tim. Review of *Power Encounters: Reclaiming Spiritual Warfare*, by David Powlison. *Christianity Today* 39.10 (1995) 48.

Stewart, J. S. "On a Neglected Emphasis in New Testament Theology." *Scottish Journal of Theology* 4 (1951) 292–301.

Story, J Lyle. "Jesus' 'Enemy' in the Gospels." *American Theological Inquiry* 6.1 (2013) 43–63.

Surin, Kenneth. "The Impassibility of God and the Problem of Evil." *Scottish Journal of Theology* 35.2 (1982) 97–115.

Swartley, Willard M. "Biblical Faith Confronting Opposing Spiritual Realties." *Direction* 29.2 (2000) 100–113.

Swinburne, Richard. *The Coherence of Theism*. Oxford: Clarendon, 1977.

———. "Is God All-Powerful?" Accessed February 23, 2025, (https://closertotruth.com/video/swiri-037/?referrer=8285#video-4271)

Tanner, Kathryn. *Christ the Key*. Cambridge: Cambridge University Press, 2010.

———. *Jesus, Humanity and the Trinity: A Brief Systematic Theology*. Minneapolis: Fortress, 2001.

Tennant, Agnieszka. "Many Christians Say They are in Need of Deliverance." *Christianity Today* 45 (September 2001) 46–56.

Theron, Jacques. "A Critical Overview of the Church's Ministry of Deliverance from Evil Spirits." *PNEUMA: The Journal of the Society for Pentecostal Studies* 18 (1996) 79–92.

Thielicke, Helmut. *Between God and Satan*. Grand Rapids: Eerdmans, 1963.

Thomas, John Christopher. *The Devil, Disease and Deliverance: Origins of Illness in New Testament Thought*. Sheffield: Sheffield Academic, 1998.

Thompson, Thomas R. and Cornelius Plantinga Jnr. "Trinity and Kenosis." In *Exploring Kenotic Christology: The Self-Emptying of God*, edited by C. Stephen Evans, 165–89. Oxford: Oxford University Press, 2006.

Torr, Stephen C. *A Dramatic Pentecostal/Charismatic Anti-Theodicy: Improvising on a Divine Performance of Lament*. Eugene: Pickwick, 2013.
Torrance, Alan. "Does God Suffer? Incarnation and Impassibility." In *Christ in Our Place: The Humanity of God in Christ for the Reconciliation of the World*, edited by Trevor A. Hart and Daniel P. Thimell, 345–68. Exeter: Paternoster, 1989.
Torrance, T. F. *The Apocalypse Today*. London: James Clarke & Co., 1960.
Tripole, S.J., Martin R. Review of *The Creative Suffering of God*, by Paul S. Fiddes. *Theological Studies* 50.2 (1989) 380–82.
Twelftree, Graham H. *Christ Triumphant: Exorcism Then and Now*. London: Hodder & Stoughton, 1985.
———. *In the Name of Jesus: Exorcism Among Early Christians*. Grand Rapids, Baker, 2007.
———. *Jesus the Exorcist: A Contribution to the Study of the Historical Jesus*. Tubingen: J.C.B. Mohr (Paul Siebeck), 1993.
———. *Jesus The Miracle Worker*. Downers Grove, IVP Academic, 1999.
Van Den Heuvel, Albert H. *These Rebellious Powers*. London: SCM, 1966.
Van Riessen, Renee D.N. *Man as a Place of God: Levinas' Hermeneutics of Kenosis*. Dordrecht: Springer, 2007.
Vanstone, W. H. *Love's Endeavour, Love's Expense: The Response of Being to the Love of God*. London: Darton, Longman and Todd, 1977.
Virkler, Henry and Mary. "Demonic Involvement in Human Life and Illness." *Journal of Psychology and Theology* 5 (Spring 1977) 95–102.
Volf, Miroslav. *After Our Likeness: The Church as the Image of the Trinity*. Grand Rapids: Eerdmans, 1998.
Wagner, C. Peter. "Spiritual Warfare." In *Territorial Spirits: Practical Strategies for How to Crush the Enemy through Spiritual Warfare*, edited by C. Peter Wagner, 33–54. Shippensburg: Destiny Image, 2012.
———. *Spiritual Warfare Strategy: Confronting Spiritual Powers*. Shippensburg: Destiny Image, 1996.
———. "Territorial Spirits." In *Territorial Spirits: Practical Strategies for How to Crush the Enemy through Spiritual Warfare*, edited by C. Peter Wagner, 67–74. Shippensburg: Destiny Image, 2012.
———. (ed.). *Territorial Spirits: Practical Strategies for How to Crush the Enemy through Spiritual Warfare*. Shippensburg: Destiny Image, 2012.
Wagner, C. Peter and Rebecca Greenwood. "Response to Gregory Boyd." In *Understanding Spiritual Warfare: Four Views*, edited by James K. Beilby and Paul Rhodes Eddy, 169–72. Grand Rapids: Baker Academic, 2012.
———. "Response to Walter Wink." In *Understanding Spiritual Warfare: Four Views*, edited by James K. Beilby and Paul Rhodes Eddy, 84–87. Grand Rapids: Baker Academic, 2012.
———. "The Strategic-Level Deliverance Model." In *Understanding Spiritual Warfare: Four Views*, edited by James K. Beilby and Paul Rhodes Eddy, 173–98. Grand Rapids: Baker Academic, 2012.
Ward, Keith. *The Christian Idea of God: A Philosophical Foundation for Faith*. Cambridge: Cambridge University Press, 2017.
———. "Cosmos and Kenosis." In *The Work of Love: Creation as Kenosis*, edited by J. Polkinghorne, 152–66. London: SPCK, 2001.

———. "The World as the Body of God: A Panentheistic Metaphor." In *In Whom We Live and Move and Have Our Being: Panentheistic Reflections on God's Presence in a Scientific World*, edited by Philip Clayton and Arthur Peacocke, 62–72. Grand Rapids: Eerdmans, 2004.

Ware, Bruce. *God's Lesser Glory: A Critique of Open Theism*. Wheaton: Crossway, 2001.

———. Review of *The Creative Suffering of God*, by Paul S. Fiddes. *Trinity Journal* 16NS (1995) 233–39.

Warren, E. Janet. *Cleansing the Cosmos*. Eugene: Pickwick, 2012.

———. Review of *Understanding Spiritual Warfare: Four Views*, edited by James K. Beilby and Paul Rhodes Eddy. *PNEUMA: The Journal of the Society for Pentecostal Studies* 36.1 (2014) 166–68.

———. "'Spiritual Warfare': A Dead Metaphor?" *Journal of Pentecostal Theology* 21 (2012) 278–97.

Watson, David C. K. *Discipleship*. London: Hodder and Stoughton, 1981.

———. *God's Freedom Fighters*. London: Movement, 1972.

Webster, John. "Non ex aequo: God's Relations to Creatures." In *Within the Love of God: Essays on the Doctrine of God in Honour of Paul S. Fiddes*, edited by Anthony Clarke and Andrew Moore, 95–107. Oxford: Oxford University Press, 2014.

Weinandy, Thomas G. *Does God Change? The Word's Becoming in the Incarnation*. Still River: St Bede's, 1985.

———. *Does God Suffer?* Notre Dame: University of Notre Dame Press, 2000.

———. "Does God Suffer?" *First Things* 117 N (2001) 35–41.

Weingart, Richard E. *The Logic of Divine Love: A Critical Analysis of the Soteriology of Peter Abailard*. Oxford: Clarendon, 1970.

Whitehead, Alfred North. *Process and Reality: An Essay in Cosmology*. New York: Free; London: Collier Macmillan, 1979.

Wierenga, Edward R. *The Nature of God: An Inquiry into Divine Attributes*. Ithaca: Cornell University Press, 1989.

Williams, Thomas. "Sin, grace and redemption." In *The Cambridge Companion to Abelard*, edited by Jeffrey E. Brower and Kevin Guilfoy, 258–78. Cambridge: Cambridge University Press, 2004.

Wink, Walter. "Demons and DMins: The Church's Response to the Demonic." *Review and Expositor: An International Baptist Journal* 89.4 (1992) 503–13.

———. *Engaging the Powers: Discernment and Resistance in a World of Domination*. Minneapolis: Fortress, 1992.

———. *Jesus and Nonviolence: A Third Way*. Minneapolis: Fortress, 2003.

———. *Naming the Powers: The Language of Power in the New Testament*. Philadelphia: Fortress, 1984.

———. *The Powers that Be: Theology for a New Millennium*. New York: Doubleday, 1998.

———. *Unmasking the Powers: The Invisible Forces that Determine Human Existence*. Philadelphia: Fortress, 1986.

Wink, Walter and Gareth Higgins. "The World Systems Model." In *Understanding Spiritual Warfare: Four Views*, edited by James K. Beilby and Paul Rhodes Eddy, 47–71. Grand Rapids: Baker Academic, 2012.

Wink, Walter and Michael Hardin. "Response to C. Peter Wagner and Rebecca Greenwood." In *Understanding Spiritual Warfare: Four Views*, edited by James K. Beilby and Paul Rhodes Eddy, 199–203. Grand Rapids: Baker Academic, 2012.

Working Party, Church of England. *A Time to Heal: A Contribution Towards the Ministry of Healing*. London: Church House, 2000.
Wray, T. J. and Gregory Mobley. *The Birth of Satan: Tracing the Devil's Biblical Roots*. New York: Palgrave Macmillan, 2005.
Wright, Nigel G. "Charismatic Interpretations of the Demonic." In *The Unseen World: Christian Reflections on Angels, Demons and the Heavenly Realm*, edited by Anthony N. S. Lane, 149–63. Grand Rapids: Baker, 1996.
———. *The Fair Face of Evil: Putting the Power of Darkness in its Place*. London: Marshall Pickering, 1989.
———. *A Theology of the Dark Side: Putting the Power of Evil in its Place*. Downers Grove: InterVarsity, 2003.
Wright, N. T. "*arpagmos* and the meaning of Philippians 2:5–11." *Journal of Theological Studies* 37.2 (1986): 321–52.
———. *Evil and the Justice of God*. Downers Grove: InterVarsity, 2006.
Wuest, Kenneth S. "When Jesus Emptied Himself." *Bibliotheca Sacra* 115.458 (1958) 153–158.
Yoder, John Howard. *The Politics of Jesus*. Grand Rapids: Eerdmans, 1994.
Yong, Amos. *Discerning the Spirit(s): A Pentecostal-Charismatic Contribution to Christian Theology of Religions*. Sheffield: Sheffield Academic, 2000.
———. *The Spirit of Creation: Modern Science and Divine Action in the Pentecostal-Charismatic Imagination*. Grand Rapids: Eerdmans, 2011.
Young, Frances. "*Apathos Epathen*: Patristic Reflection on God, Suffering and the Cross." In *Within the Love of God: Essays on the Doctrine of God in Honour of Paul S. Fiddes*, edited by Anthony Clarke and Andrew Moore, 79–94. Oxford: Oxford University Press, 2014.
———. *Face to Face: A Narrative Essay in the Theology of Suffering*. Edinburgh: T&T Clark, 1990.
Young, Francis. *A History of Anglican Exorcism: Deliverance and Demonology in Church Ritual*. London: T&T Clark, 2018.